Juran on Planning for Quality

Juran on Planning for Quality

J. M. Juran

THE FREE PRESS
A Division of Macmillan, Inc.
NEW YORK

Collier Macmillan Publishers
LONDON

The Free Press
A Division of Macmillan, Inc.
866 Third Avenue, New York, N. Y. 10022

Collier Macmillan Canada, Inc.

Printed in the United States of America

printing number

7 8 9 10

Library of Congress Cataloging-in-Publication Data

Juran, J. M. (Joseph M.)

Juran on planning for quality.

1. Quality control. 2. Quality assurance.
I. Title.
TS156.J85 1988 658.5′62 87–21234
ISBN 0–02–916681–0

Contents

Preface

The quality crisis of the 1980s has forced many Western companies to reexamine their approach to managing for quality. An important finding of that reexamination has been that *our quality problems have been planned that way.*

That arresting statement is meant to emphasize the fact that many of the deficiencies in our products and processes have had their origin in deficient planning for quality. Despite that fact, the subject of planning for quality has received only limited priority in companies and in the literature. *Juran on Planning for Quality* has been designed to help companies master the quality planning process and thereby to avoid creating deficient products and processes in the first place.

The book is organized to show how the quality planning process applies to various levels of company activity. The chapters deal with:

Quality planning as a basic managerial process (Chapter One)

Quality planning for interdepartmental projects (Chapters Two to Ten)

Quality planning as part of companywide quality management (Chapter Eleven)

Departmental quality planning (Chapter Twelve)

Introducing *Planning for Quality*[1] into a going company (Chapter Thirteen.)

[1]This book underwent an earlier publication (September 1986) under the shorter title. The shorter title is occasionally retained in the text, especially to refer to the total instrumentality set forth in the book, as here and in the title of Chapter Thirteen.

EVOLUTION OF *JURAN ON PLANNING FOR QUALITY*

This book had been in incubation for some years, but the first draft was published in April 1985. Copies were sent to about fifty organizations in the United States and abroad for critique. The response was gratifying; the critiques were forthright and constructive.

The critiques were summarized to serve as the main agenda for a two-day conference held at Stamford, Connecticut, during August 1985. That conference was attended by forty persons, representing twenty-five different organizations. The presence of so many leading authorities and incisive thinkers in the field of managing for quality, made it a memorable event.

One consensus of the Stamford conference was that the text should be designed to be universally applicable. I accepted that without reservation. In consequence, the concepts, the associated case examples, the tools and the techniques are all structured to be applicable universally:

To products in general—both goods and services

To all levels in the hierarchy, from the chief executive officer to the workforce

To all functions: general management, product development, operations (office, factory, service), human relations, and so on

To all industries: service as well as manufacture, public sector as well as private sector

A further step in the evolution of this book was field testing of the structured approach. The field testing was made possible through the continuing cooperation of the organizations that had participated in the critiques and in the Stamford conference. Field tests were set up at organizations as follows:

Automotive Division, American Society for Quality Control

Bureau of Labor Statistics, U.S. Department of Labor (two projects)

Caterpillar, Inc. (three projects)

General Motors Advanced Engineering Center

Juran Institute, Inc.

Packaging Corporation of America (a Tenneco Company)

Instrument Group, Perkin–Elmer Corporation (two projects)

The field tests served to try out the second draft of the text, along with a draft workbook. The field test projects covered an astonishing variety of subject matter. Such variety provided insights as to the applicability of the structured approach to a wide variety of products, industries, organization levels, and functions. In addition, the field tests provided valuable inputs relative to the problems of introducing the structured approach into a going organization. (The subject matter of the field test projects, along with the names of the project team members, are listed in the Appendix.)

The critiques and field tests also served to clarify the functions to be served by *Juran on Planning for Quality.* Those functions have emerged as follows:

1. As a source of subject matter for seminars on planning for quality
2. As a self-training road map for those seeking a structured approach to planning for quality
3. As a textbook for in-house training in the concepts, tools, and methodology needed to acquire mastery of the quality planning process.

From prior experience with *Juran on Quality Improvement,* I realize that for many companies, function 3 requires an added array of of training materials such as:

Video cassettes to provide summarized instruction in interesting, digestible form

Workbooks that can help teams of company managers to tackle pilot projects in planning or replanning

Manuals to enable facilitators and instructors to assist the project teams to carry out their assignments

In all likelihood those materials will be published by the end of 1987.

In its final form, *Juran on Planning for Quality* includes the experience and ideas of those who actively participated in the critiques, the Stamford conference and the field tests. I am proud to be able to list their names as active collaborators. However, I am unable to list the far greater number of sources who, over the decades, have provided me with invaluable case examples and ideas during training courses, consultations, conferences, committee meetings, and other encounters.

Florida Power and Light Company provided help of a special sort in our search for case materials in the service sector. They were generous in providing liberal access to their internal processes and experiences. Our special thanks go to Larry Alderman, Bob Averitt, Jerry Kinsey, and W. Kent Sterrett.

I am also proud to acknowledge the assistance of the staff of Juran Institute, Inc., in preparing the drafts and in organizing for the critiques, the Stamford conference, and the field tests. Robert E. Hoogstoel, Vice President of Juran Institute, Inc., contributed significantly to the conceptual approach, the supporting research, the editing of the text and the preparation of the visual aids. Other staff members directly involved were, in alphabetical order:

Harris M. Brokke
Margaret A. Cutrona
Debra Walters Rider
Marilyn M. Schmid
Laura A. Sutherland

A NOTE ON "SEXIST" LANGUAGE

The 1970s brought a wide movement to revise the language so as not to be so blatantly masculine, e.g., the use of chairperson, not chairman. I agree with the concept, but I fear I was born too early to comply fully—it is a lot of work to change the habits of eight decades. So I have decided to stay with my traditional vocabulary—for the most part. However, I plead with the readers to translate for me. When I use the word "chairman," it really means "chairperson."

Wilton, Connecticut
September 1987

J. M. JURAN

] *1* [

Introduction to Quality Planning

WHY SHOULD WE SPEND TIME LEARNING ABOUT QUALITY PLANNING?

Many companies are facing serious losses and wastes that have their main origin in deficiencies in the quality planning process:

1. *Loss of sales* due to competition in quality. In recent years, many key industries (automobiles, color television sets, computer chips, and so on) have lost more than over 25 percent of their sales to foreign competitors. A leading reason has been quality of product.

2. *Costs of poor quality,* including customer complaints, product liability lawsuits, redoing defective work, products scrapped, and so on. The total of those costs is huge. In most companies they run at about 20 to 40 percent of sales. In other words, about 20 to 40 percent of the companies' efforts are spent in redoing things that went wrong because of poor quality.

3. *The threats to society.* The products of an industrial society have the potential to lengthen the human life span; relieve people of drudgery; provide opportunities for educational, cultural, and entertainment activities; and so forth. However, the continuity of those benefits depends absolutely on the continuing and proper performance of those products, that is, on their quality. In a sense, people in industrialized societies live behind protective quality dikes. Yet we have numerous breaks in those dikes. Mostly they are small breaks such as failure of household appliances. Each is disruptive and annoying. Each requires time and money to mend. However, some of those breaks have been terrifying: the drug Thalidomide; the Three Mile Island nuclear reactor; the deadly gas

cloud at Bhopal; the space shuttle *Challenger;* the Chernobyl nuclear reactor.

Collectively, the losses in sales, the costs, and the threats to society all add up to a crisis in quality. The crisis has stimulated many companies to reexamine their approach to quality. A principal finding has been that *their quality problems are planned that way,* which means that the quality problems are largely traceable to deficiencies in the methods used to plan for quality. *Those deficiencies are still in place.* To get rid of those deficiencies we must revise the quality planning process and then learn how to acquire mastery over that revised process.

THE MISSION OF *JURAN ON PLANNING FOR QUALITY*

That brings us to the mission of this book, which consists of the following:

- Create awareness of the quality crisis; the role of quality planning in that crisis; and the need to revise the approach to quality planning
- Establish a new approach to quality planning
- Provide training in how to plan for quality, using the new approach
- Assist company personnel to replan those existing processes which contain unacceptable quality deficiencies (March right through the company.)
- Assist company personnel to acquire mastery over the quality planning process, a mastery derived from replanning existing processes and from the associated training
- Assist company personnel to use the resulting mastery to plan for quality in ways that avoid creation of new chronic problems

AWARENESS

During the early 1980s, many upper managers became alarmed by the emerging quality crisis. Some had experienced considerable damage to their companies, and they wanted to regain the lost ground. Others had not yet reached the damage state, but they wanted to keep the crisis from reaching their doors. Still others had always felt that quality should have top priority because it is "the right thing to do." They saw the quality crisis as a timely opportunity to get their message across.

Collectively, those and other perceptions resulted in a widespread move to raise "quality awareness." Many, many companies undertook "drives" to "make quality number one." The drives were mounted with the usual exhortations and fervor: exhibits, slogans, posters, banners, and the colorful rest. The hope and expectation were that the increased awareness would somehow result in changed behavior—that everyone would "do it right the first time."

Generally those drives did increase awareness to the extent that quality awareness is now largely a solved problem. However, the increased awareness seldom resulted in changed behavior. The reason is that there was so little substance behind all the exhortation. The drives did not identify the deeds to be done—the specific projects to be tackled. They established no clear responsibility for doing the needed deeds. They provided no structured process for "how to go from here to there." They made no revision in the system for judging the performance of managers.

The lesson is: Put the emphasis on the results to be achieved—the deeds to be done. The recipe for action should consist of 90 percent substance and 10 percent exhortation, not the reverse. The formula for getting results is to:

Establish specific goals to be reached

Establish plans for reaching the goals

Assign clear responsibility for meeting the goals

Base the rewards on results achieved

Awareness can certainly play a useful role in this sequence, but efforts to change behavior solely by exhortation are doomed to failure. Those on the receiving end of such exhortations tend to become cynical—"Here comes another one." Many tend to conclude that their superiors are not leading but cheerleading.

WHAT IS QUALITY?

Before we can get into our subject of quality planning we must first agree on what is meant by the word "quality." Here it is very tempting to settle for some short descriptive phrase and then to move on to the next topic. There are many short phrases to choose from, but *the short phrase is a trap.* There is no known short definition that results in a real agreement on what is meant by quality. Yet a real agreement is vital; we cannot plan for quality unless we first agree on what is meant by quality.

So we will avoid that trap. We will take enough time to define quality in a way that enables us to agree on what is to be the subject matter for our planning.

PRODUCT PERFORMANCE AND FREEDOM FROM DEFICIENCIES

The word quality has multiple meanings. Two of those meanings are critical, not only to quality planning but to strategic business planning as well.

Product Performance: Product Satisfaction

In the sense of performance, quality refers to such features as:

Promptness of a process for filling customer orders

Fuel consumption of an engine

Effectiveness of an advertising campaign

Millions of instructions per second (MIPS) of a computer

Inherent uniformity of a production process

Such features are decisive as to product performance and as to "product satisfaction." Such features compete with each other in the market place. External customers, especially ultimate users, compare the competing performances. Their comparisons then become a factor in deciding whose product will be bought. Because of the competition in the market place, a primary goal for product performance is to be equal or superior to the quality of competing products.

Freedom from Deficiencies: Product Dissatisfaction

The word "quality" also refers to freedom from deficiencies, which take such forms as:

Late deliveries

Field failures

Incorrect invoices

Cancellation of sales contracts

Factory scrap or rework

Engineering design changes

Deficiencies result in complaints, claims, returns, rework, and other damage. Those collectively are forms of "product *dis*satisfaction."

Some deficiencies impact external customers and hence are a threat to future sales as well as a source of higher costs. Other deficiencies impact internal customers only and hence are mainly a source of higher costs.

For quality in the sense of freedom from deficiencies, the long-range goal is perfection.

Note that product satisfaction and product dissatisfaction *are not opposites*. Product satisfaction is why customers buy the product. Product dissatisfaction is why they complain. It is quite possible for a product to have no deficiencies and yet be unsalable because some competing product has better product performance.

THE SPIRAL OF PROGRESS IN QUALITY

A simple definition of quality is "fitness for use." That definition must quickly be enlarged, because there are many uses and users.

A convenient way to show some of the many uses and users is through the "spiral of progress in quality" (Figure 1–1). We shall refer to that simply as The Spiral.

The Spiral shows a typical sequence of activities for putting a product on the market. In large companies we departmentalize those activities. As a result, each department carries out an operating process, produces a product, and supplies that product to other departments or to clients. Those recipient departments can

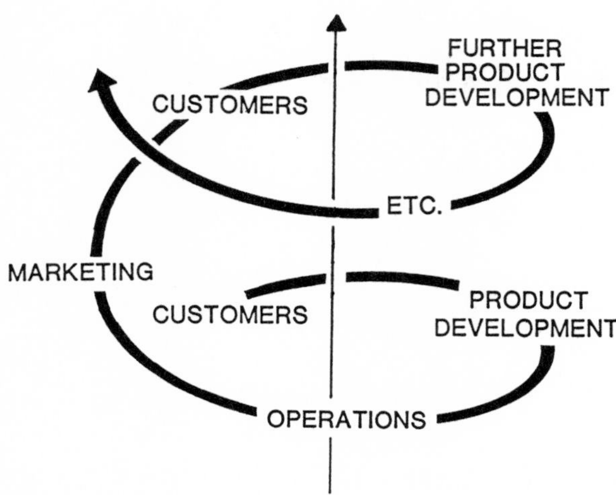

FIGURE 1–1 The spiral of progress in quality

be regarded as "customers" who receive products from the supplying departments. The table below shows some of the relationships evident from The Spiral:

SUPPLIER	PRODUCT (GOODS AND SERVICES)	CUSTOMER
Client	Information on needs	Product development
Product development	Product designs	Operations
Operations	Goods, services	Marketing
Marketing	Goods, services	Clients

Note that some of the customers are "internal," that is, members of the same company as the suppliers. Other customers are external.

The Spiral is a greatly simplified version of what goes on in a large company. If we go into elaboration we soon see that there is a great multiplicity of uses and users:

> For example, in Company A an important end product of the Purchasing Department is the purchase order, which is sent to supplier companies. In Company B (a supplier), the Customer

Order Department is obviously a key user of the purchase order. But look at some other users and uses of the purchase order:

USER DEPARTMENT	PURCHASE ORDER USED TO:
In purchaser's company:	
Production	Confirm progress on purchase requisition; provide input for production scheduling
Quality Control	Provide quality standards for receiving inspection
Accounts Payable	Provide basis for verification of supplier's invoice
In supplier's company:	
Production	Provide input to production scheduling, routing; trigger bill of materials explosion for component parts/material
Quality Control	Provide quality standards for product as produced
Material Control	Trigger inventory transfers to accomplish production of purchased goods

Conventional "hardware" products also involve multiple users and uses.

For the company that makes color TV sets, the consumer is the end user. However, there are other users and uses:

USER	USE
Within the company:	
Assembly Department	Assemble from components
Test Department	Test in final assembled form
Shipping Department	Pack for shipment and load on carrier vehicle

USER	USE
In the distribution chain:	
Freight carrier	Transport to next destination
Wholesaler	Store, break bulk
Retailer	Store, display, sell
During maintenance:	
Service shop	Service, diagnose, repair

"PRODUCT" INCLUDES GOODS AND SERVICES

Note that we have been using the word "product" as a generic term for whatever is produced, whether goods or services. Goods are physical things, whereas service is work performed for someone else. Most companies produce both.

We shall have many occasions to refer to both goods and services. To shorten the reference it is convenient to use a generic term. We shall use the word "product" for that purpose, so "product" includes both goods and services.

WHO ARE THE CUSTOMERS?

In the dictionary sense, "customers" usually means those who buy from us, that is, clients. Our use of the word "customer" includes clients, but we go further. We stretch the word "customers" to include *all persons who are impacted by our processes and our products*. Those persons include internal as well as external customers. Let's look more closely, starting with the external customers.

External Customers

The term "external customers" is used here to mean persons who are not a part of our company but who are impacted by our products. The term "internal customers" means persons or organizations who are a part of our company. Those definitions are not 100 percent accurate, but they are valid to a high degree.

The table below lists some important categories of external customers, along with what they need from us and what we need from them.

CATEGORY	WHAT THEY NEED FROM US	WHAT WE NEED FROM THEM
Clients	Quality products	Income, respect
Owners	Income, stability	Broad support
The media	Newsworthy stories	A good image
The local communities	Jobs, taxes, good corporate citizenship	Recruits, services
Government regulatory bodies	Conformance to regulations	Protection against unfair competition, peace and quiet
The public	Product safety, environmental protection	Respect, support

Internal Customers

In a large company there are a lot of internal customers. We saw some examples on The Spiral, where internal departments are customers of other internal departments. The internal customer–supplier relationship also extends to every *person* in the company:

Clerical employees in department A supply data to employees in department B.

Factory employees in department C supply components to employees in department D.

And so on to supervisors, managers, and top executives.

Earlier, we tabulated some specific customer–supplier relationships derived from The Spiral (see p. 6). There are many other such relationships, involving activities not shown on The Spiral. For example:

SUPPLYING DEPARTMENTS	PRINCIPAL PRODUCTS	SOME INTERNAL CUSTOMERS
Finance	Financial statements	Managers
Employment	Recruits	All departments
Order Editing	Edited orders	Operations
Office Services	Office space, supplies, maintenance	All office departments
Legal	Legal advice	All departments

Customers as Suppliers

Note that there is two-way communication between suppliers and customers. Customers provide their suppliers with requisitions, specifications, feedback on product performance, and so on. As to such communication the conventional roles are reversed. The customer becomes a supplier and the supplier becomes a customer.

Customers and Users

The word "customer" has a popular appeal. That is why we adopt it to designate those who are impacted by our processes and products, even if they are not clients. (In this context "customer" includes innocent bystanders.) We will adopt the word *"user"* to designate *anyone who carries out positive actions* with respect to our product—actions such as further processing, sale, ultimate use, and so on.

SUMMARY (Interim)

We are now poised to proceed with development of our subject of quality planning. Before we do, let us pause to summarize what we have covered so far:

Our past ways of quality planning are inadequate for today's competition and for the needs of society.

To meet modern needs for quality requires that we revise our approach to quality planning, and that we bring everyone to a state of mastery over the new approach.

"Quality" has multiple meanings.

One meaning of quality is product performance. Product performance results from product features that create product satisfaction and lead customers to buy the product.

Another meaning of quality is freedom from deficiencies. Product deficiencies create product dissatisfaction and lead customers to complain.

Product satisfaction and product dissatisfaction are not opposites.

A simple definition of quality is "fitness for use."

There are many uses and users.

"Customer" includes all who are impacted by our processes and products.

Customers include persons internal as well as external to our company.

"Product" includes both goods and services.

THE JURAN TRILOGY®

Quality planning is one of three basic managerial processes through which we manage for quality. The three processes (The Juran Trilogy) are interrelated. It is useful to look at that interrelationship before going specifically into what is quality planning. A simple diagram (Figure 1–2) shows the interrelationship.

It all begins with quality planning. The purpose of the quality planning is to provide the operating forces with the means of producing products that can meet customers' needs, products such as invoices, polyethylene film, sales contracts, service calls, and new designs for goods.

Once planning is complete, the plan is turned over to the operating forces. Their job is to produce the product. As operations proceed, we see that the process is deficient: 20 percent of the operating effort is wasted, as the work must be redone because of quality deficiencies. That waste then becomes chronic because *the process was planned that way.*

Under conventional responsibility patterns the operating forces are unable to get rid of that planned chronic waste. What they do instead is carry out *quality control* to prevent things from getting worse. Control includes putting out the fires, such as that sporadic spike in Figure 1–2.

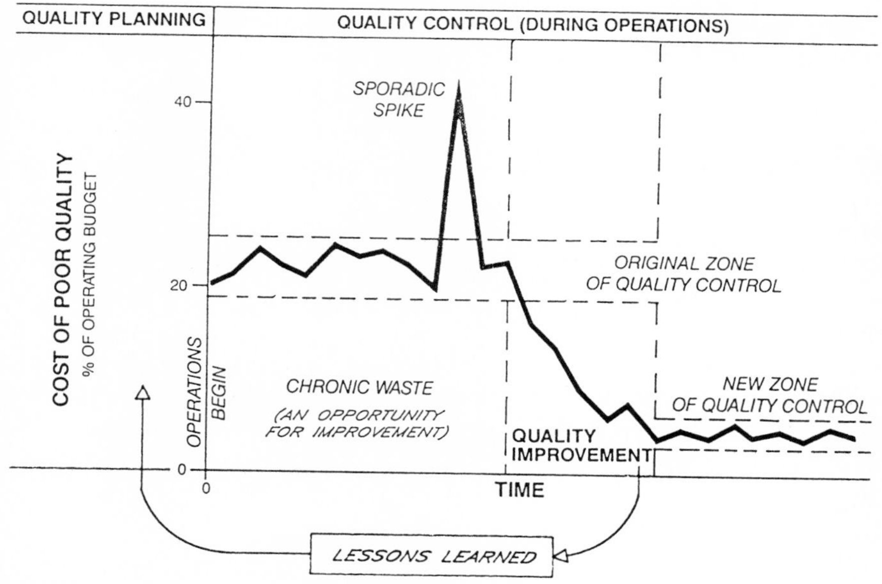

FIGURE 1–2 The Juran Trilogy

The chart also shows that in due course the chronic waste was driven down to a level far below that planned originally. That gain was achieved by the third process in the trilogy: "quality improvement." In effect, it was realized that the chronic waste was also an opportunity for improvement, so steps were taken to seize that opportunity.

THE TRILOGY IS NOT SO NEW

If we look sideways we soon see that those three processes—planning, control and improvement—have been around for some time. They have been used in finance for centuries—long enough to evolve some standardized terminology. The table below gives some examples:

TRILOGY PROCESSES	FINANCIAL TERMINOLOGY
Quality planning	Budgeting, business planning
Quality control	Cost control, expense control, inventory control
Quality improvement	Cost reduction, profit improvement

What is new is applying the trilogy concept to managing for quality and doing so with a structured approach.

QUALITY PLANNING COMPARED WITH QUALITY IMPROVEMENT

Managers who have engaged in quality improvement on a project-by-project basis have raised the question: Just how does going into a new approach to quality planning differ from project-by-project quality improvement?

An answer in popular terms is found in the case of the manager who is up to his waist in alligators. He undertakes to slay alligators, one by one—a reptilian version of project-by-project improvement. But there will never be an end to it, because more and more alligators keep emerging from the swamp. The ultimate answer is to drain the swamp.

In that analogy, project-by-project improvement amounts to slaying alligators one by one. The new approach to quality planning consists of draining the swamp.

A more realistic example is seen in the process for putting new products on the market. In some industries (e.g., automobiles) a large class of chronic quality problems has for years been the inability of factory processes to meet the tolerances set by the design engineers. The two key events are (1) setting tolerances and (2) trying to meet those tolerances in the factory. The two events are not directly consecutive. They are separated by a time interval that often extends to a year or two. Each inability to hold tolerances becomes a chronic quality problem. Collectively those problems have created huge chronic wastes.

Many companies have meanwhile gone into project-by-project improvement. The projects chosen have included cases of inability of factory processes to meet design tolerances. Such projects have generally been successful. The project team diagnosed the symptoms, found the causes, and provided remedies. The benefits have been considerable, and everyone has cheered. Yet the remedies provided in all those individual improvement projects did not remedy the basic cause, which created that entire class of quality problems. That basic cause was the fact that at the time of setting tolerances, the designers were unilaterally and unwittingly creating subsequent chronic problems for the factory. A remedy for that basic cause requires a revision of the new product *planning* process.

THE QUALITY PLANNING ROAD MAP

In broad terms, quality planning consists of developing the products and processes required to meet customers' needs. More specifically, quality planning comprises the following basic activities:

Identify the customers and their needs

Develop a product that responds to those needs

Develop a process able to produce that product

When we look more closely, it turns out that we can generalize *a road map for quality planning*—an invariable sequence of steps, as follows:

Identify who are the customers

Determine the needs of those customers

Translate those needs into our language

Develop a product that can respond to those needs

Optimize the product features so as to meet our needs as well as customers' needs

Develop a process which is able to produce the product

Optimize the process

Prove that the process can produce the product under operating conditions

Transfer the process to the operating forces

Figure 1–3, the quality planning road map, shows those steps in graphic form. The sequence is stitched together through several commonalities:

1. The interlocking input–output chain, in which the output for any step becomes the input for the next step
2. The triple role concept, under which every activity plays the triple role of customer, processor, and supplier
3. The establishment of common units of measure for evaluating quality

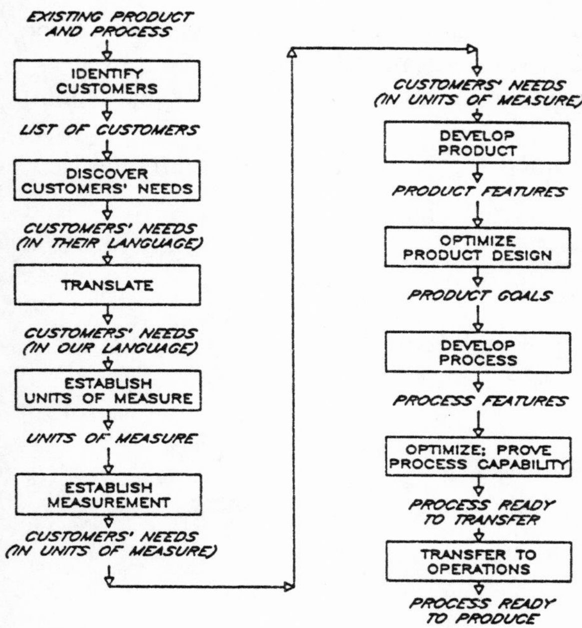

FIGURE 1–3 The quality planning road map

4. The establishment of means (“sensors”) to evaluate quality in terms of those units of measure

In the remaining chapters we shall examine each of those steps on the road map, as well as each of the ways through which the whole sequence is stitched together.

SUMMARY (Concluded)

Managing for quality is carried out through a trilogy of managerial processes:

Quality Planning

Quality Control

Quality Improvement

The trilogy parallels a trilogy long used in financial management.

Quality planning consists of developing the products and processes required to meet customers' needs.

Quality planning consists of an invariable series of specific planning activities.

Those activities are joined together by several commonalities:

An interlocking input–output chain

The triple role concept

Common units of measure

Common means of evaluating quality

] 2 [

Who Are the Customers?

THE MISSION FOR THIS CHAPTER

This chapter takes the first step on the quality planning road map (Figure 1–3). The mission on that first step is to identify who are the customers. The input–output diagram is shown in Figure 2–1.

The figure is of course the same as the first step on the road map.

Any input–output diagram consists of three elements: the input, the process, and the output. In this first step on the quality planning road map:

The *input* is the subject matter of our quality planning/replanning—the existing product and process.

The *process* consists of construction of a *flow diagram* to discover who is impacted by the product.

The *output* is the resulting list of customers.

Note that those who carry out this first step are actually engaged in three roles:

Customers: They receive input from suppliers, so we call them *customers.*

Processors: They convert the inputs into products, so we call them *processors.*

Suppliers: They supply the products to customers, so we call them *suppliers.*

In chapter twelve we shall examine in detail the application of the triple role concept to departmental quality planning. However, the triple role concept applies universally, at all levels: corporate, divisional, departmental, and so, ultimately, to each person.

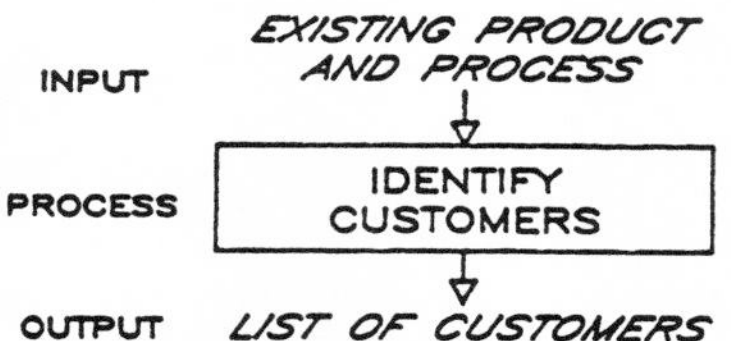

FIGURE 2–1 The input–output diagram for "Who are the customers?"

THE PRODUCT

The subject matter of quality planning can be anything at all. During Chapter One we noted a wide variety of products (goods and services) as well as some processes. A quick look back will emphasize the variety of possible subject matter for quality planning.

> *Products* information, product designs, financial statements, legal advice, automotive engines, recruits, edited customers' orders, office space, computer chips, office supplies, maintenance service, advertising campaigns
>
> *Process* for filling customers' orders, for factory production

The list is not limited to industrial subjects; it extends to all human endeavor.

> A family has just returned from a disastrous vacation. Many things went wrong, mainly due to poor planning. They conclude not to let that happen again, so they start out on the quality planning road map. The product—the subject matter of the planning—is vacations.

THE FLOW DIAGRAM

The most effective way to identify customers is to follow the product to see whom it impacts. Anyone who is impacted is a customer. To follow the product we make use of a fundamental planning tool, *the flow diagram.*

The flow diagram is a graphic means for depicting the steps in a process. Figure 2–2 is a simple example.

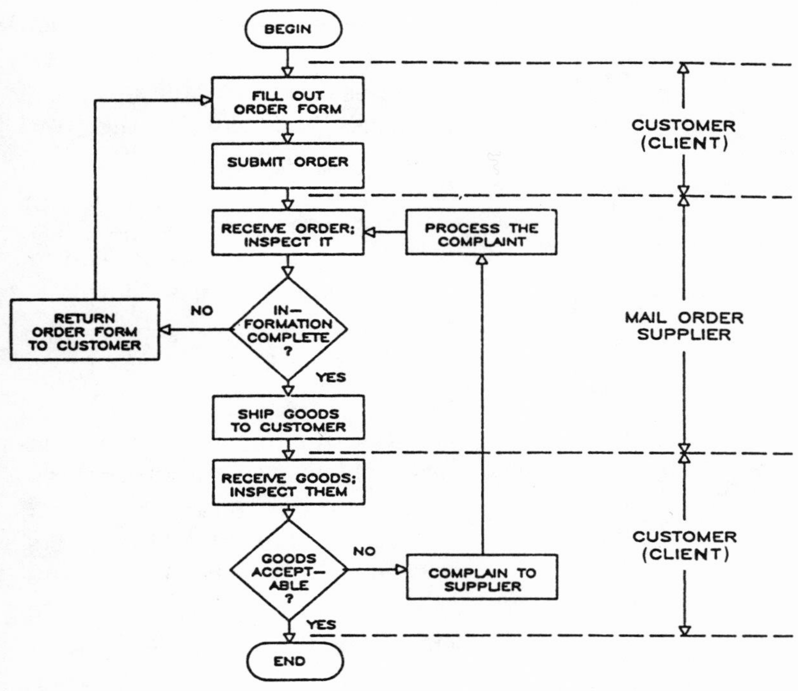

FIGURE 2–2 A simple flow diagram: The mail order process

Basic Symbols

Most flow diagrams are built up out of a few basic symbols:

The *activity symbol* is a rectangle, which designates an activity. Within the rectangle is a brief description of that activity.

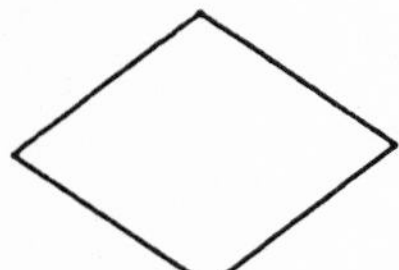

The *decision symbol* is a diamond, which designates a decision point from which the process branches into two or more paths. The path taken depends on the answer to the question that appears within the diamond. Each path is labeled to correspond to an answer to the question.

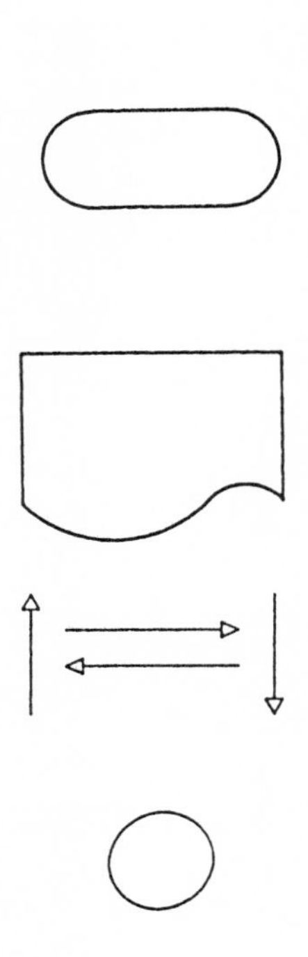

The *terminal symbol* is a rounded rectangle, which unambiguously identifies the beginning or end of a process, according to the word within the terminal. "Start" or "begin" are used to designate the starting point of process flow; "stop" or "end" are used to designate the end of process flow.

The *document symbol* represents a document pertinent to the process.

The *flow line* represents a process path, which connects process elements, e.g., activities, decisions, and so on. The arrowhead on a flow line indicates direction of process flow.

The *connector* is a circle, which is used to indicate a continuation of the flow diagram.

When flow diagrams become complex, it is helpful to prepare a schematic to show the broad flow. Figure 2–3 shows such a flow for the process of preparing invoices in a large power company. Such a schematic helps readers to visualize the interrelationships among the more detailed subdiagrams.

Benefits of Flow Diagrams

The value of the flow diagram was demonstrated during the field tests of this textbook. Prior to publication, many teams of managers undertook to plan/replan some process, using the quality planning road map. Virtually all teams reported that they derived multiple and essential benefits from preparing the flow diagram. They reported that the flow diagram accomplishes the following:

PROVIDES UNDERSTANDING OF THE WHOLE. Each team member was fully knowledgeable about his segment of the process but not

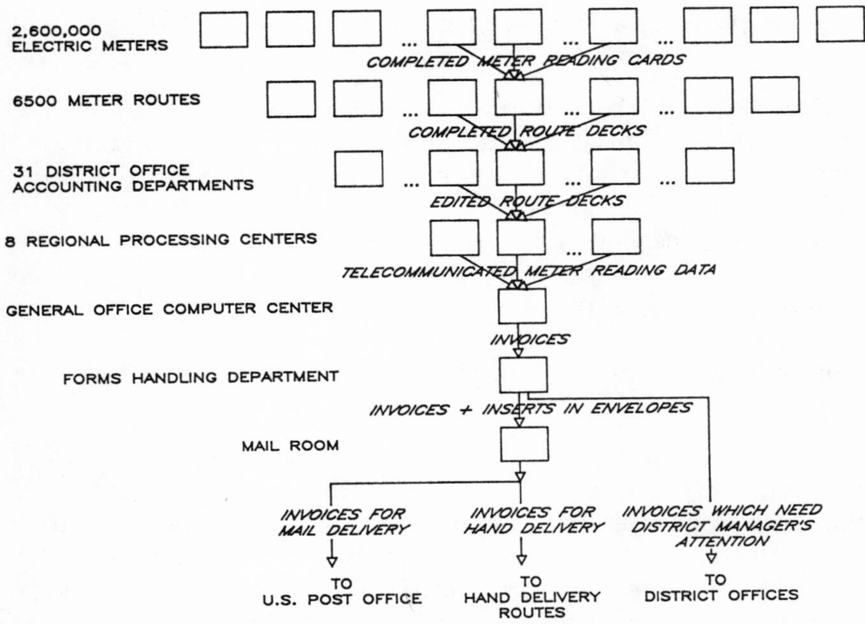

FIGURE 2–3 Schematic diagram of invoicing process information flow
Courtesy: Florida Power & Light Co.

fully knowledgeable about the complete process. The flow diagram supplied the missing knowledge to an unprecedented degree.

PROVIDES CLEARER EXPLANATIONS. The team found that the flow diagrams made it easier to explain the process to managers who were not on the team.

IDENTIFIES CUSTOMERS PREVIOUSLY NEGLECTED. A surprising finding by some test teams was that much planning was being done without first identifying all the important customers. It had been widely assumed that "everyone knows" who are the customers. But it turned out that without the discipline of preparing the flow diagram some essential customers were being neglected or even overlooked. In the case of one very important process, it became necessary to make a substantial revision in strategy because a great deal of planning had already been done without a clear knowledge of who were the customers. Lacking that knowledge the planners also lacked the knowledge of what the needs of some important internal customers were.

IDENTIFIES OPPORTUNITIES FOR IMPROVEMENT. Most flow diagrams exhibit subprocesses or "loops," which are needed to take care of nonstandard events. For example, the product of step A undergoes an inspection before being sent on to step B. Any errors found during inspection are routed back to step A for correction. We saw two examples of such loops in the mail order flow diagram (Figure 2–2). One of those loops is reproduced in Figure 2–4. The existence of the loop proves the existence of an opportunity. If we could eliminate the cause of the errors, we could avoid all that extra work.

MAKES IT EASIER TO SET BOUNDARIES. When we set out to plan/replan some process, we soon realize that we must establish a boundary to our mission. The reason is that every process interacts with some of the other processes in and out of the company. Those others interact with still other processes. Ultimately every company process is affected, but the effects keep diminishing as we get farther and farther from our specific mission. It is out of the question to pursue those interactions to the bitter end—we would wind up replanning the work of the entire company. So we establish a boundary based on our judgment. The test teams found that the flow diagram provided a graphic aid for setting the boundary.

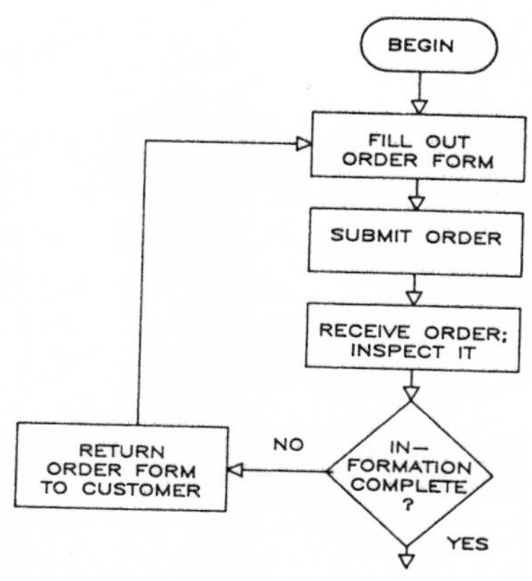

FIGURE 2–4 A loop—an opportunity for improvement

Sources of Flow Diagrams

Many companies make use of flow diagrams to depict process flow. Examples abound in prior planning projects and reports of all kinds. However, it is likely that most process flow information exists either in narrative form (e.g., in written procedures) or is unwritten—it exists in the heads of the managers and workers.

When we undertake a quality planning project, the prior process flow studies can be helpful, especially if they reflect the discipline of flow diagram analysis. However, each planning project requires updating the old as well as providing for the new. There are two widely used methods for creating the flow diagram:

1. *The investigator.* In this approach a trained investigator "makes the rounds" and confers with the personnel who preside over the various steps in the process. From those inputs the investigator prepares the flow diagram along with an analysis and recommendations. Those are then discussed with the pertinent heads, either collectively or individually. Revisions are made, and the final version goes through recognized channels for approval.
2. *The team.* In this approach a multidepartmental team is appointed to do the quality planning. The team members are generally from the organizations responsible for the various steps in the process. The team then proceeds to develop the flow diagram and the associated analysis.

In this connection we have some useful inputs from the teams who field-tested this text. The main conclusion of the teams was that *participation* is the key to good quality planning. The team members all relished being party to a planning project that impacted their responsibility. Many of those same team members related prior experiences in which their participation had been too late—the key decisions had already been made and had become irreversible. It was refreshing to be brought in at the outset so that their contribution would be influential.

THE "PROCESSOR TEAM"

Let us now take a moment to define a term we shall be using now and then: "processor team."

The input–output diagram consists of three basic elements: input, process, and output. We have some standardized names for the persons who are closely associated with those basic elements. Those who provide the inputs are usually called *suppliers*. Those who receive the output are usually called *customers*. Those who run the processes are sometimes called *processors,* but this term is not well standardized.

We need a generic term to describe any organization unit that carries out a prescribed process. We shall adopt *"processor team"* as such a generic term.

A processor team can be any organization unit: the company, a division, a department, a crew, an individual. (We sometimes refer to an individual as a one-man gang.) As we move on to identifying customers, we shall see more clearly why we took time out to define that term "processor team."

TO IDENTIFY CUSTOMERS, FOLLOW THE PRODUCT

One of the basic methods for identifying customers is to follow the product to see whom it impacts. Anyone who is impacted is a customer.

> For example, a processor team produces invoices in six copies. These invoices end up in six different final destinations. Along the way the invoices may impact some intermediate steps. Each of the six final destinations, as well as each intermediate step, is a customer.
>
> Another processor team conducts the process of cutting gears. It receives "blanks" from a supplier and operates machines that cut gear teeth into the blanks. It then sends the cut gears on their way to subsequent processor teams, who cut keyways, heat treat, grind and lap, store, ship, assemble into gear boxes, assemble gear boxes into vehicles, sell the vehicles, operate the vehicles, maintain the vehicles, and so on. Each of those subsequent processor teams is a customer.

CATEGORIES OF CUSTOMERS

There are many categories of persons and organizations who are impacted by our processes. The number is often so great that we must "prioritize," that is, allocate the bulk of our resources to those customers who are most significantly impacted.

Significant Impacts

The tabulation below shows some categories of processor teams and the associated significant customer impacts.

PROCESSOR TEAM	EXAMPLES OF CUSTOMERS WHO ARE SIGNIFICANTLY IMPACTED
Our company	*Clients.* They buy from us and are the source of our income.
	Ultimate users. Even though they may not make the buying decision, their feedback on use of the product strongly influences those who do the buying.
	Investors. They buy our securities.
	Regulators. Their rules are a form of mandated needs to be met.
	The public. They influence the climate in which we operate.
Marketing Research	Marketing, Product Development
Product Development	Process Development
Process Development	Operations
Order Editing	Operations
Accounts Receivable	Clients
Any person	The supervisor
Any supervisor	The subordinate
Any stage on The Spiral	Later stages; *also earlier stages* (They are customers for data-feedback.)

Two of the categories listed warrant some elaboration:

1. *The supervisor–subordinate relationship.* The supervisor is obviously a customer who is impacted by the activities of the subordinate's process. Those activities influence the ability of the supervisor to meet his own assigned responsibilities. But the subordinate is also a customer of the supervisor. From the supervisor the subordinate receives training, information, orders, advice, decisions, and other essentials needed to carry out the subordinate's process.

2. *Earlier stages on The Spiral as customers.* Here the customer status is created by data feedback. Any processor team needs data feedback from subsequent processor teams if it is to plan its operations effectively.

Key Interfaces

Companies and their clients interface in multiple ways. The most familiar examples are seen in service companies. A hotel guest may have occasion to interface with multiple hotel employees: doorman, reception clerk, bellman, telephone operator, housekeeper, dining room waiter, cashier, and so on. Among such multiple contacts some may be *key interfaces.* To illustrate:

INDUSTRY	EXAMPLE OF KEY INTERFACE
Banking	Bank teller and depositor
Restaurant	Waiter and diner
Hotel	Reception clerk and guest
Market	Salesperson and shopper
Telephone	Operator and subscriber

As we develop the list of who are our customers it is very useful to identify such key interfaces.

CLASSIFICATION BASED ON IMPORTANCE

Customers exhibit differences in various ways: in their importance to us, in the way they use our products, in the way they are impacted by our processes, and so on. We respond to those differences by classifying customers and then designing ways to deal specially with the different classifications.

One of the most critical classifications is that of *importance* of the customer. To respond to differences in importance we make use of the Pareto principle. Under that principle we classify customers into two basic categories:

1. A relative few ("vital few"), each of whom is of great importance to us.
2. A relatively large number of customers, each of whom is only of modest importance to us (the "useful many").

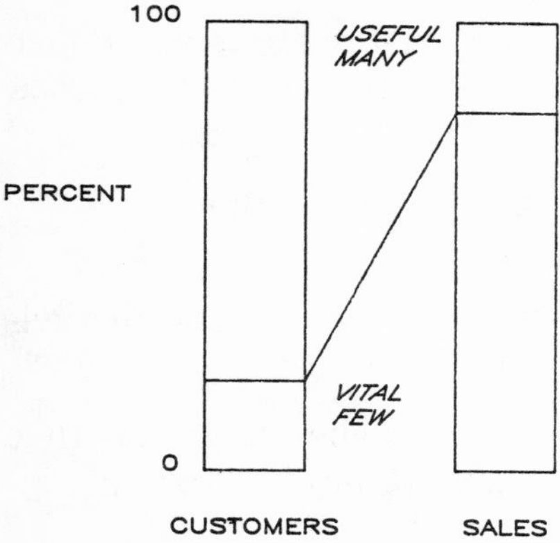

FIGURE 2–5 Pareto analysis of customers and sales volume

Figure 2–5 shows the relationship graphically.

Hotel rooms are booked by two types of clients:

1. Travelers who arrive one by one at random
2. Planners of meetings and conventions who book blocks of rooms far in advance

The planners of meetings and conventions constitute the vital few customers. They receive special attention from the hotel. The travelers are the useful many, and they receive standardized attention.

VITAL FEW CUSTOMERS

A common example is large original equipment manufacturers (OEM) or large merchants. Such customers will of course demand that our product meet their needs as to product satisfaction. In addition they will demand that product dissatisfaction be minimal.

Those same major customers also have an interest in needs that are not "hardware-related," e.g., timeliness of deliveries, level of technical service, accuracy of billing. They may even demand that we modify our practices to incorporate certain new elements, e.g., new training programs, statistical process control, just-in-time delivery.

An *in-house* example of the vital few customers is the *upper managers* within our company. They are concerned with needs such as:

Our quality versus that of competitors in the market place

Cost of poor quality

Quality of work of various organization sectors: corporate, division, suppliers, major activities around The Spiral

The great importance of the vital few customers demands that we contact them in depth, using (usually) any of several approaches:

1. "Make the rounds" to visit each customer and to secure that customer's perception of needs.

A quality manager undertook to update the company's package of managerial reports on quality. A part of his planning consisted of sitting down with each corporate officer to raise such questions as "What information do you need on quality in order to carry out your responsibility as a corporate officer?" The resulting inputs were helpful in establishing a consensus on what should be the contents of the report package.

2. Conduct an in-depth review of proposals with a sample of the customers.

From time to time the Bureau of Labor Statistics (BLS) proposes changes in the basis for computing the consumer price index (CPI). For example, BLS may propose to reflect population shifts by revising the list of cities from which price information is gathered; or BLS may propose to measure the cost of housing by rental cost rather than asset cost. As the BLS prepares its proposal for revisions, it meets with a number of its customers (users of the CPI) to review the proposed revisions.

3. Convene a conference of a few such customers at a time to discuss in depth their perception of the needs.

While preparing this book, the author convened a conference or trainers and quality managers from some twenty-five companies. Each of the companies was a potential customer for the completed text; each invitee was a potential trainer/facilitator. An agenda, distributed in advance of the conference, consisted of a large number of specific questions on the content and its application. The questions were designed to elicit specific information and to stimulate discussion. The conference proved to be a valuable aid to discover the needs of potential customers and to shape the text to meet their needs.

Whatever the method, the contacts with vital few customers should be preceded by careful planning, e.g., identifying the questions to which answers are needed, soliciting customers' nominations for agenda topics, and sending the agenda out in advance.

There are also other categories of vital few customers, e.g., government regulators, the media, and labor union officials. Their concepts of needs and priorities reflect their perceptions of their responsibilities, which may be markedly different from the perceptions of other customers. However, the method of approach for securing their perceptions remains essentially the same.

At a meeting of the board of directors of a major airline some members voiced objections to the military style of the new uniforms for flight attendants. A recent addition to the board was the head of the flight attendants' union. He pointed out that in the few months since the introduction of the uniforms there had been a significant reduction in assaults against flight attendants. That reduction was attributed to the new uniforms. The style remained unchanged.

USEFUL MANY CUSTOMERS

There are several categories of useful many customers.[1]

Consumers

We define "consumer" as a small-volume buyer for personal use. That definition applies to the great majority of the population—it involves very large numbers of people. Those people supply the purchasing power that supports many of our industries, including

[1]*A note on marketers' terminology:* Any marketer knows that a relatively few "key" customers account for most of his sales volume. Each such customer may be designated as "primary," "vital," "major," or the like. However, marketers avoid openly designating any of the remaining (non-key) customers as "minor," "secondary," and so on. The stated position of the marketers is that every customer is important and should be treated as such.

some of the giants. Those same people are in a unique position to contribute information relative to customer needs. No one is better informed about the conditions under which the product is used, neglected, or misused. No one has accumulated as much experience in use of the product. No one is more qualified, by experience, to make judgments as to likes and dislikes.

Naturally, consumers also reach conclusions (perceptions) from all that experience. They then make use of their perceptions in various ways:

They reach decisions on what to buy or not to buy in the future.

They communicate their perceptions to others.

They generate ideas that might help us to improve matters.

The Workforce

The term "workforce" usually refers to nonsupervisory employees in nonprofessional work categories. In manufacturing companies many of those employees are production workers on the factory floor. Another large segment of the workforce is the clerical and administrative employees in various office departments. In service companies, the workforce is almost exclusively clerical and administrative.

As in the case of consumers, workers have knowledge in depth with respect to needs for quality. That knowledge is derived from extensive "residence" in the workplace and from the repetitive performance of numerous cycles of processing in that workplace. As a consequence of all that residence and processing, they develop expertise in such matters as condition of the facilities, environmental variations in the workplace, support provided (or denied) by service departments, variations in inputs to the process, and consistency of management actions.

Such expertise is a useful input to many planning projects. For some projects the input is indispensable. All of this means that the workforce should be regarded as internal customers who can tell us a great deal about quality needs.

Middle Managers and Professionals

Middle managers and professionals have special strategic roles to play with respect to quality. They may be too numerous to be called the "vital few," but their roles are so important that they properly constitute a special category of customers.

On-time departure of aircraft is a key quality need for an airline. To maintain on-time departure requires the coordination of many activities, conducted by many departments. Examples of activities and the departments responsible are:

ACTIVITY	DEPARTMENT
Clean cabin	Cabin Service
Inspect aircraft, refuel	Maintenance
Load meals	Dining Service
Check in ticketed passengers; check baggage; accommodate standbys	Passenger Service
Load baggage	Ramp Service

Each of those departments has a mission to perform. That mission takes time. If routinely conducted, it may delay departure. None of those departments has the added mission of expediting on-time departure.

At one airline, the departmental managers collectively were unable to achieve a satisfactory rate of on-time departures within this traditional departmental structure. One recommendation was to create a gate manager whose prime objective was the attainment of an on-time departure. The recommendation was accepted; it contributed to a dramatic rise in the rate of on-time departures.

CLASSIFICATION BASED ON USE

A second system of classifying customers is based on what they do with our product.

Processors

Processors use our product as inputs to their process. They then perform additional processing after which they sell the resulting product to *their* customers. In consequence our product impacts multiple levels of customers:

The processor (our client)
The processor's clients

The impact may then extend to subsequent customers in the progression of the product to the ultimate user.

Merchants

Merchants buy our product for resale. As part of the resale they may perform some processing along with breaking bulk, repackaging, and so on. As with the processors, our product impacts multiple levels of customers: the merchant, the merchant's clients, and so on through the distribution chain.

Ultimate Users

The users are the final destination of the product. In some product lines there is a market for used products, so there are multiple tiers of ultimate users.

Some ultimate users are *consumers* who buy for their own use. Other ultimate users are *employees*—the office worker who uses the copier, the soldier who uses the weapon. Either way, the ultimate user is a most important category of customer and hence must be identified.

The Public

Members of the public may be impacted by us even though they do not buy our products. The most obvious impacts relate to product safety or to damage to the environment. There are other impacts as well. The public keeps an eye on our company and judges our behavior as a citizen in the community. Its judgment is based on such inputs as:

What our employees have to say about our personnel policy
What our suppliers say about our business practices
The appearance of our facility
Our responsiveness to community activities and problems

Those judgments then contribute to a climate, which can help or hinder our operations. In extreme cases the climate can become a critical influence on our ability to meet our goals.

Accordingly, the public is to be regarded as a customer despite the fact that its members may not be clients. So in looking at the needs of our customers, we must not overlook the needs of the public.

ON TO CUSTOMERS' NEEDS

Up to now we have concentrated on identifying customers. The next step on the quality planning road map is to determine the needs of those customers. That step is the subject of Chapter Three, "What Are the Customers' Needs?"

SUMMARY

The first step in quality planning is to identify who are the customers.

To identify customers, follow the product to see whom it impacts. Anyone who is impacted is a customer.

To follow the product, prepare a flow diagram of the process that produces the product.

Under the Pareto principle, customers can be classified into two basic categories:

A relative few ("vital few"), each of whom is of great importance to us.

A relative large number of customers, each of whom is of modest importance to us ("useful many").

"Vital few" customers include large original equipment manufacturers (OEM), large merchants, upper managers.

"Useful many" customers include consumers, merchants, the workforce, processors, and the public.

] 3 [

What Are the Needs of Customers?

THE MISSION FOR THIS CHAPTER

The mission is to determine what the needs of the customers are. Figure 3–1 shows the input–output diagram.

The *input* is the list of customers as developed in Chapter Two.

The *process* is a sort of marketing research applied internally as well as externally.

The *output* is the list of needs of the customers.

VARIETIES OF CUSTOMERS' NEEDS

The subject of human needs is quite complex, because human beings are complex. As we dig into the subject, we soon discover a lot below the surface.

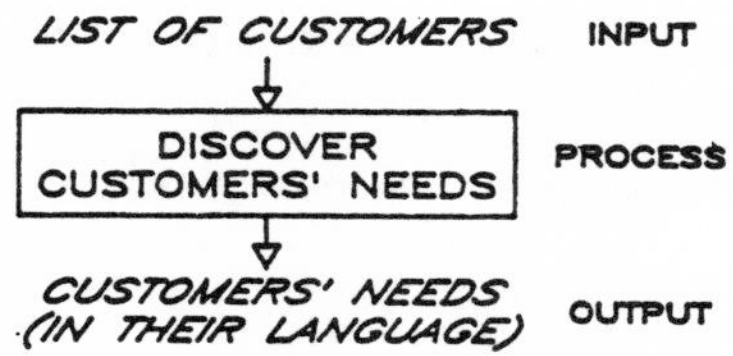

FIGURE 3–1 The input–output diagram for "What are the needs of customers?"

Stated Needs and Real Needs

Customers commonly state their needs as seen from their viewpoint, and in their own language. That is especially the case with those external customers who are also clients. A common example involves the purchase of goods.

Clients may state their needs in terms of the goods they wish to buy. Their real needs, however, are for the services those goods can provide. To illustrate:

CLIENT WISHES TO BUY	CLIENT REALLY WANTS
Food	Nourishment, pleasant taste
Automobile	Transportation
Color TV	Entertainment
House	Living space
House paint	Colorful appearance, freedom from maintenance

Understanding the needs of clients requires answers to questions like this:

Why are you buying this product?

What service do you expect from it?

How to raise such questions is a subject in its own right. We shall look at that subject later in this chapter under the heading "Communicate with Customers."

Perceived Needs

Customers understandably state their needs based on their perceptions. Some of those perceptions are product-related. Others have little to do with the product—they have their origin in some mysterious world which we will call the "cultural pattern." We shall refer to the resulting needs as "cultural needs." Either way, the perceptions of our customers often differ from our perceptions. Our view of the product differs. We live in a different world of cultural patterns. The differences in perception are perennial troublemakers.

Perceived Needs, Product Related

We have numerous cases in which products are "alike," but the customers' perceptions are otherwise.

> A man in need of a haircut has the option of going to (1) a barbershop inhabited by barbers or (2) a "salon" inhabited by "hair stylists." The end result is the same. Either way he is shorn by a skilled artisan. Either way he emerges with the same outward appearance. What differs is (1) his remaining assets and (2) his sense of well-being.
>
> What applies to services also applies to physical goods.
>
> There are factories in which chocolate-coated candies are carried by a belt to the packaging department. At the end of the belt are two teams of packagers. One team packs the chocolates into modest cardboard boxes destined for budget-priced merchant shops. The other team packs the chocolates into satin-lined wooden boxes destined to be sold in deluxe shops. The resulting price for a like amount of chocolate can differ by severalfold. The respective purchasers encounter other differences as well: the decor, the extent of service, the box. However, the chocolates are identical. In fact, when any chocolate reaches the packers, it has no way of predicting whether it will end up in the budget shops or in the deluxe shop.

In both cases—the haircut and the chocolates—some customers pay handsomely for perceived differences. The chocolate company accepted that reality and organized its business so as to take advantage of it. Some suppliers may consider the customers' perceptions as "unreal," but in such cases it is the suppliers who may pay handsomely.

> A steel mill lost some of its sales of stainless steel for reasons unrelated to the quality of the steel. The client in question was a machine shop that made stainless steel fittings to be sold to companies in the aerospace industry. Those companies stressed cleanliness in the workshops. (Some of those fittings were on the moon.) The machine shop observed that the stainless steel as received was dirty, oily, and wrapped in a nondescript manner. In contrast, a competing steel mill delivered its steel in a clean, neatly wrapped condition. When the steel com-

pany's salesmen explained all that to the factory, the reaction was: "The steel will make good fittings. The customer is crazy."

In other cases the supplier who learns of customers' perceived needs designs a new approach to mutual advantage.

A fish merchant who displayed his fish in transparent wrappings encountered consumer resistance. All clients wanted fresh fish, but some were suspicious—to them wrapped fish were less than fresh. The merchant then created an additional display case in which unwrapped fish were displayed on ice. That satisfied the resistant customers. Other customers preferred the wrapped fish. But all the fish, wrapped and unwrapped, had been bought the same morning at the Fulton Fish Market.

In this case the real need was fresh fish. Some customers had the perception that only unwrapped fish were fresh. Other customers accepted on faith that the wrapped fish were fresh. The merchant designed his affairs to satisfy all customers' perceptions.

Cultural Needs

The needs of customers, especially internal customers, go beyond products and processes. They include needs for job security, self-respect, respect of others, continuity of habit patterns, and still other elements of what is broadly called cultural values. While such needs are real, they are seldom stated openly. Instead they are stated in disguised form.

A widespread example is "turf"—that is, the "ownership" of some area of responsibility, expertise, or the like. Such ownership confers status; a threat to the ownership is a threat to that status.

A proposed new process threatens to eliminate the need for some human expertise; the expertise will be built into the technology. The present human experts will resist introduction of the new process. Their reasons will be on plausible grounds—the effect on costs, on other customer needs, and so forth. The one reason they will not give is: "This change will reduce my status."

Similarly, there may be resistance to the creation of teams to conduct analyses in areas formerly regarded as a monopoly of some expert. (The "Not Invented Here" syndrome is traceable to this same fierce protection of turf.)

The lesson is that we should be alert to the possibility of real needs behind the stated needs. In the case of cultural resistance, the real needs are seldom obvious—the disguises are usually subtle. What we must learn to do is look beyond the stated needs to understand what are the potential threats to the subsurface needs of the human beings who are impacted. It is often possible to invent ways of meeting most of those personal needs while meeting company needs. However, we must first learn what those personal needs are.

Needs Traceable to Unintended Use

Many quality failures arise because the customer uses the product in a manner different from that intended by the supplier. The practice takes many forms. Untrained workers are assigned to processes requiring trained workers. Equipment is overloaded or is allowed to run without adherence to maintenance schedules. Documents are misfiled. Priorities are given to nonquality parameters.

The critical point in all this is whether the quality planning should proceed based on intended use or on actual use. The latter requires adding a factor of safety during the planning. That adds to the cost. Yet it might be the optimal result, in view of the higher cost arising from actual use or misuse. (The analysis might find that the optimum lies somewhere between these extremes.)

In any event, the need is to learn what will be the actual use (and misuse) and what are the associated costs. Also, what are the consequences of adhering to intended use? Acquiring such information obviously requires close teamwork between supplier and customer.

SYSTEMATIC ORGANIZATION OF NEEDS

In industrial societies the needs of customers become quite numerous. Of course, various industries arise to meet those needs. But even within any one industry the needs are still so numerous that planners have evolved systematic approaches to deal with such large numbers. One of those systems organizes customers' needs into a logical interrelated pyramid of needs: primary, secondary, tertiary, and so forth.

THE PYRAMID OF NEEDS

Health is obviously a primary human need. As seen by many "customers," health consists of meeting such secondary needs as alertness, not getting tired, enjoying meals, sleeping well, prompt recovery from ailments, and looking good.

In turn, the secondary need of "alertness" breaks down into tertiary needs such as good vision, good hearing, quick reflexes, and others. We can show the pyramid of needs for health care with a graphic model (Figure 3–2).

Such proliferation extends to goods as well as to services. The automobile is a widely understood example. The primary customer needs are safety, comfort, economy, spaciousness, durability, appearance, and so on (not necessarily in that order). One of those needs—economy—gives rise to such secondary customer needs as low purchase price, high trade-in value, low financing cost, low operating and maintenance cost, and high resale value.

In turn, the secondary need of low operating and maintenance cost breaks down into such tertiary needs as warranty coverage, fuel efficiency, dependability, and adequate service.

Figure 3–3 shows the pyramid of needs for the automobile in graphic form.

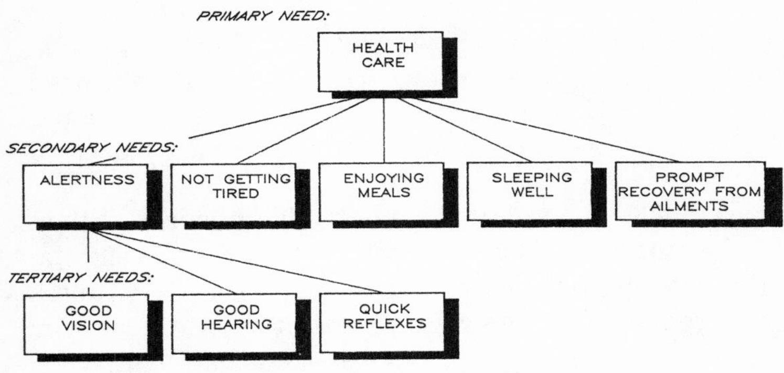

FIGURE 3–2 Pyramid of needs (health care example)

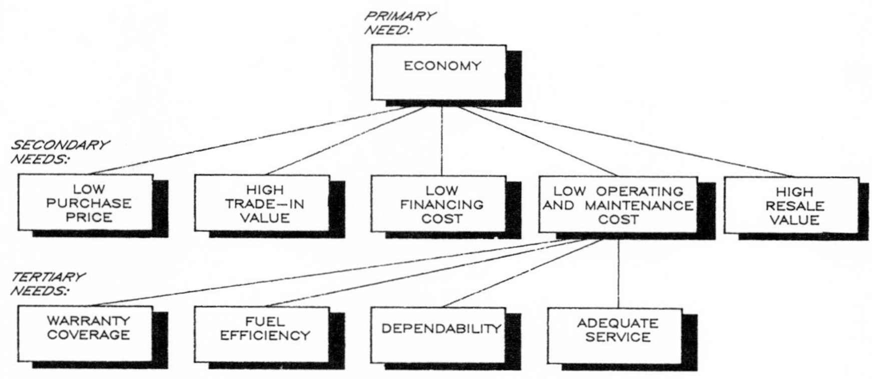

FIGURE 3–3 Pyramid of needs (an automobile example)

In planning for quality, it is necessary to analyze customer needs down to secondary, tertiary and, in complex cases, still further. The reason is that the analysis has value. It adds to our knowledge of customer needs. There is also an end point to the subdivision. It does not go on and on ad infinitum. An end point is reached whenever customer needs become known with such precision that further subdivision provides no added knowledge of customer needs.

Despite the fact that customer needs can become very numerous, each requires specific quality planning. Each requires means of measurement, a goal, a product design, and a process design. To simplify life for the planner, and to make sure that nothing is missed, the needs are arrayed in some orderly fashion.

Graphic Model

One such arrangement is a graphic model, as in Figures 3–2 and 3–3. In each case, the top block shows a primary customer need. That need is then "exploded" into secondary needs, as shown in the middle row of blocks. Then one of those secondary needs is exploded into tertiary needs.

The graphic model is "user friendly," but only for small numbers of needs. As the numbers grow, the blocks proliferate. To show all the blocks then requires wall-sized maps or, alternatively, miniaturized (and illegible) blocks. To make matters worse, there is no convenient space for marking in the subsequent planning activities.

THE SPREADSHEET

A second form of orderly arrangement is the spreadsheet. In the spreadsheet, the customers' needs are listed in the left-hand column so that each horizontal row is devoted to a single need. Distinction among primary, secondary, and tertiary needs is made by differences in the amount of indentation from the left-hand margin. Figure 3–4 is a spreadsheet listing some customer needs for health care. Figure 3–5 similarly lists some customer needs for automotive travel.

In each case only the left-hand columns of the spreadsheet have been filled in. The remaining (vertical) columns are then filled in as the quality planning progresses. The columns will show such information as product features, process features, units of measure, and goals. The intersections of rows and columns are in due course filled in to show the planning decisions. (All this will evolve in subsequent chapters of this textbook.)

The spreadsheet gets around the limitations of the graphic model (Figure 3–2) by adding more and more spreadsheets. A large planning project will accumulate quite a large book of spreadsheets. A personal computer with a spreadsheet program is a useful aid to building and maintaining a spreadsheet. The spreadsheet illustrations in this chapter (Figures 3–4 and 3–5) and in following chapters were prepared on an IBM PC using the program called LOTUS 1-2-3.

Note: Spreadsheets must be prepared for the needs of *internal* customers as well as external customers. Many quality planning projects are concerned with internal processes and procedures whose impact is mainly on internal customers.

THE PROCESSES FOR DISCOVERING CUSTOMERS' NEEDS

The chief processes are the following:

Be a customer

Communicate with customers

Simulate customers' use

Let's look at each of them more closely.

WHERE WE ARE ON THE SPREADSHEET:

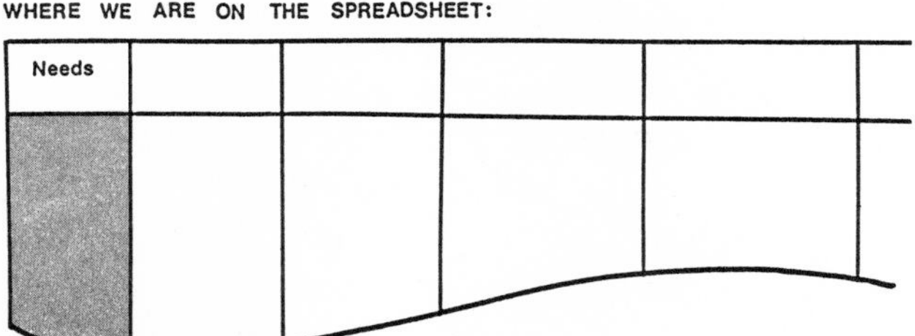

NEEDS		
PRIMARY	SECONDARY	TERTIARY
Health care	Alertness	Good vision
		Good hearing
		Quick reflexes
	Not getting tired	
	Enjoying meals	
	Sleeping well	
	Prompt recovery from ailments	
	Looking good	

FIGURE 3–4 The quality planning spreadsheet: Customer needs (the health care example)

The Cooper

Here is a village craftsman, a cooper. He starts with an oak tree and ends up with a barrel. Let's give him a nickname: Coop. If we look back at The Spiral (Figure 1–1), we see that *Coop does everything.* He performs every activity except ultimate use of the

WHERE WE ARE ON THE SPREADSHEET:

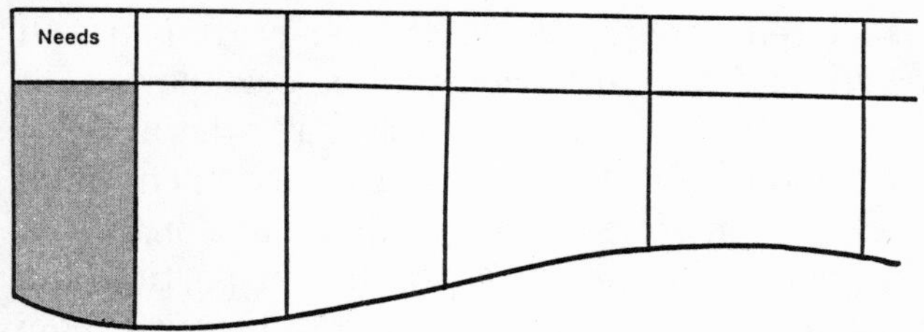

NEEDS		
PRIMARY	SECONDARY	TERTIARY
Economy	Low purchase price	
	High trade-in value	
	Low financing cost	
	Low operating and maintenance cost	Warranty coverage
		Fuel efficiency
		Dependability
		Adequate service
	High resale value	

FIGURE 3–5 The quality planning spreadsheet: Customer needs (the automobile example)

product. Even there, Coop personally sells the barrel to the ultimate user, and he receives any feedback direct from that ultimate user.

All this throws much light on how Coop manages to attain high quality and the associated reputation of a good craftsman. Of course, he had learned his trade and acquired experience in that trade. But Coop also participates widely in the many detailed activities around The Spiral: feedback from ultimate users; choice of product design; selection of materials; design and maintenance of tools; conduct of the production process; product inspection and test; marketing; customer service. As Coop works his way from phase to phase of The Spiral *he becomes his own customer, over and over again.* There is no surer way of discovering what are the needs of customers. And there is no shorter feedback loop. All those direct, multiple feedbacks go far to explain why Coop has become so surefooted in meeting customers' needs.

The Innkeeper

In the same way that Coop attains high product quality in the manufacturing sector, the Village Innkeeper—let's call him Hearthside—is able to accomplish the same thing in the service sector. To a considerable extent, Hearthside is his own customer. He lives on the same premises as his guests. He is served by the same staff. His meals and beverages come from the same pots and kegs as are used to serve his guests. His horses are housed in the same stables as those of his guests. Of course he gets considerable feedback from his clients, but being his own customer adds a good deal to his understanding of customers' needs.

Training

Obviously, if we could arrange matters so that everyone in the company participated as widely around The Spiral as Coop and Hearthside, it would help us a lot in identifying needs of customers. Some companies do expose certain key managers and professional specialists directly to multiple activities around The Spiral. For example, some hotel chains require prospective hotel managers to work successively in the various hotel departments—dining room, housekeeping, finance, reception, and so on. Similar rotational practices are followed by some members of other chains, e.g., banks, supermarkets. Certain Japanese manufacturing companies give their product designers training that includes the following participation:

In the factory they spend time at various production stations so that they *make* the kinds of product they will be designing.

In retail stores they *sell* the kinds of products they will be designing.

In service shops they *repair* the kinds of product they will be designing.

Two Ways to "Be a Customer"

So far we have looked at two ways to "be a customer":

1. Design jobs so that, like the village cooper or innkeeper, a person is directly exposed to many customers' needs.
2. Establish a training course that temporarily exposes people to many needs beyond those directly visible within their respective jobs.

Now let us turn to the second of those processes for discovering needs of customers.

COMMUNICATE WITH CUSTOMERS

Communication with customers is the most widely used way of discovering customers' needs. It is adaptable to a great many types of supplier–customer relationships.

Customer-Initiated Communication

A good deal of the communication takes place at the initiative of customers. In the case of external customers it takes the forms of complaints, returns, claims, and others (including lawsuits). Each of those product *dissatisfactions* requires individual redress. Collectively they can also be a threat to the marketability of our product.

Internal customers also take the initiative to communicate cases of product dissatisfaction. Those are usually stimulated by costs and delays traceable to poor quality received from supplier departments. Each such case demands redress. Collectively they can add up to a shockingly high cost of poor quality. They are also a threat to morale—to the ability of company personnel to work together as a team.

Most companies take seriously the reported instances of product dissatisfaction. They do provide redress and otherwise try to retain the customer and his good will.

It is otherwise with the dissatisfactions collectively. Many companies fail to summarize the data so as to identify the vital few chronic problems. Those that do so often lack the organization machinery needed to attack and eliminate the chronic problems. In consequence, many failure-prone product features are carried over from model to model. Many incapable processes are likewise carried over. That should not go on, but it does, mainly because the planning process fails to deal adequately with the dissatisfactions collectively.

Supplier-Initiated Communication

Beyond communication on product *dissastisfaction,* suppliers also need communication on product *satisfaction*—why customers buy the product. Note that product dissatisfaction and product satisfaction *are not opposites.* Information about product dissatisfaction (complaints, returns, claims) comes to us mainly because customers take the initiative. Information about product satisfaction seldom comes to us through customers' initiatives. Instead, *we* must take the initiative to conduct the necessary marketing researches. (A product may give no product dissatisfaction and yet not be salable because a competing product gives better performance or greater value.)

Communication Through Behavior

Communication with customers is not limited to verbal methods, oral or written. Some of the most revealing communication is derived from study of behavior.

> Marriott Hotels observed that guests were ignoring complimentary bath crystals. So the company dropped them in favor of another free feature—cable television—which was far better received.

MARKETING RESEARCH—EXTERNAL

To discover the quality needs of customers we make use of the tools of marketing research. As a minimum we need answers to the following questions:

Which product features are of primary importance to you?

As to those key features, how does our product compare to that of our competitors?

What is the significance of those quality differences to you, in money or in other ways that might be important to you?

Beyond those basic questions we need to establish an atmosphere that permits a free flow of open-ended, supplemental questions as well.

In market research it is quite common to discover the existence of needs that are important to customers but are not on the list of the companies supplying the goods or services. The case of the housewives who were unhappy with certain nonrepair aspects of service calls is an example (page 49). In other cases such hidden needs can affect salability of the product. An example is the steel mill that lost some of its sales of stainless steel for reasons unrelated to the quality of the steel itself (pages 36–37).

The key questions above are basic to all marketing research. However, the research must be specially tailored to the various kinds of customer. A number of such special applications are discussed below.

Vital Few Clients

Normally the vital few are contacted individually to determine their quality needs. Often such clients take the initiative to define their needs. The definition may consist of broad performance requirements. Alternatively, the definition may consist of detailed product specifications. Either way, the supplier should try to go below the surface, to determine what will be the actual use, and what the real needs are.

Some suppliers are tempted to avoid the added effort of going below the surface. They reason that if they meet the clients' stated needs, they are "covered." That may well be true from a legal standpoint, but it is not true from the standpoint of long-range client relations.

Every client wants fitness for use—product satisfaction and freedom from failure. The supplier who has conformed to requirements but failed to achieve fitness for use may stand his ground: "I met the terms of the contract." However, that does not solve the client's problem, and the client does not cheerfully go "back to the drawing board." If the client is unable to get fitness for use from his supplier, next time around he will be looking for a supplier whose policy is to meet the real needs of clients.

Nonclients

It is easy to be fooled if we confine our marketing research to clients.

> A chemicals manufacturer asked its clients to rank the company relative to its competitors on various aspects of performance: product innovation, quality, promptness of delivery, technical assistance, and so on. The company was quite pleased to learn that it was ranked first, second, or third in virtually all aspects of performance.
>
> Then someone noted that the study was biased—it included no nonclients. So a supplemental research was conducted, with special attention to former clients: Why had they stopped buying? This time the research findings were less than pleasing.

Processors

Processor customers are also *users*. They employ our product in their processes. In their capacity as users their needs include worker safety, high productivity, low waste, and still other forms of internal goals. The processors then sell their products to *their* customers, whose needs may be quite different. In effect there are two lists of customer needs, and our product may impact some of the items on each list. In cases involving successive processing companies, our product may impact multiple lists.

Our customer usually supplies us with some information relative to certain of his customers' needs that must be met by our product. However, this information is sometimes limited to product dissatisfaction or is otherwise incomplete. In such cases we may need to go beyond our customer and conduct research to determine more fully the needs of the subsequent levels of customers.

Merchants

As with processors, our product impacts multiple levels of customers: our clients, our clients' clients, and so forth. If we also sell to many small merchants, it can become prohibitive to contact each one in depth. Instead, resort can be had to sampling. A common form of sampling is through an "advisory council" or "dealers' council."

In other cases the "merchants" buy for ultimate use, e.g., hospitals who buy medical devices and supplies. There the council typically consists of specialists—e.g., physicians, nurses—from a variety of disciplines and is designated by a broad name such as professional council.

Ultimate Users—Consumers

To a degree, we can secure information about consumer reaction from such intermediaries as merchants or salespersons. However, those intermediate sources are themselves impacted by their own needs. The impacts can and do introduce bias into the views of the intermediaries. In consequence, if there is enough at stake, we should arrange to secure information directly from consumers.

> In a large service department an in-depth sampling of consumers disclosed dissatisfactions that were not being reported to the company. Housewives were irritated by servicemen who smoked cigars, left mud on the floors, and failed to clean up their own debris. While the housewives did not complain to the company, they had a lot to tell their friends.

Contact with consumers is carried out in a variety of ways: questionnaires, phone calls, consumer panels. All of those ways require the use of sampling, and that in turn, requires special techniques (see "The Sampling Concept," pages 56–57).

An example of such contact is a Qantas Airways survey of 2,500 passengers to secure their views on priority of "essential needs." The results contained surprises as well as confirmations. For example, the company managers had given high ranking to on-time departures and arrivals. It came as a surprise that those needs were not given high priority by the passengers surveyed.

QANTAS AIRWAYS
Survey of Passenger Needs: Order of Priority

"Essential Needs"

1. No lost baggage
2. No damaged baggage
3. Clean toilets
4. Comfortable seats
5. Prompt baggage delivery
6. Ample leg room
7. Good quality meals
8. Prompt reservation service
9. Friendly/efficient cabin crew
10. Clean and tidy cabin
11. Comfortable cabin temperature/humidity
12. Assistance with connections
13. Being kept informed of delays
14. Transport to cities
15. Accurate arrival information to relatives/friends
16. Well-organized boarding
17. Quick/friendly airport check-in
18. Self-service baggage trolleys
19. On-time arrival
20. Provision of pillows/rugs
21. Assistance with customs/immigration
22. On-time departures

Consumers rely heavily on their own *human senses* to arrive at perceptions about quality. The resulting perceptions are obviously influential in consumers' decisions on what to buy. It therefore becomes important for industrial companies to learn what those perceptions are and, as far as possible, to discover the detailed cause-and-effect relationship between consumer perceptions and the decisions to buy.

It is well known that the unaided human senses are unable to evaluate or even to sense many of the technological properties of complex products. Nevertheless, consumers make decisions as to whether to buy complex products, and as to which of the competing products to buy. Those decisions are based in part on perceptions derived from human sensing. Such perceptions can easily be erroneous, but consumers rely on them all the same.

It is tempting for technologists to discount the value of consumer perceptions, which can so easily be biased by technological illiteracy. The perceptions are indeed biased, but since they influence sales they are realities to be understood and faced, not ignored.

Companies face these realities in various ways, namely:

1. They accept some consumer perceptions, bias and all, and then design products and practices to respond to those consumer perceptions.

Thomas Edison tried to anticipate a degree of technological illiteracy on the consumer's part when he designed the first electrical lighting system in New York City in 1882. In every way possible the unfamiliar electrical system was made to look like the familiar and trusted gas lighting system—the appearance of the lighting fixtures, the quality and intensity of the light, the nomenclature, and so on.

2. They try to change consumer perceptions by such methods as providing consumers with new experiences that will result in changes in perceptions. For example, they provide low-cost (or no cost) opportunities for trial use of products.

In 1983, as part of its program to market the IBM PC (Personal Computer), IBM Corporation displayed the PC in the concourse areas of a number of large airports. A passing traveler could stop and experiment with the PC via a simple keyboard on the outside of the display case.

3. They publish technological data and propaganda to stimulate changes in perception.

Makers of microwave ovens maintained a propaganda campaign for many years to gain public acceptance of a novel process for food preparation.

Children are a special case of consumers and are the source of some delightful marketing researches.

> An architect who specializes in designing playgrounds begins each design project with a lengthy interview with a group of children from the community in which the playground will be built. He emphasizes to the children that they are the experts. In a highly interactive session the children offer many suggestions as to what their ideal playground would contain.
>
> Later that day the children can view the preliminary sketch for the project and offer comment on it. The project plan includes securing donations of material from the community. On an appointed day community volunteers, including parents and children, meet to construct the playground.
>
> In like manner, toy designers use children as a source of inputs on customer needs. Some of the children are not yet able to speak, so it is necessary to create an environment (a playroom) that permits the behavior of children at play to answer such questions as:
>
> Is the toy safe?
>
> Is the toy fun?
>
> Can it be thrown about without breaking?
>
> Is it easy to handle?
>
> Will it spark imaginative play?
>
> Does it have extended play value?
>
> What ages is it best suited for?

Ultimate Users—Others

Other ultimate users are mostly employees of organizations that buy products to be used by employees. The products are goods and services of every imaginable sort: utility services, equipment, supplies. As repetitive users, the employees (like consumers) become experts in many aspects of product performance, environmental influences, and so on. Their expertise is obviously a valuable source of information about customer needs.

Some, perhaps most, of the information works its way up the customer's organizational hierarchy to the technical specialists and purchasing managers. They in turn are in a position to transmit the information to the suppliers. However, the transmission is seldom complete. Many suppliers have devised ways to secure supplemental information directly from the ultimate users and have been amply rewarded. An example is the "professional council" of doctors and nurses, created by manufacturers of health products used in hospitals.

The Public

To some degree we can learn of the public's perceptions through study of the outward evidence: complaints directly to us, letters to the editor, protest meetings. In some cases that evidence may give a distorted picture: It represents only a small, vocal minority. However, in other cases the evidence may suggest that a broad problem is in the making. In that event it may be well to conduct a structured public opinion survey to secure a more balanced, quantified understanding of the public's perception. (Some companies do not wait for matters to reach a problem state. They conduct periodic public opinion surveys to discover trends long before they grow into crises.)

Public opinion surveys are carried out in much the same way as marketing research. We identify the questions to which we need answers. We then contact a sample of the public to secure the answers. The sampling methods follow those used for discovering the needs of large populations: consumers, employees, and so forth.

"MARKETING RESEARCH"—INTERNAL

To carry out quality planning we must also learn what the needs of internal customers are. To do so we make use of the same tools as we use for getting information about needs of external customers: sampling, questionnaires, interviews, conferences. However, we seldom apply the term "marketing research" to internal customers. Instead we use such terms as "survey" or "study."

Middle Managers and Professionals

As internal customers, middle managers and professionals usually make up about 10 percent of the employee population, but their influence on quality is considerable. Their great influence demands that such customers be consulted in depth as to the needs of their respective organizations with respect to quality. Determining the needs of managers is done in two principal ways:

A MULTIDEPARTMENTAL TEAM. Teams are often set up to conduct joint planning. It is quite effective. Every team member is of course an expert as to his area of the flow diagram: the inputs to that area, the process carried out in that area, the resulting product, the immediate customers for that product. However, he is not necessarily expert with respect to other areas of the flow diagram and the resulting mutual interactions. The multidepartmental team makes it possible for all members to broaden their view. In doing so they are able to propound questions that, when answered, clarify the mutual needs.

MAKING THE ROUNDS. A specialist is assigned to contact those departments which are significantly impacted by the project undergoing planning. Based on the findings, the specialist prepares a draft, which is then sent to the managers for review.

Quite often the impacted departments are in *different companies*. In theory the same concept of joint planning should be applied. In practice that is difficult, especially in an adversary environment. The most common forms of such collaboration include:

Joint teams of supplier and customer personnel

Customers' visits to suppliers' locations to learn about suppliers' problems of processing while providing information about customers' needs

Suppliers' visits to customers' locations to acquire information concerning needs

Trained specialists' visits to the locations of both suppliers and customers and later publication of a report for the information of all

The Workforce

The workforce is a large body of internal customers with much expertise relative to their jobs (see page 30). That expertise can be a valuable input to quality planning, but special steps are needed to acquire and transmit the information.

To acquire such information from the workforce we often must overcome certain inherent biases that may be present:

An atmosphere of blame If present, it always inhibits the free flow of communications.

The supervisor–subordinate relationship The fact that the boss asks the question tends to influence the answer the subordinate gives.

Conflict in loyalties Workers may be wary of communicating information that might create problems for their colleagues, the union, or someone else.

Overcoming such biases requires the use of special tools and precautions in data collection and analysis. A case example will make this clear.

At a manufacturing plant, a joint committee of managers and workmen held regular meetings to discuss quality and productivity. At one meeting a grinding machine operator complained of oversize parts coming to him from an earlier process in the lathe department. The plant superintendent answered by saying, "The lathe operators know they're supposed to make that part on the low side of the allowable size range. I'll tell them again." In one sentence, he managed to invoke three biases:

1. He created an atmosphere of blame: "It's the lathe operators' fault."

2. He cut off further discussion of a genuine problem by "pulling rank," that is, using his status as boss. The implication was, "Don't bring it up again."

3. He made the grinding machine operator feel that to open his mouth further would make more trouble for the lathe operators.

That was a remarkable negative accomplishment, considering that the plant climate was sufficiently informal to support such a promising meeting in the first place.

Happily, an observer managed to bring together the two operators of the respective machines—grinder and lathe. They soon determined that the real cause of the trouble was *conflicting engineering drawings.*

Note that in the above case a key element of the solution was creation of a *team*. The two machine operators were in a supplier–customer relationship. Once they were able to join forces, their communication and their ability to find common ground rose remarkably.

THE SAMPLING CONCEPT

In our efforts to identify customer needs we do not contact each member of the "useful many" in depth. Instead, we contact them on a limited basis. For example, we may contact all of the useful many customers through a questionnaire focusing on selected quality needs. Alternatively, we may select a sample of the useful many customers, contact each in depth, and then draw broad conclusions from the results of the sampling.

The sampling approach offers a practical, cost-effective way for securing information from the useful many. However, valid application of the sampling concept requires the use of certain special tools and skills in matters such as:

Choice of sample (the "panel"), whether at random, stratified, or otherwise

Conditions prevailing during collection of information, whether natural or controlled

Sample sizes that ensure statistical significance

Avoidance of bias during data collection

To illustrate, during the 1970s, AT&T operated a telephone survey program called TELSAM (telephone service attitude measurement). TELSAM measured customer attitude toward the residential telephone service as provided by the operating companies of the Bell System.

The sample of persons interviewed was drawn, with the aid of computers, from residential customers of all of the operating companies. It included only persons who had recently dialed a call or had recent contact with an operator, a business office, a repairman, an installer, or a salesperson. The questions pertained only to their latest encounter with the telephone company.

Each interview was conducted by a trained interviewer, by telephone; the customer was always telephoned at home. The questions were standardized; responses were fed to a computer for analysis. A summary of responses was prepared each month and distributed to the managers.

SIMULATE CUSTOMERS' USE

A third way to identify needs of customers is to simulate customers' use.

The early phases of training airline pilots are carried out in cockpits which have no wings.

Numerous product quality comparison tests are conducted by trained specialists under controlled laboratory conditions, rather than by a consumer panel under conditions of actual use.

Automobiles undergoing crash tests are inhabited by lifeless dummies.

Many product design ideas are first worked out through mathematical simulation. Then a model is constructed in the model shop to be tested in the laboratory.

Simulation has certain advantages over study during actual use. During simulation we are able to exclude unwanted variables. Such exclusion enables us to determine with greater precision the effect of specific quality features on overall fitness for use. In addition, simulation is less costly than market research under actual field conditions.

Simulation also has limitations. Laboratory conditions do not fully represent operating conditions; they are "an imitation of the real thing." (That is the literal meaning of simulation.)

We shall have a closer look at simulation in future chapters. In those chapters we shall also see that there are ways of reducing the risks we take when we deal with an imitation instead of the real thing.

CUSTOMERS' NEEDS—A MOVING TARGET

Customers' needs do not remain static. There is no such thing as a final list of customers' needs.

We are beset by powerful forces that keep coming over the horizon and are ever changing directions: new technology, market competition, social upheavals, international conflicts. Those changing forces create new customers' needs or change the priority given to existing ones.

> In the early 1970s an international cartel was able to raise the price of crude oil nearly tenfold. As a result, the need for "low fuel consumption" rose remarkably in the scale of priorities. In turn, this cascaded down to raise the priority of such customers' needs as fuel efficiency of engines, weight of motor vehicles, weight of components, and so on.

The same powerful forces usually affect the company in more ways than merely the effect on quality. The strategic business planners know this; their planning process includes a study of those forces to judge their likely impact on the company and to take responsive measures.

There is a corresponding need to conduct periodic strategic planning for quality. A critical element in that planning is identifying those powerful forces and examining their impact on customers' needs and their priorities. In the absence of such strategic planning, we overlook essential early warning and thereby encounter unpleasant surprises and crisis situations, with resulting urgencies, wastes, and irritations. In a later chapter we shall look at strategic quality planning in some detail.

ON TO TRANSLATION

Once we "know" what the customers' needs are, the next steps would seem to be: Develop the products and processes required to meet those needs. We shall take those steps in later chapters of this book, but first we must take some essential intermediate steps:

Translate customers' needs into *our* language

Establish units of measure so we can communicate with precision

Establish systems of measurement (sensors) so we can express quality in terms of those units of measure

The next chapter therefore deals with the translation process.

SUMMARY

To understand customers' needs we should go beyond stated needs and discover the unstated needs as well.

Customers' perceptions may seem "unreal" to us, but they are a reality to customers and hence must be taken seriously.

Customers' needs include cultural needs, which are seldom stated openly.

Some customer needs are traceable to uses unintended by the supplier.

Customers' needs are so numerous as to require an orderly arrangement.

The spreadsheet is the chief mechanism for such orderly arrangement.

Methods of discovering customers' needs include:

Be a customer

Communciate with customers

Simulate customers' use

Communication on product dissatisfaction is usually at the initiative of customers, through complaints and the like.

Communication on product satisfaction is usually at our initiative, through marketing research.

Product dissatisfaction and product satisfaction are not opposites.

Marketing research to discover customers' needs requires, as a minimum, answers to the following questions:

Which product features are most important to you?

As to those key features, how does our product compare to that of our competitors?

What is the significance of those quality differences to you, in money or in other ways that might be important to you?

Marketing research must also be specially tailored to fit the various kinds of customer.

Sampling is a practical, cost-effective way of securing information from the "useful many" customers.

To acquire information from consumers requires recognition of the importance of consumer perceptions and of consumer reliance on human senses.

To acquire information from the workforce requires overcoming inherent biases: an atmosphere of blame, the superior–subordinate relationship, conflict in loyalties.

Customers' needs are a moving target.

] *4* [

Translation

THE MISSION FOR THIS CHAPTER

The mission for this chapter is to express customer needs in our (supplier's) language. Figure 4–1 shows the input–output diagram.

The *input* is the list of customer needs as expressed in customers' languages.

The *process* is the translation.

The *output* is the list of customer needs expressed in our language.

THE LANGUAGE PROBLEM

Customer needs may be stated in any of several languages:

The customer's language

Our language

A common language

When customer needs are stated in the customers' language, it becomes necessary to translate such needs into either our language or a common language. That necessity applies to internal customers as well as to external customers.

Vague Terminology

Every day we run into cases in which the identical word has multiple meanings, even within the same company. To some people the word quality means the grade of a product—the features that distinguish the deluxe hotel from the budget hotel. To others the word quality means freedom from errors and failures. To still others the word means good workmanship.

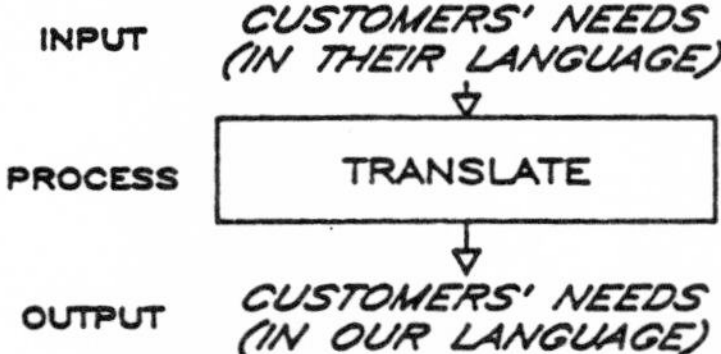

FIGURE 4–1 The input–output diagram for "Translation"

An everyday example of vague terminology is that faced by physicians when examining patients. Diagnosis of ailments requires understanding of the symptoms. In some cases the diagnostic instruments provide extensive and even conclusive information as to the nature of the ailments. In other cases some essential information must come from the patient. The patient must describe in words phenomena that to him may be unprecedented, and for which descriptions in words seems hopelessly inadequate. Yet the physician is faced with translating such vague descriptions into useful information.

At a different level is the translation problem faced by designers of aircraft during debriefing of test pilots. The engineers need information in technological, quantified language. The test pilots (who are the advance guard for ultimate users) describe the performance in terms of human sensing: vibration, bounce, yaw. Together the designers and test pilots can have some memorable dialogues.

Multiple Dialects

Within any company there are multiple functions: finance, personnel, technology, operations. Each function exhibits its own dialect. The company also has multiple levels in the hierarchy, and again there are multiple dialects. At the bottom is the common language of things; at the top is the common language of money. Those in the middle need to be bilingual. Figure 4–2 shows the hierarchy in graphic form.

The situation becomes worse when *multiple companies* are involved.

> The frequent traveler soon learns that his concept of "medium" as applied to a cooked steak is not the same as that of various restaurant chefs.

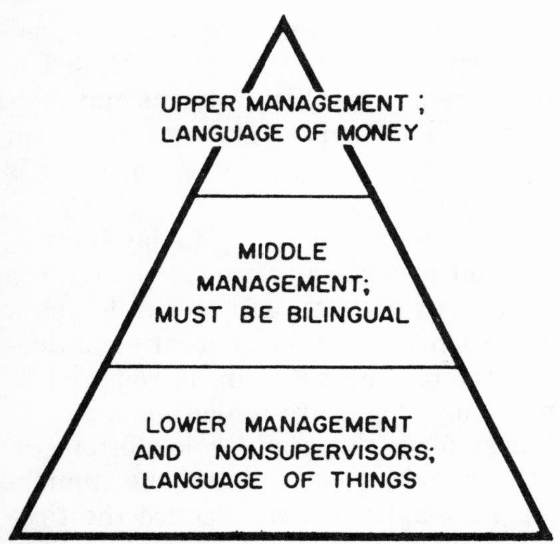

FIGURE 4–2 Common languages in the company

Some industrial companies require that suppliers adopt "self-certification," "just-in-time," "statistical process control," or the like. Such terms have widely different meanings in various companies.

The language problem becomes still more complex when *multiple industries* are involved. It is quite common for industries to evolve, standardize, and perpetuate a unique dialect. Members of the industry are comfortable with that dialect; it was created to help them communicate with each other. However, that dialect becomes an obstacle to communication with outsiders. (The problem is at its worst at multinational levels. We shall stay out of that.)

Remedies

Numerous forms of remedy are available to bridge across languages and dialects. The most usual are listed here:

The glossary
Samples
Special organization to translate
Standardization
Measurement

THE GLOSSARY. One remedy consists of agreeing on the precise meanings of key terms and then publishing the agreements. The publication takes the form of a glossary—a list of terms and their definitions. The publication may be embellished by other forms of communication: sketches, photographs, videotapes. An example is the glossary at the end of this book.

A glossary does not evolve as a by-product of day-to-day communication. Instead, it is the result of a specific project to create a glossary. (Typically, the vagueness goes on and on until such a project is set up.) In addition, such a project is inherently multidepartmental in nature. A multidepartmental team is required to help assemble complete inputs and to ensure full agreement.

The organizational machinery for such a team project often employs a specialist to make the rounds, secure inputs, and summarize them for team review. That approach can reduce the time spent in team meetings while still securing the essential benefits of the team approach.

SAMPLES. Samples take such forms as textile swatches, colored chips, and audio cassettes. They serve as specifications for such product features as appearance of textiles, color of printing, and noise of room air conditioners. They make use of human senses beyond those associated with word images. There are many cases in which such human senses provide better communication than is possible through words.

The concept of samples is not limited to physical goods. Some service companies use video recordings to demonstrate "samples" of good service—courtesy, thoughtfulness, and so on.

As with the glossary, creating samples normally requires specific projects and multidepartmental teams. Some require industry teams and even multi-industry teams.

SPECIAL ORGANIZATION TO TRANSLATE. Another approach is to create a department to do translating on a continuing basis. A common example is the Order Editing Department, which receives orders from clients. Some elements of the orders are in client language. Order Editing translates those elements into our language, e.g., product code numbers or our acronyms. The translated version is then issued as an internal document within our company.

A second example is the Technical Service Department. The specialists there are knowledgeable as to our products. Through their contacts with customers they learn of customer needs. That combined knowledge enables them to assist both companies to communicate, including assistance in translation.

Those and other organized forms of translation serve essential purposes. However, they are costly and, in varying degrees, error-prone. The costs and errors can be reduced by standardization and by establishing units of measure.

STANDARDIZATION. As industries mature they adopt standardization for the mutual benefit of customers and suppliers. Standardization extends to language, products, processes, and so on.

> An air traveler needs to fly from Cleveland to Chicago late in the evening, in economy class, in a nonsmoking area, in a window seat if possible. The airline translates that into flight 455 Y, seat 8A. Here the stated needs consist of departure date and time, class of service, seat location. Not stated but implied are other needs: safety, on time arrival, comfort, courteous service.

In the case of physical goods, standardization is very widely used. Without it a technological society would be a perpetual Tower of Babel.

> A consumer needs illumination for a dark room; the electric bulb has burned out. The dead bulb is marked 110 volts, 60 watts. Armed with that information, the consumer can secure an equivalent replacement.

All organizations make use of short designations for their products: code numbers, acronyms, words, phrases, and so forth. Such standardized nomenclature makes it easy to communicate with internal customers. If external customers adopt the nomenclature, the problem of multiple dialects disappears.

> The airline flight guide publishes flight information for multiple airlines. The information is well standardized. Some clients learn how to read the flight guide. For such clients, communication with the airlines is greatly simplified. In effect, the client translates from his dialect into that of the airlines.

MANAGERIAL PRODUCTS. A critical problem in translation is "products" of a managerial nature. They include: policies, objectives, plans, organization structure, orders (commands), advice, reviews, incentives, and audits. The customers are mainly internal, across all functions and all levels. The problem is to ensure

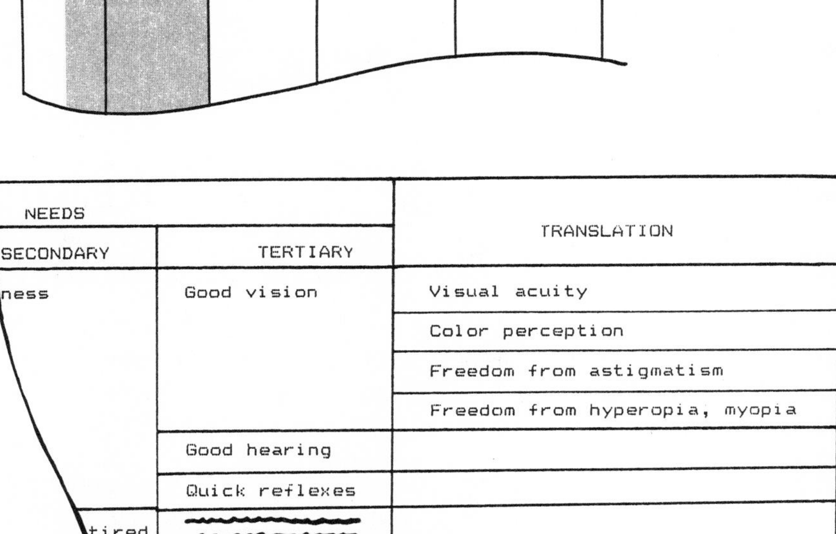

FIGURE 4–3 The quality planning spreadsheet: Translation added (the health care example)

that the internal customers interpret the products in ways intended by the internal suppliers. In turn, there is the problem of ensuring that the responses are made in ways that minimize misunderstanding. The remedies are "all of the above," as summarized on page 69.

MEASUREMENT. The most effective remedy for the language problem is to establish measurement. We shall discuss this approach in the next two chapters.

FITTING THE TRANSLATIONS INTO THE SPREADSHEET

Translations can be fitted into the spreadsheet by entering them into the vertical column adjacent to the list of customer needs. (In some cases no translation is needed—the customer needs are already stated in our language.)

In the case of human health (page 39), the tertiary customer need of good vision might translate into: visual acuity; color perception; freedom from astigmatism, hyperopia, myopia; etc. All of those elements of translation would be entered into the spreadsheet, since they have different units of measure and require different responses in the form of product features. Figure 4–3 updates the health care spreadsheet to show the translations.

Let us go into more detail relative to the case of the automobile (page 42) since we shall be following that example through all of our steps along the quality planning roadmap. The spreadsheet, Figure 3–5 listed some of the primary, secondary and tertiary needs of the customer. Figure 4–4 is a section of a spreadsheet showing certain of those customer needs along with the associated translation into supplier's language.

SUMMARY

Customer needs, expressed in customer's language, are often unclear to us because of vague terminology and multiple dialects.

To assure effective communication, customer needs must be translated into our language.

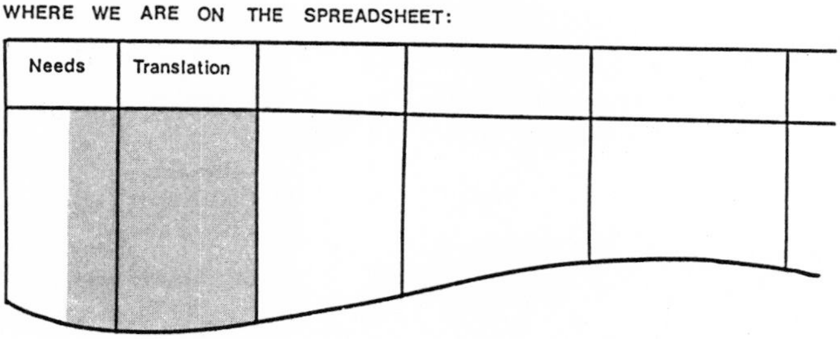

WHERE WE ARE ON THE SPREADSHEET:

Needs	Translation				

NEEDS		TRANSLATION
ECONDARY	TERTIARY	
chase price		
e-in value		
g cost		
and st	Warranty coverage	Length of warranty Extent of coverage
	Fuel efficiency	Distance covered per quantity of fuel
	Dependability	Reliability (freedom from failures)
	Adequate service	Promptness
		Competence
		Courtesy
value		

FIGURE 4–4 The quality planning spreadsheet: Translation added (the automobile example)

The need for translation extends to internal customers as well as external customers.

Remedies for the language problem include:

The glossary
Samples
Special organization to translate
Standardization
Measurement

] 5 [

Establish Units of Measure

THE MISSION OF THIS CHAPTER

The mission is to express customer needs in units of measure. Figure 5-1 shows the input-output diagram.

> The *input* is customer needs as translated into our language.
>
> The *process* is establishment of units of measure.
>
> The *output* is units of measure for the translated customer needs.

THE NEED TO MEASURE

Good quality planning requires precise communication among customers and suppliers. Some of the essential information can be adequately conveyed by words. However, an industrial society increasingly demands higher and higher precision for communicating quality-related information. That higher precision is best attained when we "say it in numbers."

> A widespread customer need is "prompt" service. When promptness is expressed in hours or days (or whatever), precision of communication rises remarkably.

To "say it in numbers" requires that we create a system of measurement consisting of:

> *A unit of measure*—a defined amount of some quality feature, which permits evaluation of that feature in numbers.
>
> *A sensor*—a method or instrument, which can carry out the evaluation and state the findings in numbers, in terms of the unit of measure.

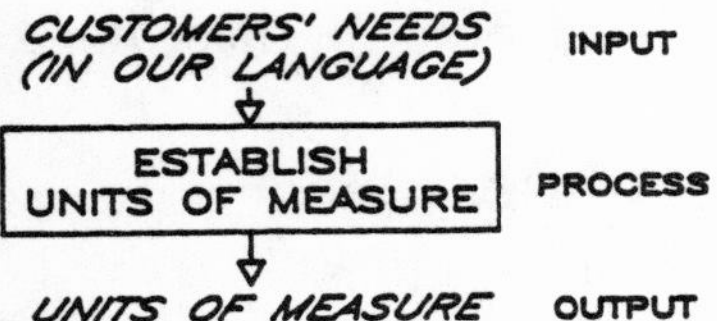

FIGURE 5–1 The input–output diagram for "Establish units of measure"

We shall deal with the unit of measure in this chapter. We shall deal with the sensor in the next chapter.

A Wide Range of Use

Once we have established a system of measurement, we have a common language. We can use that language to help us at each and every step of the quality planning road map:

Evaluation of customer needs and our needs
Evaluation of product and process features
Establishment of optimal product and process goals

The system of measurement is also a great help in the other two processes of the quality trilogy: quality control and quality improvement. In addition, measurement helps us to deal with such other phenomena as economic considerations related to quality:

Value of quality
Salability of quality
Quality of competing products
Cost of attaining quality
Cost of poor quality

THE SPECTRUM OF UNITS OF MEASURE

Quality features must serve a wide spectrum of quality needs: technological, departmental, managerial, and so on. That same variety in turn demands that we establish a wide spectrum of units of measure, each appropriate for the corresponding quality need. Let us have a look at a few species of units of measure contained within the spectrum.

The first species is at the *technological* level. Some of these units of measure are quite familiar to the layman:

QUALITY FEATURE	UNIT OF MEASURE
Distance	Kilometers, miles
Weight	Grams, ounces
Time	Hours, minutes
Electrical current	Amperes
Temperature	Degrees

Other technological units of measure are unfamiliar to most laymen but are well known to the technologists:

QUALITY FEATURE	UNIT OF MEASURE
Heat	Joule
Electric capacitance	Farad
Inductance	Henry
Magnetic flux	Tesla
Angular acceleration	Radians per second squared

A second species of units of measure concerns *product performance.* Here are a few examples:

QUALITY FEATURE	UNIT OF MEASURE
Fuel efficiency	Miles per gallon Kilometers per liter
Timeliness of service	Minutes, hours, days
Continuity of service	Percent "uptime"

A third species of units of measure is associated with *errors and failures:*

QUALITY FEATURE	UNIT OF MEASURE
Defect content in goods	Percent defective; parts per million (ppm); demerits per unit
Field failures	Mean time between failures; maintenance hours per 1,000 operating hours
Service interruption	Percent downtime (the opposite of uptime)
Error content of services	Percent error in billing (or transport, warehousing, etc.)

A fourth species of units of measure includes *functional department performance measures.* To illustrate:

FUNCTIONAL DEPARTMENT	EXAMPLES OF UNITS OF MEASURE
Product Development	Months required to launch new products
Purchasing	Cost of poor quality (from suppliers) per dollar of purchases Percent of reorders due to poor quality
Manufacture	Cost of poor quality per dollar of manufacturing cost
Materials Management	Percent stock-outs
Sales	Percent of orders canceled
Credit	Ratio of bad debts to sales
Finance	Percent of documents containing errors
Field Service	Percent of service calls requiring second call

A fifth species of units of measure involves quality features at the *upper management level.* Interest in this species is a comparatively recent phenomenon, so the subject is still in the early stages of evolution. Here are some examples:

QUALITY FEATURES	UNIT OF MEASURE
Competitiveness in the market place	Ratio of product performance to that of leading competitors
Cost of poor quality	Ratio of cost of poor quality to sales

A sixth species of units of measure concerns *evaluation of managers' performance* on quality-related activities. Often these units of measure are identical with those used to measure departmental quality performance, e.g., percent of error-free product, cost of poor quality versus cost of operations. But sometimes the measures of managers' performance also include evaluation of specific deeds done. For example, during a program to extend training in quality-related matters, measures of managers' performance may include the proportion of subordinates trained.

PRECISE DEFINITION

For all units of measure we need precise definition. In the case of the technological units of measure a good deal of research has gone into defining with extreme precision what is a meter of length or a second of time. For most other units of measure we need not go to extremes, but we do need enough precision to ensure good communication.

Most of what we measure comes in subspecies. Errors may be critical, major, or minor; they may be avoidable or unavoidable; they may be traceable to customer error, product design, purchased services or components, worker error, and so on. If a unit of measure contains the word "error," we must define the word "error" with enough precision to enable us to agree on what to count and what to omit.

UNITS OF MEASURE FOR ABSTRACTIONS

Some quality features seem to stand apart from the world of physical things. Quality of service often includes courtesy as a significant quality feature. Even in the case of physical goods we have quality features such as beauty, taste, aroma, feel, sound. How do we establish units of measure for such abstractions?

One answer is to quantify the number of violations of the abstraction. Safety is an abstraction, but we can count the known instances of lack of safety, that is, the number of accidents. Similarly we can count the instances of lack of courtesy, lack of beauty (presence of blemishes), and so forth. In such cases it is quite common to go a step further and establish an index—a ratio of the number of such instances of "lack of," to the opportunity for such instances, e.g., accidents per million man-hours of exposure.

Note that in such kinds of quantification there is still need to define what an instance of "lack of" is.

Another approach for dealing with abstractions is to break them up into identifiable realities. Hotel room "appearance" is certainly a quality feature, but it also seems like an abstraction. However, we can dig in and identify those specifics which collectively constitute "appearance": the condition of the carpet, lavatory, linens, windows, ashtrays, and so on. Identifying those specifics also simplifies the job of establishing units of measure. (One of the airlines undertook to quantify "aircraft interior appearance." That is obviously a quality feature for an airline.)

THE PYRAMID OF UNITS OF MEASURE

The various units of measure are all interconnected; they constitute a sort of pyramid (Figure 5–2). If we dissect the pyramid, the layers are somewhat as follows:

> At the base of the pyramid are the myriad technological units of measure on individual units of product and on individual elements of service.
>
> In the second layer of the pyramid are units of measure that serve to summarize the basic data, e.g., percent defective for specific processes, documents, product components, service cycles, persons.
>
> Next are units of measure that serve to express quality for entire departments, product lines, classes of service. In large organizations there may be multiple layers of this category of units of measure.

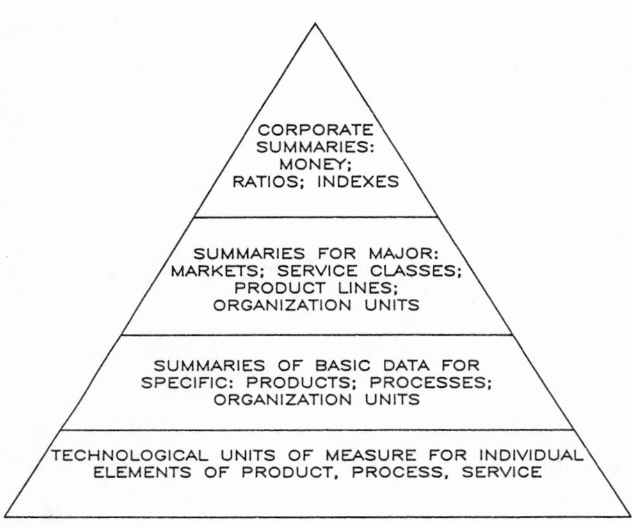

FIGURE 5–2 The pyramid of units of measure

At the top of the pyramid are the financial measures, indexes, ratios, and so on, which serve the needs of the highest levels in the organization: corporate, divisional, functional.

In Chapter Eleven we shall look at the application of the concept of units of measure to Companywide Quality Management.

THE IDEAL UNIT OF MEASURE

Our extensive experience in establishing units of measure enables us to list the main criteria to be met by the ideal unit of measure. The ideal unit of measure:

1. *Provides an agreed basis for decision making.* One purpose of measurement is to provide factual assistance for decision-making by diverse human minds. The greater the validity of the measurement concept, the greater is the likelihood of securing a meeting of those minds.

In the frozen food industry an important crop is peas. For years the food processors bought the peas by weight, but with the proviso that the peas must be tender. Weight could be measured precisely, but there were endless debates about tenderness. A serious complication was the fact that during the ripening period of several days, peas double their weight but lose their tenderness. The solution was to evolve a new instrument—a "tenderometer," which could measure tenderness. Thereafter peas were purchased by weight, but on a sliding scale of price based on tenderometer readings.

2. *Is understandable.* Understandability is seldom a problem at the technological level. However, many units of measure at the managerial level have involved words that lack standardized meanings or have involved formulas of undue complexity. Any such vagueness or complexity becomes a natural source of divisiveness. Those who lack understanding of the unit of measure become suspicious of those who possess that understanding.

A statistical control chart is a tool for monitoring the stability of a process, thereby helping attain uniformity of the resulting product. In the absence of thorough training and involvement of workers and supervisors, there is a danger that when control charts are introduced to the operating area, control chart limits will be mistakenly seen as an unofficial tightening of official specifications.

3. *Applies broadly.* Measures of quality features are widely used as a basis for comparative analysis. Whether at the technological level or the managerial level, we need to answer such questions as: Is our quality getting better or worse? Are we competitive with others? Which one of our operations provides the best quality? How can we bring all operations up to the level of the best? Units of measure that have broad applicability can help us answer such questions.

Percentages and ratios are broadly applicable and facilitate comparison. For example:

Percent of service calls requiring a repeat call

Percent of overfill in packages

Ratio of good tons to total tons

Percent of sales contracts canceled

At the managerial level we have further need for breadth of application. We would like to apply common units of measure for evaluating the quality performance of various segments of the organization: divisions, offices, factories, laboratories, warehouses, managers, and so on. In the case of financial performance we do have such common units of measure—they have been evolved over the centuries. We are now in the early stages of a similar evolution in common units of measure for quality.

Again, ratios and percentages facilitate comparison, even across functions. For example:

Percent of man-hours devoted to rework and repair

Ratio of cost of poor quality to sales

4. *Is susceptible of uniform interpretation.* Identical numbers can nevertheless result in widely different interpretations. What is critical is whether the units of measure have been defined with adequate precision.

A report on quality of teller transactions in a bank includes number of errors per thousand transactions. Does the failure of a teller to say "thank you" carry the same weight in the report as a key entry error that results in a $500 shortage in a customer account? "Error" must be defined so that its meaning in the report is unambiguous.

5. *Is economic to apply.* It is obvious that a balance must be struck between the cost of making evaluations and the value of having them. In part, the application of this criterion relates to the basic question: *Should we measure or not?* More usually the application relates to "precision" of measurement. The unit of measure should be established at that level of precision which enables us to make valid decisions from the data. To go beyond that level of precision usually adds cost without adding value.

To measure arrival and departure time of commercial airlines to the nearest minute is close enough. To extend the precision to the nearest second would mean extra effort in definitions, measurement, and so forth, with doubtful value.

6. *Is compatible with existing designs of sensors.* Measurement of quality is wonderfully simple if a ready-made instrument exists, one that we can plug in to read the result in terms of the unit of measure. Such simplicity is widely prevalent at the technological level of the pyramid. At the upper levels we encounter numerous instances of designs of units of measure for which we have no readily available instruments or "sensors." Clearly, a unit of measure for which we have no sensor does not meet the criterion of an ideal unit of measure. However, the unit of measure may be important enough to require that we invent a new sensor. At the technological level that may involve costly research. However, at the managerial level it can be surprisingly simple. Once we publicize the need, human ingenuity has a way of responding to the challenge.

One aircraft manufacturer computes the cost of hours lost due to poor quality of purchased parts. The company computes for each supplier an index, which relates cost of lost hours to dollar volume of purchased parts. They rate suppliers as "excellent," "acceptable," or "in need of immediate attention and improvement," according to the index value.

CREATING A NEW UNIT OF MEASURE

Periodically we run into situations that require creating a new unit of measure. For example, some companies have undertaken to estimate (or evaluate) the cost of poor quality (COPQ) and to publish the results in order to:

Observe trends

Compare performance of multiple organization units

To publish such information requires creation of a unit of measure—in this case, some sort of index or ratio. There have been many nominations for structuring the ratio. In all cases the numerator is the same: the dollars of COPQ. The denominators proposed include:

Operating hours

Dollars of operating labor

Dollars of standard operating cost

Dollars of processing cost

Dollars of sales

Units of product produced

Each such denominator has a logic to support it. What is decisive, however, is the judgment of the managers after they have been exposed to the various units of measure. To provide managers with such exposure, indexes are published in several of the nominated versions. Then, based on the experience of the managers, the most meaningful units of measure are retained, and the rest are discarded.

UNIT OF MEASURE FOR VARIABILITY

We have not yet discussed one of the most important units of measure in the entire area of quality: the unit of measure for variability.

We could logically discuss this subject during any of several steps on the quality planning road map. What we will do is discuss it when we get to the process development step, since variability plays so vital a role during that step.

UPDATE OF THE QUALITY PLANNING SPREADSHEET

Establishment of a unit of measure makes it possible to enter the unit of measure in the quality planning spreadsheet. That is done in the vertical column to the right of the column headed "Translation."

In the case of the automobile, the prior spreadsheet (Figure 4–4, page 68) included several customer needs, each translated into supplier's language. The associated units of measure are typically as follows:

TRANSLATION	TYPICAL UNIT OF MEASURE
Length of warranty	Years, months
Coverage of warranty	List of subsystems covered or excluded, list of costs covered or excluded
Distance traveled per quantity of fuel	Miles per gallon, kilometers per liter
Reliability	Failure rate, mean time between failures
Promptness	Days, hours
Competence	Percent of repeat calls for service
Courtesy	Frequency of complaints about lack of courtesy

Figure 5–3 shows the updated spreadsheet.

ON TO MEASUREMENT

To "say it in numbers" we need not only a unit of measure; we need also to measure quality in terms of that unit of measure. So measurement is the next step on our quality planning road map, and is the subject of the next chapter.

SUMMARY

Precision in matters of quality requires that we "say it in numbers."

To say it in numbers requires, for each quality feature, a unit of measure and a sensor.

WHERE WE ARE ON THE SPREADSHEET:

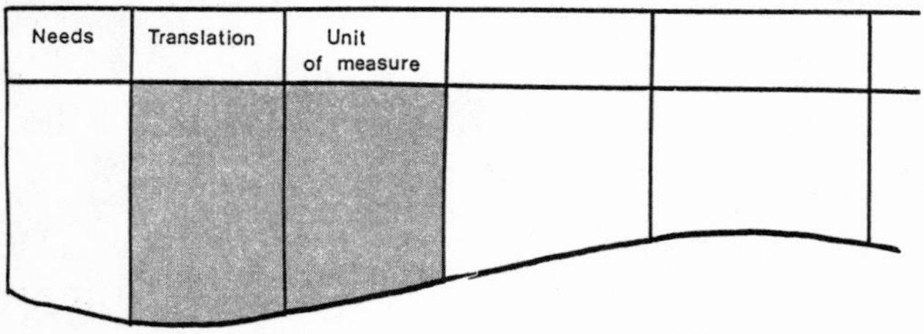

Needs	Translation	Unit of measure		

TIARY	TRANSLATION	UNIT OF MEASURE
ge	Length of warranty Extent of coverage	Years; months List of subsystems covered or excluded; list of costs covered or excluded
	Distance covered per quantity of fuel	Miles per gallon; kilometers per liter
	Reliability (freedom from failures)	Failure rate; mean time between failures
e	Promptness	Days; hours
	Competence	Percent of repeat calls for service
	Courtesy	Frequency of complaints about lack of courtesy

FIGURE 5–3 The quality planning spreadsheet: Unit of measure added (the automobile example)

There are multiple species of units of measure:

Technological
Product performance
Errors and failures

Departmental performance

Corporate performance

Managerial performance

For all units of measure we need precise definition.

Units of measure for abstractions may be established by (1) counting the violations, or (2) breaking the abstraction up into identifiable realities.

Units of measure form a pyramid, starting with technological units at the base and ending with financial units, indexes, and ratios at the top.

An ideal unit of measure:

Provides an agreed basis for decision making

Is understandable

Applies broadly

Is susceptible to uniform interpretation

Is economic to apply

Is compatible with existing designs of sensors

] *6* [

Establish Measurement

THE MISSION OF THIS CHAPTER

The mission is to evaluate customer needs in terms of the units of measure. Figure 6–1 shows the input–output diagram.

The *input* for this chapter is units of measure.

The *process* is establishment of means of measurement.

The *product* is customer needs expressed in terms of the units of measure.

THE SENSOR

To "say it in numbers" we need not only a unit of measure. We need also to evaluate quality in terms of that unit of measure. A key element in making that evaluation is the sensor.

A sensor is a specialized detecting device. It is designed to recognize the presence and intensity of certain phenomena and to convert that sensed knowledge into "information."

APPLICATIONS OF SENSORS TO QUALITY PLANNING

Sensors are widely used in the quality planning process. The table below lists some examples of:

Persons whose work includes some extent of quality planning

Quality features that are the subject of quality planning

Sensors used to evaluate the quality features

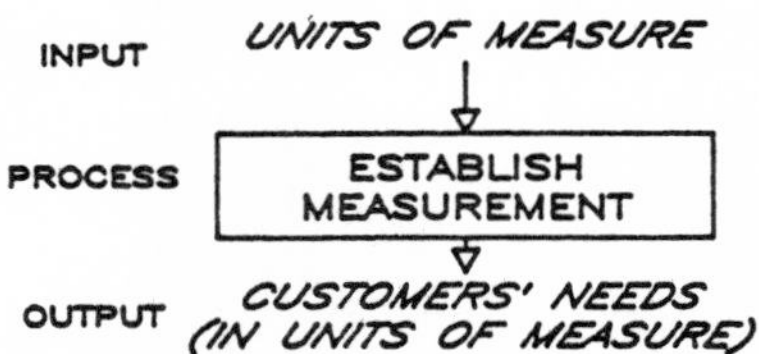

FIGURE 6–1 The input–output diagram for "Establish measurement"

PLANNERS	QUALITY FEATURES	SENSORS
Anyone	Personal health	Physical examination
Corporate planner	Economic trends	Economic indicators
Any supervisor or manager	Performance of individual workers, machines; performance of departments, divisions, corporation	Data sheets; summaries; reports
Design engineer	Failure rate	Model test laboratory
Design engineer	Producibility, maintainability	Design review team
Process engineer	Process precision	Process capability evaluation

VARIETIES OF SENSORS

Even in primitive societies there are numerous kinds of phenomena to be detected: odors, tastes, feel, time, temperature, etc. In our technological societies this list grows remarkably, requiring a corresponding growth in the variety and precision of sensors.

In the biological organism, some of the more well-known sensors are the myriads of tiny sense organs which transform heat, light, mechanical energy (pressure, touch), and chemical energy (smell, taste) into nerve impulses. In the company, the more familiar sensors are the clock cards, materials requisitions, inspectors' gages, salesmen's call records.

The sensor may consist of technological means for sensing stimuli which cannot be detected by the unaided human being (magnetism, radiation). It may be a means for amplifying the human sense organs (thermometer, microscope). In any case, the detected stimuli must be converted into "on or off" signals, scale measurements, beeps, or other things the human senses can detect.

The sensor may also consist of a human being who is "plugged in" to do what, as yet, no technological instrument is able to do. The patrol inspector, the watchman on the beat, and the field auditor are all examples of human beings used as sensory devices.

The industrial sensor is not necessarily located within the company. The sensors which detect changes in prices of materials, in business activity, or in cost of living may be maintained by a trade association, a government bureau, a business magazine. Through publication, the resulting stimuli energize various readers into action.

The sensor may be on a heroic scale. A wind tunnel creates an artificial environment. A "test town" is used to discover the probable effect of marketing a new product. A national test panel, of thousands of consumers or television viewers, is used to the same effect. The "polls" serve a related test purpose.[1]

FUNCTIONS OF SENSORS

The basic function of the sensor is to evaluate the presence and intensity of the phenomena the sensor is designed to detect. In recent decades additional functions have been added to many sensors:

Evaluating the results of sensing *on a scale of measurement.* This evaluation produces "variables data" as contrasted with the simpler data on presence or absence of the phenomenon, that is, "good or bad"; "in or out"; "go or no-go."

Recording the resulting data to permit data processing.

Data processing to arrive at summaries, trends, and so forth.

During quality planning the sensor has two principal uses:

To provide *early warning* of problems ahead.

To evaluate *process capability*—the ability of the quality plan to meet goals under operating conditions.

[1]J. M. Juran, *Managerial Breakthrough* (New York: McGraw-Hill, 1964), p. 258.

We need sound decisions in such matters; a good deal is at stake. Making such sound decisions depends in part on the credibility of the sensors: Can we rely on what they tell us? This credibility depends largely on the precision, accuracy, and maintenance of the sensor.

PRECISION, ACCURACY, AND MAINTENANCE OF SENSORS

Precision

The precision of a sensor is a measure of the ability of the sensor to reproduce its results on repeat test. For most technological sensors, reproducibility is high and also easy to quantify.

At the other end of the spectrum are the cases in which we use human beings as sensors: inspectors, auditors, supervisors, appraisers. Human senses are notoriously less precise than technological sensors. Human senses are also subject to serious biases. However, it is usually feasible to evaluate the ability of the human sensors to reproduce their results. It is also feasible to plan the use of human sensors in ways that bring the biases down to acceptable levels.

The more critical the quality features that are the subject of quality planning, the greater is the need to evaluate the precision of the sensor (whether technological or human). Similarly, on critical quality features there is great need to design the plan of human sensing in ways that minimize biases.

> During the 1940s a manufacturer of razor blades made extensive use of human beings as sensors. Many male employees would forgo their morning shave at home. Instead, they shaved themselves in special washrooms on the company premises. They recorded the results of those shave tests on data sheets like the one in Figure 6–2.
>
> Under the prevailing procedure the panelist was issued a razor blade to be tested. (The blade might be a sample from current product, a competitor's blade, or a new product under development.) The panelist used the blade day after day, recording his rating after each shave. Once the rating reached "poor" the panelist would discard the blade.

NAME ______________________ DEPT. ______________

TYPE OF BLADE ______________________

STARTING DATE ______________________

SHAVE RATINGS

SHAVE NUMBER	EXCELLENT	GOOD	FAIR	POOR
1				
2				
3				
4				
5				
6				
7				
8				
9				
10				
11				
12				
13				
14				
15				
16				

FIGURE 6–2 Data sheet on shave tests

A critical analysis of the resulting data sheets disclosed the existence of two serious deficiencies in the shave test:

1. For any blade the ratings invariably either declined from day to day or remained the same. No rating ever improved. That invariability was challenged by those who doubted that human evaluation of a shave could discriminate so precisely.

2. Every blade reached the rating of "poor" on or before the fifth shave, that is, no blade was ever used more than five times. Again the skeptics doubted the ability of human sensors to appraise ultimate blade life so precisely.

The theory of the skeptics was that the panelists' data were biased due to their prior knowledge of how many times the blade had been used. A new shave test was then so designed that the panelists would be unaware of the number of prior uses of the blade. The resulting shave test data differed radically from the past in two respects:

1. Shave test ratings wavered more widely. It was not unusual for ratings to improve during successive shaves with the same blade.
2. The life of the blades rose remarkably. Blades were often used ten times or more instead of the prior maximum of five. The previous life of the blade had been determined by psychological considerations, not by metallurgical capability.

Accuracy

The accuracy of a sensor is the degree to which the sensor tells the truth—the extent to which its evaluations of some phenomenon agree with the "true" value as judged by an agreed standard. The difference between the observed valuations and the true value is the "error," which can be positive or negative.

The relationship between accuracy and precision is evident from Figure 6–3.

For technological sensors it is usually easy to adjust for accuracy—to recalibrate. A simple example is a clock or watch. The owner can listen to the time signals provided over the radio. (In this case the time signals are the standard.) The owner then makes a correction, that is, a change that offsets the error. In industrial dialect, the owner has "recalibrated the instrument."

In contrast, the precision of a sensor is not easy to adjust. The upper limit of precision is inherent in the basic design of the sensor. To improve precision beyond the upper limit requires a redesign. (The sensor may be operating at a level of precision below that of its capability because of misuse, inadequate maintenance, or other reasons. In that event removal of those causes can allow the sensor to regain its inherent precision.)

Maintenance

Sensors deteriorate during use (and even during nonuse). To guard against errors, biases, and so on, it is necessary to establish systematic means for maintaining the integrity of the sensing. The

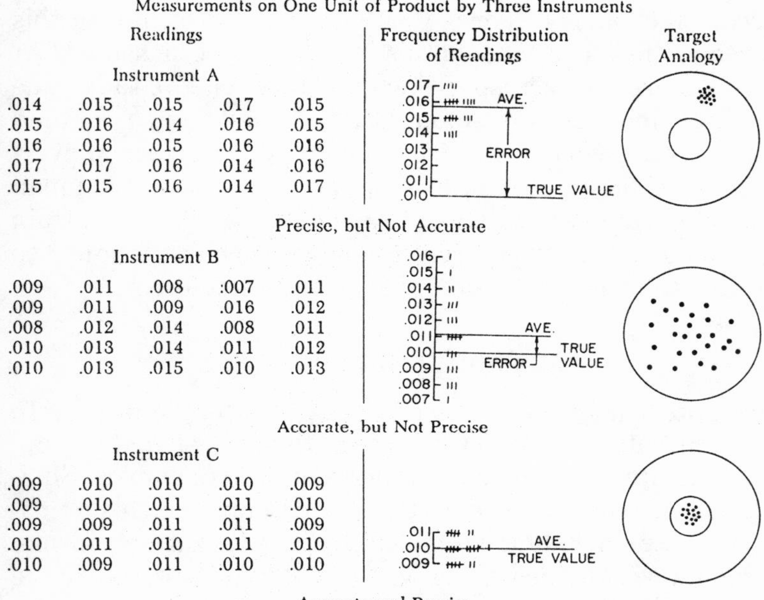

FIGURE 6–3 Accuracy and precision

systematic means is centered on a plan for maintenance of the sensors. Such a plan comprises:

1. A *schedule* for maintenance of sensors. The schedule sets out how often the sensor is to be checked. The determination of how often may be based on calendar time, extent of use, or some other measure.
2. A *checklist* or countdown. The checklist sets out what actions are to be taken during the check.

Human sensing also deteriorates during use, as a result of fatigue, monotony, and so forth. In critical sensing (e.g., the military sentry or watchtower), it is common to limit the length of watch in order to minimize deteriorations.

HUMAN SENSORS

Human sensing takes place at all levels of the hierarchy of measurement. At the basic data level, human beings must decide:

Which accounts should be charged with these hours of time or this material requisition? How should this field failure be classified? At higher levels there are corresponding questions relative to preparing summaries, indexes, and so on. In addition, we must contend with human errors, which arise from a variety of causes: inadvertence, lack of technique, conscious errors. The extent of human sensing is so great that we should take positive steps to attain credible sensing. Those steps are well known. Each is designed to be responsive to some particular species of human error.

Misinterpretation

Words are notoriously subject to a variety of interpretations. To secure uniform interpretations, precise definitions should be supplied, supplemented by such aids as checklists and examples. Similarly, detailed instructions should be provided on how to summarize and calculate, including examples. In critical matters, formal training should be provided along with examinations to verify the "process capability" of the human sensors-to-be.

Inadvertent Errors

Inadvertent errors are unintentional, unpredictable, and often unwitting. The person making the error is not at the time aware of having done so.

> A depositor receives his monthly statement from the bank and discovers that his computed balance differs from that reported by the bank. Analysis then shows (usually) that the depositor had unwittingly made some inadvertent error through a lapse of attention.

The unpredictability of inadvertent errors produces a randomness in the data. (We cannot predict which depositor will have the next unbalance, when it will take place, or what type of error will be involved.) The random feature of such errors does help us to identify that they are of the inadvertent species. However, we are limited in choice of remedy, because the root cause of the errors is an inherent weakness in the human organism—an inability to maintain attention indefinitely. (If the inattention is intentional, that is a conscious error.)

To a degree, inadvertent errors can be reduced by:

Aptitude testing to identify persons best suited for the tasks in question

Organizing work so as to reduce fatigue and monotony, e.g., rest periods, task rotation

However, in those cases where we cannot endure inadvertent errors, e.g., matters affecting human safety, we must resort to technological solutions: fail-safe designs, foolproofing, automated processes, redundancy.

Lack of Technique

One widespread species of human error is traceable to incomplete knowledge on the part of the human sensor. Some persons have acquired a knack—a small difference in method that accounts for a large difference in results. Those who possess the knack get superior results; those who lack the knack get inferior results.

The remedy is to study the methods used by both superior and inferior performers. Usually such study discovers the knack, which can then be transferred to all workers through training. Alternatively, it may be feasible to incorporate the knack into the technology.

An interesting example of a knack was that devised by the late eminent cardiologist Dr. Paul Dudley White. (He was the leader of the team appointed to treat President Eisenhower's heart attack.)

Early in his career Dr. White established a spreadsheet system of record keeping to assist him in follow-up of the progress of his patients. He described the system in his autobiography.

> I had printed for me large sheets. . . . These sheets contained two horizontal lines for each patient, divided by vertical columns with the serial number, the name, the age, the sex, the diagnosis arranged according to etiology (both cardiac and noncardiac), the structural change and the functional condition of the circulation, and a special column at the end of the lines devoted to some unusual reason why this patient might be particularly important to be followed up. Now, after all these fifty years, I find these volumes of great value; they hardly require a computer, because of the organization of this original tabulation, which has proved so useful. This type of follow-up can apply to any particular field in medicine

> or surgery, or any science as a matter of fact, or any other activity of life, but as the years have gone by and the organization of my material has become so helpful, I have emphasized more and more the importance of this relatively simple technique in the practice of medicine and in the collection of information otherwise.[2]

In the dialect of practitioners in quality, Dr. White's knack consisted of a structured system of data recording to facilitiate finding relationships between process variables (patients' symptoms) and product results (treatment and subsequent progress).

Conscious Errors

Conscious errors are intentional and witting. The person making the error knows it at the time and intends to keep it up. Conscious errors come in a variety of subspecies:

Defensiveness against real or imagined grievances (For example, an atmosphere of blame stimulates subordinates to hide information that might become the occasion of blame.)

Coloration, which is a deliberate distortion of the sensed data for a variety of (usually) self-serving human purposes: reduction of workload, avoidance of unpleasant tasks, self-aggrandizement, fear of being punished as the bearer of bad news

The following is an example of coloration that took place in a company whose product line included electric and gas ranges.

> The Vice President at Headquarters phoned the Works Manager in the hinterlands. "How many ranges are you shipping today?" The Works Manager asked the Production Manager, who asked the Assembly Superintendent, who asked the Shipping Room Foreman, who asked Pete. Pete, being low man on the totem pole, had no one to ask. So he went out to the shipping platform and counted the ranges—in the freight cars, in the trucks, and on the platform. There were 400 in all.
>
> Pete was no fool. He remembered that yesterday they had shipped 440 ranges. He also knew someone would ask "Why is today below yesterday?"
>
> He found the answer. There were 40 more ranges in a hold area. They had been assembled today, but they couldn't be shipped,

[2]Paul Dudley White, *My Life and Medicine* (Boston: Gambit, 1971), pp. 195–196.

> because they lacked electric clocks. "We're just out of electric clocks. A truckload is on the road now, and is due here at 11 A.M. tomorrow." In Pete's mind everything dropped into place. Those 40 ranges in the hold area were as good as shipped.
>
> So he reported—440 ranges. And this information sped up the line. 90 percent message and 10 percent coloration.[3]

Reduction in coloration can be achieved in part by establishing a climate that favors forthright communication. Creating such a climate demands leadership from upper management—leadership by setting the example. A good deal can also be done to convert to nonhuman channels of communication. The computer has opened up extensive possibilities for processing basic data and communicating the results directly to the users with minimal human coloration.

Bias

Bias is one of the most troublesome sources of error in human sensing. Bias has some resemblance to coloration, but there are subtle differences. In coloration the human sensor knows the facts but consciously adds distortion. In bias the distortion is not necessarily conscious. There may be inner forces that influence the response of the human sensor. The bias may even be inherent in the design of the sensing plan. In the razor blade shave test example (pages 86–88), the panelists' reports were certainly biased by their knowledge of the number of shaves previously taken with the razor blades undergoing test. However, the test plan was so designed that each panelist was bound to know the prior history of each blade he was using.

"Mind set" is a form of bias, and it can be a hindrance in quality planning.

> In a project to improve the yield of a wave solder process it was proposed to run the solder bath at a higher temperature. The process engineer objected on the ground that while the higher temperature was beneficial in some respects, it would make matters worse in other respects. On being challenged, the process engineer produced data that had been taken ten

[3]Juran, *Managerial Breakthrough,* p. 271.

> years before on a different process. A restudy then showed that the process engineer "knew" something that wasn't so. However, his belief had been stated so often that it became a mind set. (It is difficult for any of us to deny what we have been contending for years.)

The need to avoid bias is greatest in those cases where we look to a special study to provide a major input to planning. Here are two examples:

> A bank undertook to upgrade its customer service. As part of its planning it conducted marketing research: interviews with a sample of clients. One of the areas of customer service was that of the loan department. In that area it became evident that clients were most reluctant to provide comment, even on the assurance of confidentiality. Clearly, those clients were afraid of jeopardizing their relationship with the loan officers on whom they had a degree of dependence. The bank could and did conduct "exit interviews"—interviews with former clients who had gone elsewhere out of dissatisfaction with the bank's service. The exit interviews, of course, carried the risk of being biased in the opposite direction.

> A chemicals company (page 48) conducted a survey among a sample of clients to learn their perception of the company's performance relative to that of competitors. The survey showed that for most elements of performance, the company was ranked among the best. However, the survey was biased: The sample contained no *non*clients. Hence there was a risk that the conclusions were misleading.

Futility

Yet another source of human bias is a sense of futility. In many industries the workforce is potentially a sensor relative to conditions in the workplace. Through their daily, intimate contacts with those conditions, the workers are in a position to identify opportunities as well as deficiencies. For example, in a hotel the housekeepers, bellmen, and others are in a position to report on the conditions prevailing in the hotel rooms, reactions of hotel guests, and so forth. If the workers discover that their reports are not acted on, they stop reporting.

The situation of futility is at its worst if the workers learn that their reward for acting as sensors is unwarranted blame.

> For years the hospital industry had only the vaguest idea of the extent of errors in the process of giving medication to patients. All hospitals posted rules requiring nurses to report medication errors promptly to the hospital administrator. However, in many hospitals the nurses had learned that when they made such reports they were often subjected to unwarranted blame. Hence they stopped making such reports. In due course a classic study made by a qualified outsider showed that (1) about 7 percent of the medications involved errors, some quite serious, and (2) the bulk of the errors were management-controllable, not worker-controllable.

The case examples suggest the means to be used to minimize the bias of human sensors:

Provide for a design review of the data collection plan. In complex designs the design review team should include someone who is skilled in statistical designs and in communicating with persons who lack such skills.

Approach the occurrence of errors constructively: What can we do together to reduce such errors in the future? Above all, avoid instant blame.

When urging employees to act as sensors, either take action on their reports or explain why not.

Figure 6–4 summarizes the various types of human error and the usual associated remedies.

TIME OF SENSING

Sensing is done in three time frames relative to operations:

Before operations

During operations

After operations

ERROR TYPES	REMEDIES
Misinterpretation	Precise definition, glossary
	Checklists
	Examples
Inadvertent errors	Aptitude testing
	Reorganization of work to reduce fatigue and monotony
	Fail-safe designs
	Redundancy
	Foolproofing (error-proofing)
	Automation, robotics
Lack of technique	Discovery of knack of successful workers
	Revision of technology to incorporate the knack
	Retraining
Conscious errors:	Design review of data collection plan
coloration	Removal of atmosphere of blame
bias	Action on reports, or explanation of why not
futility	Depersonalize the orders
	Establish accountability
	Provide balanced emphasis on goals
	Conduct quality audits
	Create competition, incentives
	Reassign the work

FIGURE 6–4 **Human error types and remedies**

The purposes and uses of these forms of sensing are shown below:

	BEFORE OPERATIONS	DURING OPERATIONS	AFTER OPERATIONS
Purpose of sensing	To secure early warning of impact of quality planning on subsequent operations	To keep operations in a state of conformance to goals	To discover "lessons learned" as an input to future planning
Type of sensor	Special, early warning sensors	Usually, the "regular" sensors needed to generate data for control of operations	Mainly a summary of data that are a by-product of prior cycles of operation
Analysis of the sensed information is by:	The quality planners	The operating forces	"Historians" who may be planners or full-time analysts
Use of the sensed information is by:	The quality planners	The operating forces	The quality planners

SENSING TO SECURE EARLY WARNING FOR QUALITY PLANNERS

Quality planning is often done by persons who later will *not* have the responsibility to conduct operations. Here are some common examples of the widespread separation of planning from execution.

> A systems analyst designs a data processing system to deal with the various aspects of accounts receivable: customers' orders, order editing, shipping, billing, collections, and so on. After approval, this plan will be executed by numerous persons in multiple "line" departments.

A market manager prepares a marketing plan involving advertising, sales promotion, selling, warranties, and so forth. This plan likewise will be carried out by numerous persons in multiple departments.

A design engineer prepares a design for a new product. To make that new product then requires execution by multiple departments: Purchasing to buy the materials, Process Engineering to plan for manufacture, Production to run the manufacturing processes, Customer Service to carry out field maintenance, and so on.

There are advantages to the separation of planning from execution, but there are also risks. A serious risk has been that the plans, while usually meeting the needs of external customers, do not meet the needs of internal customers. In the dialect of managing for quality, the plans lack process capability. To make matters worse, the calendar time consumed by the planning cycle may be so considerable that lack of process capability will create costly crises for the operating forces. In such cases we need some special design of sensor to provide *early warning* of a crisis in the making. There are several principal forms of such special early warning sensors.

The Planner as Sensor

The planner "makes the rounds" to learn the operating conditions at first hand. The learning may come from structured training courses, from temporary assignment to carry out operating tasks, or from discussion with operating supervisors and workers. The intention is to install the early warning system into the planner.

"Design Review" Team as Sensor

A team is formed of managers or specialists drawn from those operating areas which will be heavily impacted by the plan. The design review team studies the plan and tells the planner, in effect: "If you plan it this way, the consequences will be as follows." The responsibility for making the planning decisions continues to rest with the planner. However, the findings of the sensor (the design review team) are influential.

Note: The term "design review" in the past has usually been

associated with review of designs of physical goods. However, the concept is applicable to all types of designs: systems design, organization design, and so on.

Joint Planning

The joint planning approach has much in common with design review, but there is a big difference: The responsibility for approval of the plan is joint. A widespread formula used to assign responsibility is as follows:

ACTIVITY	OPERATING DEPARTMENTS	PLANNING AND CONTROL DEPARTMENTS
Design plan	X	X
Execute plan	X	
Audit to see if execution follows plan		X

In the case of complex systems (e.g., aerospace or military programs, major electronic systems), joint planning is sometimes done by traveling teams. Under this concept a multidisciplinary team of planners remains attached to the program as it progresses through the successive phases of development, manufacture, and deployment.

Note that all of the above forms of sensing (for early warning) involve extensive use of human sensors. We have seen that human sensing is subject to a wide array of errors. Those who make use of information provided by human sensors should be well schooled in the nature of human sensing errors.

SENSORS AT MANAGERIAL LEVELS

The sensors used for quality planning at the technological level are generally well developed and well understood. In contrast the sensors used for quality planning at the supervisory and managerial levels are still in the early stages of evolution. Those sensors need further development, since the trend is more and more to make quality planning a part of the company's strategic business plan.

In Chapter Five we saw that units of measure form a pyramid that roughly parallels the organization pyramid. In general, the sensors follow a similar pyramidal structure. At the base of the pyramid the sensors include numerous technological instruments to measure the technological product and process features. As we move up the pyramid there is an associated shift to other forms of sensors.

At supervisory and middle management levels there is much interest in measures that help to establish departmental quality goals and to evaluate departmental performance against goals. Sensors for such purposes consist mostly of:

Departmental summaries of product and process performance, derived from inspections and tests, reports of nonconformance, and so on

Personal observation in which the departmental head serves as sensor

At upper management levels the interest is in measures of such broad matters as:

Quality compared to that of competitors

Cost of poor quality relative to sales

Performance of managers with respect to quality

Time required to launch new products

Sensors to evaluate such features are correspondingly broad:

Data systems, which collect and summarize information into indexes, ratios, and so forth

Reports from committees, project teams, research teams, and others

Audits conducted by "independent" observers

Personal observation by upper managers

Managerial sensors consist mostly of composites of data expressed in such forms as summaries, ratios, and indexes. Managers do not use the word "sensors" to describe those composites; they use the word "reports." Such managerial sensors have been widely and successfully used, mainly for quality control, and to a lesser degree for quality planning.

MEASURES OF ECONOMIC CONSEQUENCES OF QUALITY

Quality affects company economics in two principal ways:

The effect on costs

The effect on sales income

These are quite different conceptually, although they interact in some respects.

The Effect of Quality on Costs

Methods are available for quantifying "cost of quality." Those methods involve evaluation of various categories of costs of attaining quality as well as categories of costs of poor quality. The evaluation may be done through enlarging the accounting system (a lengthy, time-consuming process). Alternatively, the evaluation may be done by estimates.

In terms of the quality trilogy, the big *short-range* opportunity for reducing quality-related costs lies in reducing the cost of poor quality. To do so requires adopting a structured quality *improvement* process based on project-by-project improvement.

In contrast, the *long-range* opportunity for reducing cost of poor quality lies in improving the quality *planning* process. Such improvement solves the problem of chronic wastes at the source by not creating them—by planning new products and processes in ways that avoid creating new chronic quality problems.

The Effect of Quality on Sales Income

Measuring the effect of quality on sales income has very little in common with measuring the effect of quality on costs. The reason is that two kinds of quality are involved. In the case of costs, "quality" refers mainly to *conformance* to standards. In the case of sales income, "quality" refers mainly to product *features:* their presence or absence, and their competitiveness in the market place. In the dialect of the quality specialists, this form of "quality" is "grade" or "quality of design"—very different from "quality" in the sense of conformance to standards.

(While quality of design and quality of conformance are very different in their nature, they are both referred to by the word "quality," spelled the same way and pronounced the same way. That dual use of the same word has led to extensive confusion and plenty of damage.)

Interaction

The two different kinds of quality do interact with each other. Each contributes to the quality reputation of the company, positively or negatively. Products that are failure-prone can easily result in the loss of future sales. Useful, innovative product features can help sell products even though predecessor products have a history of nonconformance.

UPDATE OF THE QUALITY PLANNING SPREADSHEET

Establishment of a sensor permits a further update of the quality planning spreadsheet. An additional column can be headed "sensor" and filled in, based on the measurement method. That method will enable the planners to evaluate customer needs in terms of the unit of measure.

Applied to the case of the automobile, we can add to the table on page 80 as follows:

TRANSLATION	UNIT OF MEASURE	SENSOR
Length of warranty	. . .	Data system
Extent of coverage	. . .	Published lists
Distance covered per quantity of fuel	. . .	Odometer/fuel gage
Reliability (freedom from failures)	. . .	Data system
Promptness	. . .	Data system
Competence	. . .	Data system
Courtesy	. . .	Data system

Most of the sensors used to evaluate the above customer needs are seen to involve data systems—records to be kept and summarized. In the case of fuel consumption, the technological instruments at the filling station and on the dashboard make it possible for the motorist to sense fuel consumption both instantaneously and cumulatively.

Figure 6–5 shows the updated segment of the spreadsheet.

WHERE WE ARE ON THE SPREADSHEET:

Needs	Translation	Unit of measure	Sensor	

TIARY	TRANSLATION	UNIT OF MEASURE	SENSOR
ge	Length of warranty Extent of coverage	Years; months List of subsystems covered or excluded; list of costs covered or excluded	Data system Published lists
	Distance covered per quantity of fuel	Miles per gallon; kilometers per liter	Odometer/ fuel gage
	Reliability (freedom from failures)	Failure rate; mean time between failures	Data system
e	Promptness	Days; hours	Data system
	Competence	Percent of repeat calls for service	Data system
	Courtesy	Frequency of complaints about lack of courtesy	Data system

FIGURE 6–5 The quality planning spreadsheet: Sensor added (the automobile example)

ON TO PRODUCT DEVELOPMENT

Up to now we have taken several steps on the quality planning road map: identifying customers and their needs; translating those needs into our language, and providing the means to "say it in numbers." The next step is product development—the development of product features that are responsive to the customer needs. That step is the subject of Chapter Seven.

SUMMARY

A sensor is a device specially designed to evaluate the presence and intensity of specific phenomena.

The precision of a sensor is its ability to reproduce its results on repeat test.

The accuracy of a sensor is the degree to which it tells the truth.

Sensors are used at all levels of the company—at managerial levels as well as technological levels.

Human beings as sensors are a serious source of error.

Misinterpretation errors can be reduced by precise definitions of terminology, detailed instructions, checklists, examples, training, and qualifying examinations.

Inadvertent errors can be reduced by aptitude testing, by reorganization of work, and by use of failure-proof technology.

Errors due to lack of technique can be reduced by study of comparative work methods to discover the knack that makes superior performance possible.

Conscious errors can be reduced by abolishing any atmosphere of blame and adopting a constructive approach to error reduction.

Errors due to bias can be reduced by design review of the data collection plan.

Errors due to futility can be reduced by taking action on reports of human sensors or by explaining why not.

Sensing for early warning can be done by:

- Exposing planners directly to the activities which their plan will impact
- Creating design review teams
- Joint planning by planners and operating personnel

] 7 [

Product Development

THE MISSION OF THIS CHAPTER

The mission is to develop the product features required to meet customer needs. The input–output diagram is shown in Figure 7-1.

The *input* is customer needs expressed in units of measure.

The *process* is product development.

The *output* is product features that respond to customer needs.

Note that the end result of product development is information: a plan. The subsequent product (goods or services) will be produced by the operating forces, and then only after a process has been developed to produce the product.

WHO ARE THE QUALITY PLANNERS?

As we get into the subject of product development, it is timely to have a close look at "Who are the quality planners?" This question has relevance to every step on the quality planning road map, especially to Product Development and to Process Development (Chapter Nine).

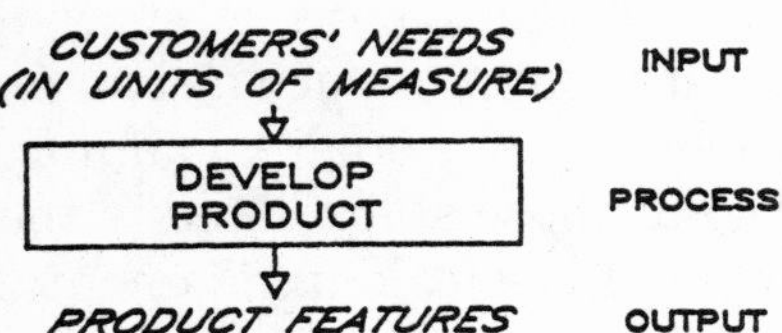

FIGURE 7-1 The input–output diagram for "Product development"

Prior to the rise of the Taylor system, virtually all planning for operations, including planning for quality, was done by the operating managers and supervisors. The Taylor system (introduced early in the twentieth century) brought about a revolutionary separation of planning from execution. In due course that revolution spread to the quality function and resulted in the creation of quality specialists, principally in two specialist categories:

Quality engineers, whose functions were associated with product quality in the factory

Reliability engineers, whose functions were associated with product quality in the field

Those quality specialists have done much to evolve concepts and tools, which are essential aids to managing for quality. However, the operating managers and line specialists (design engineers, process engineers) have been slow to adopt those aids. The lack of adoption is traceable in part to that same separation of planning from execution.

Meanwhile, during the second half of the twentieth century, Japanese industries surprised the Western world by taking over quality leadership in many important product lines. A distinguishing feature of the Japanese quality revolution was their approach to quality planning:

They assigned responsibility for quality planning mainly to the operating managers and line specialists.

They carried out massive training programs to enable the operating managers and line specialists to understand and use the new quality concepts and tools.

The Japanese results have caused Western companies to reexamine their assignment of responsibility for quality planning. Those companies are in the early stages of shifting more and more of the responsibility to the operating managers and line specialists, while providing the training needed to support such a change.

No matter how we assign the responsibility, the quality planning activities remain unchanged: to carry out those steps listed in the quality planning road map. However, when we make fundamental changes in responsibility, we also create impacts on the people involved. Some of those impacts are severe, extending to destruction of careers that had seemed secure.

In the material that follows, the emphasis will continue to be on the quality planning functions, not on who the quality planners are. The assignment of responsibility will continue to change from decade to decade, but the list of functions is timeless.

PRODUCT DEVELOPMENT DEFINED

As used here, "product development" means providing product features that respond to customer needs. There are other terms with similar meanings: product design, system design, product engineering.

The *activity* of providing product features varies widely. At one extreme it consists of applying some existing or standard design to meet customer needs. At the other extreme the activity can involve extensive research to find an appropriate response.

PRODUCT FEATURES: THE CRITERIA

Customer needs are met through product features. Each customer need is unique and requires a correspondingly unique product feature. Ideally, every such product feature should comply with the following criteria:

Meet the needs of our customers

Meet our needs (as suppliers)

Meet competition

Optimize the combined costs of our company and our customers

Let us look briefly at each of these criteria, with emphasis on the key words.

Meet the Needs of Customers

Customers here means both external and internal customers, as we saw in Chapter Two. *Needs* means not only the stated and perceived needs of customers; it includes real needs as well, as discussed in Chapter Three.

Meet Our Needs

We have numerous cases in which suppliers do not meet the needs of customers because of various restraints. An obvious class of such cases relates to the cost of meeting the needs.

> The author lives in a region of the State of Connecticut in which the dominant source of energy is electric power. The region is heavily forested and suffers occasional power outages during storms. Falling trees damage the power lines.
>
> An obvious need of customers for electric power is continuity—no outages. To meet that need the supplier might be forced to bury the power cables underground. That would be very costly, since the region is rocky and hilly as well as heavily forested. It is most unlikely that the clients of the power company would be willing to pay the price.

Meet Competition

The fact that a product meets customer needs does not ensure that customers will buy it; a competitor's product may be better or may give better value. Hence, meeting competition is an important criterion for product developers.

> An example on a large scale was the development of the Taurus-Sable models of automobiles. There the manufacturer identified about four hundred of the key features that determined product salability. The manufacturer then analyzed competing models of automobiles, both domestic and foreign, to determine their performance with respect to those key features. The goal given to the product developers was to meet the "best in class" for each of those four hundred features.[1]

Optimize the Costs

Customers and suppliers incur costs when they use or supply the product, and each tries to keep their respective costs to a mini-

[1]L. C. Veraldi, (Ford Motor Company), MIT Conference paper, Chicago, August 22, 1985.

mum. However, the true optimum as viewed by society is to minimize the combined costs.

A widespread example is that of long-life goods. For such goods, the cost to the ultimate user is made up of:

The original purchase price

The subsequent costs of operation and maintenance

The national economy would benefit enormously if the "life cycle cost" concept were made effective. Under that concept, product design is aimed at minimizing the "cost of ownership," which is the sum of the purchase price plus the subsequent costs of operation and maintenance. However, many product designs are aimed at minimizing the original purchase price. That makes it easier for the supplier to sell the product, but it is no bargain for the client.

PRODUCT FEATURES: THE DEVELOPMENT CYCLE

The work involved in providing a product feature varies widely. In many cases a suitable solution is already in existence in such forms as standardized computer software or standardized hardware components. In such cases product development consists of applying those known designs to meet customer needs.

At the other extreme it may be necessary to go through the full cycle of product development steps:

Nomination of the scientific conceptual principle to be employed (e.g., electronic, hydraulic, optical)

Study of technical feasibility

Economic evaluation

Decision on conceptual principle

Model design, construction, and test

Scale up

The full cycle can involve considerable work. Much can be done to reduce that work by using knowledge derived from similar prior cases. However, for critical, uniquely new needs, it is necessary to go through the entire cycle.

THE EFFECT OF PROLIFERATION

In its simplest form, product development is done for self-use.

> A housewife creates a new recipe for a cake, produces it with general-use kitchen utensils, and serves it to her family. Her do-it-yourself husband designs a new bookshelf and installs it in the living room. Their son, a drama student, writes an original play as part of a course assignment.

In all such cases one human mind presides over the entire series of product development steps, so the need for system is minimal.

As the scale of operations grows, everything multiplies—the numbers proliferate. A bigger market means more customers, a wider product line, and hence more product features. A bigger company employs more people and hence has more internal customers to satisfy. That same bigger market attracts more competitors and hence imposes more restraints.

The resulting combinations (of customers and needs) not only require development of large numbers of product features; they also require a systematic approach. It takes a structured approach to deal with all those numbers and the resulting complexity.

> The village cooper may produce and sell about a hundred barrels each year. He also produces "invoices," largely informally and in unwritten form. In contrast, the electric power company requires a highly structured system to produce and deliver millions of invoices annually.

Developing all those product features can involve extensive work in technology, which is *not* our subject. However, dealing with all that proliferation requires a systematic approach. This is a form of quality planning, which *is* our subject. Some of the planning is done to help the product developers get their arms around the complexities. Additional planning is done to assist the product developers to make optimal use of their technology.

THE NEED FOR STRUCTURE

If much is at stake (as is the case with automobiles), it becomes necessary to go into a structured, systematic approach to quality planning. The structure is needed mainly because:

Some of the analyses inherently require structure. We shall shortly examine those.

To go from system design down into the depths of the product hierarchy gets into a great deal of detail, again requiring a structured approach.

The structured approach makes use of a variety of planning and analysis tools, including:

Spreadsheets

The phase system

Product subdivision

Criticality analysis

Competitive analysis

Salability analysis

Analysis to avoid failures

Value analysis

THE SPREADSHEET, AGAIN

An important tool for dealing with all that proliferation is again the quality planning spreadsheet. In earlier chapters we filled in vertical columns in the spreadsheet, as follows:

Customer needs in customer language

Customer needs in our language (translation)

Units of measure

Sensors

At this point it is timely to head up additional columns to show which product features have traditionally been used to meet the customer needs listed on the spreadsheet. Figure 7–2 shows the resulting spreadsheet as applied to some aspects of quality of automobiles.

At this stage of quality planning the product features are necessarily in broad terms, which the planners often call system design. In due course those broad features must be broken down into considerable detail. However, some essential analysis takes place even at the present stage. One aspect of this early analysis is to

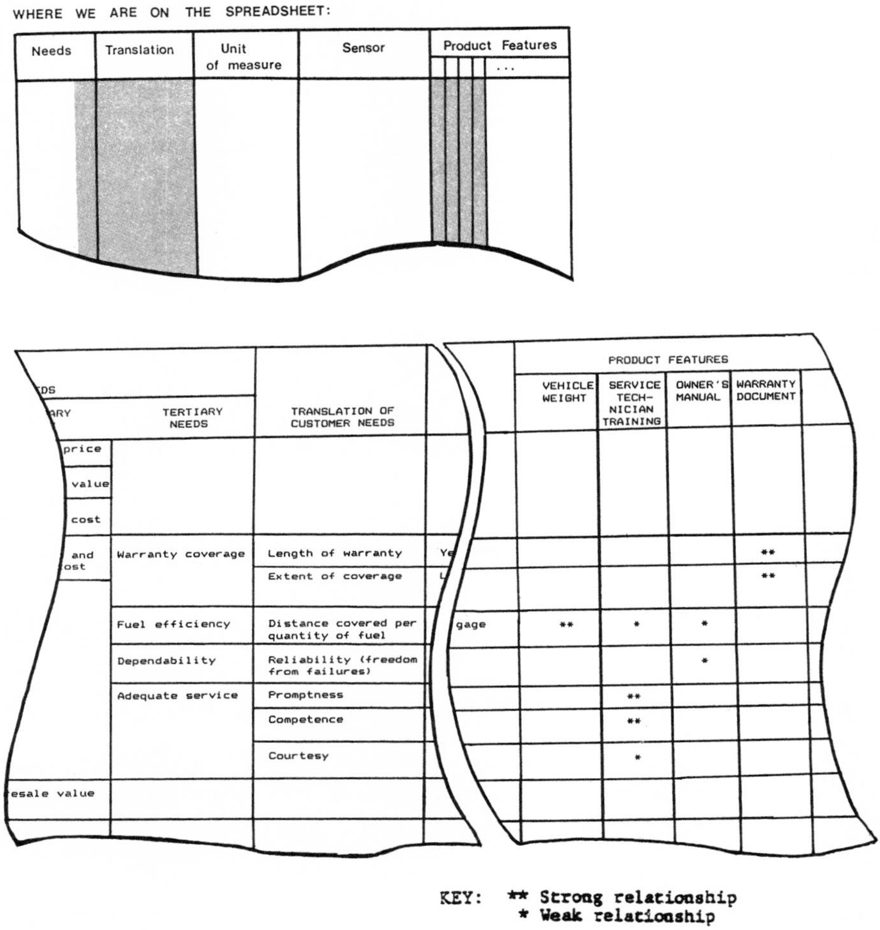

WHERE WE ARE ON THE SPREADSHEET:

Needs	Translation	Unit of measure	Sensor	Product Features ...

DS ARY	TERTIARY NEEDS	TRANSLATION OF CUSTOMER NEEDS		PRODUCT FEATURES: VEHICLE WEIGHT	SERVICE TECHNICIAN TRAINING	OWNER'S MANUAL	WARRANTY DOCUMENT
price							
value							
cost							
and ost	Warranty coverage	Length of warranty	Ye				**
		Extent of coverage	L				**
	Fuel efficiency	Distance covered per quantity of fuel	gage	**	*	*	
	Dependability	Reliability (freedom from failures)				*	
	Adequate service	Promptness			**		
		Competence			**		
		Courtesy			*		
esale value							

KEY: ** Strong relationship
 * Weak relationship

FIGURE 7–2 The quality planning spreadsheet: After adding product features and their relationships to needs (the automobile example)

identify the relationships between customer needs and present product features. The results of the analysis are entered into the spreadsheet by use of symbols. As exemplified in Figure 7–2, the symbols show at a glance (1) the existence of a relationship and (2) the intensity of the relationship.

The relationships identified (by symbols) on Figure 7–2 can help the planners to focus on two essential areas:

For those cases where there is no present provision for meeting customers' needs, what action is needed?

For those cases where provision for meeting customer needs is already in existence, is that provision adequate?

THE PHASE SYSTEM

For large development projects many companies make use of a concept known as the phase (or stage) system. Under this concept the product development cycle is divided up into segments or phases, each phase being an identifiable step in the progression of events. An example of such a division is as follows:

Market research
Preliminary design
Design evaluation
Model design, construction, and test
Pilot production model design, construction, and test
Planning for full-scale manufacture
Etc.

Each of the phases is defined in terms of the activities to be carried out and the results to be achieved. The definitions include criteria that set out the conditions to be met for completion of the phase.

In addition, the phase system provides for business decisions to be made at several key points during the progression, as for example, after model test. In that way, the phase system is a managerial tool for stimulating and controlling product development. It defines work segments, establishes criteria to be met, and provides for a business team to decide whether to continue or to stop. Figure 7–3, the flow diagram of a phased product development process, graphically illustrates the phase system.

PRODUCT SUBDIVISION (OR PRODUCT BREAKDOWN)

Product subdivision is a process for going from the system design level down to lower levels in the product hierarchy. We have seen some simple forms of this process in earlier chapters, specifically

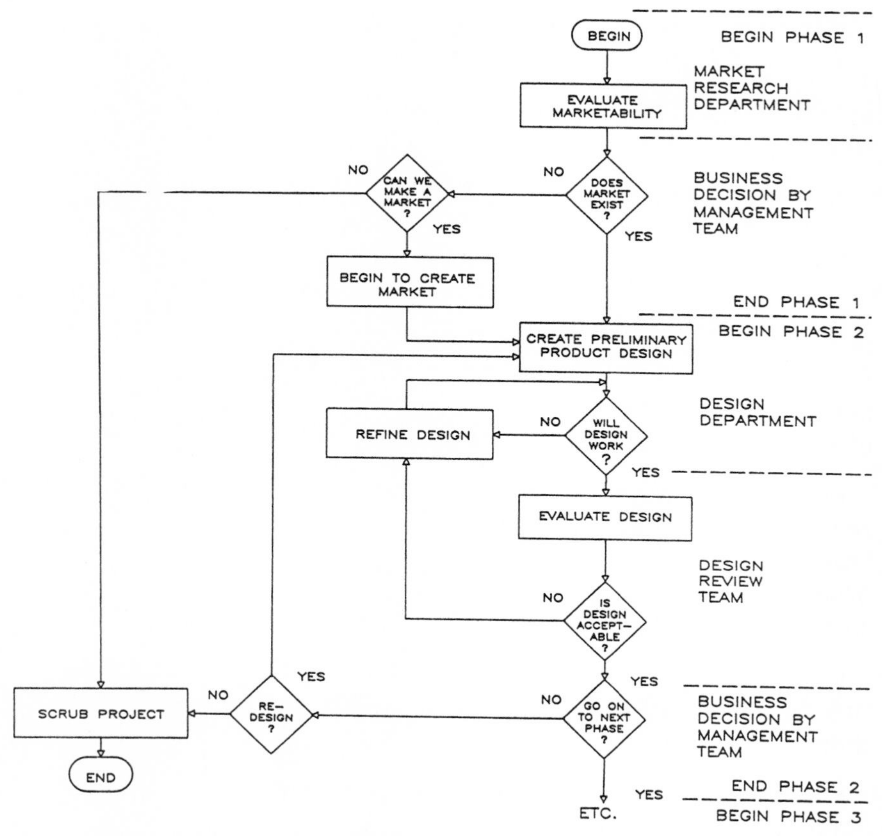

FIGURE 7–3 Flow diagram of a phased product development process

the concept of primary, secondary, and tertiary needs for automobiles (pages 40 and 43) and for health care (pages 39 and 42) in Chapter Three.

(The terminology used to designate the successive levels in the product hierarchy differs from industry to industry. In the case of physical goods the usual terms are "systems, subsystems, components, assemblies, parts," and so on.

For large systems the constituent elements can run into huge numbers—thousands and even hundreds of thousands. For such numbers, the need for structure becomes absolute.

CRITICALITY ANALYSIS

The complexity due to proliferation of customer needs goes beyond the effect of mere numbers. There is added complexity due to the degrees and variety of customer needs.

Customer needs are not equally important. Product safety or continuity of electric power supply are obviously critical customer needs.

A widely used tool for dealing with proliferation and complexity is the *criticality analysis*. The purpose is to identify the "vital few" features so that they will receive priority of attention and assets. A product feature may be classified as critical for a variety of reasons.

ESSENTIAL TO HUMAN SAFETY. Product features may pose direct threats to human health or safety or to the environment. Other threats may arise from user ignorance or misuse of the product. The aim of criticality analysis is to identify such threats so that steps can be taken to eliminate them.

LEGISLATED MANDATES. Many of our laws impact product features. Product safety is an obvious area of such legislation, but there are others, e.g., restrictions imposed to conserve energy.

ESSENTIAL TO SALABILITY. We saw in the case of the Taurus-Sable models of automobiles that about four hundred product features were judged to be critical for product salability. The total number of product features (primary, secondary, tertiary, and so on) in an automobile runs into many hundreds of thousands.

DEMANDING AS TO INVESTMENT. Some proposed product features may require substantial investment in facilities, inventories, special processes, and so on. The challenge to the product developers is to come up with alternatives that are less demanding as to investment.

DEMANDING AS TO CONTINUITY. The industrial society is dependent on the continuing performance of technological goods and services. That dependence has given birth to a new family of product features, all related to continuity of performance: reliability, failure rate, uptime (the opposite of downtime), maintainability, and others. For some goods and services those features of continuity require quite as much emphasis from product developers as the more traditional product performance features.

LONG LEAD TIME. Some product features may cause delays in subsequent processes such as developing a source of supply, establishing an adequate operating process, or training and certifying workers. Again there is a challenge to the product developers to find alternatives.

INSTABILITY. Some product features are inherently unstable because of failure-proneness (e.g., numerous components), low shelf life, susceptibility to misuse, and the like. The most economic remedies may lie in developing product features that are inherently more stable.

Criticality Reflects the Combined Views

Note that criticality is viewed from the standpoint of both the customer and the supplier. For example, in the case of salability, the priority given to product features is based on analysis of customer views and behavior. Other forms of criticality, e.g., investment, are based on realities faced by the supplier.

Criticality Analysis Spreadsheet

To ensure that appropriate action is taken with respect to all critical features, use can be made of a criticality analysis spreadsheet. Figure 7–4 shows the Critical Component Register, a form of spreadsheet used by Rank Xerox Limited. In this example the application is to product components. Each component is listed on a horizontal row. A total of twenty-seven categories of criticality are listed in the vertical columns. The analysis then identifies which types of criticality are applicable to which component.

In the same company, a more detailed analysis is then carried out for each instance of criticality. Figure 7–5 is the Component/Assembly Criticality Analysis, which shows the actions planned to respond to the several types of criticality. Some of those actions impact other processes: purchase of materials, materials transport, packaging, storage.

ISSUE NO: 1 | DATE: 9/9/83

PRODUCT: PRINTER | SHEET: 1 OF:

CRITICAL COMPONENT REGISTER

							MAKE/ASSY/VENDOR						SAFETY				TOOLING			HANDLING			INVENTORY					SOURCING			
FUNCTION: COMM OPS					•	•	•	•	•			•	•	•			•	•		•	•	•	•	•	•	•	•	•	•	•	•
FUNCTION: QUALITY					•	•	•	•	•		•	•	•	•	•	•	•	•	•	•	•				•			•			
FUNCTION: MED					•	•	•	•	•	•		•	•	•	•	•	•	•	•	•	•	•	•	•	•	•	•				
COMM CODE	PART NUMBER	DESCRIPTION	SUB SYST	ISSUE DATE	1 PROBLEM HISTORY	2 NEW TECHNOLOGY	3 TIGHT TOLERANCES	4 CRITICAL PARAMETERS	5 RIGID STANDARDS	6 OPERATOR CERT.	7 INSPECTOR CERT.	8 COMPLEX	9 MECH SAFETY	10 ELEC SAFETY	11 ENVIRONMENTAL SAFETY	12 SPEC CLOTHING/APPAR.	13 HIGH COST	14 LONG LEAD	15 REQUIRES CALIB.	16 HANDLING SENSITIVITY	17 SPECIAL TOTING	18 SPEC VENDOR PACKING	19 HIGH UMC	20 LONG LEAD	21 SHELF LIFE	22 STORAGE BULK	23 WEIGHT	24 NEW VENDOR	25 SPPS	26 IPO	27 PROPRIETARY PART
570	2S93801	BOOKWELL MLDG	17·00	8237													0	0		0 0		0 0	0	0		0		0 0			
570	2S93816	PLATEN COVER	17·00	8237													0	0		0 0		0 0	0	0		0		0 0			
180	9P90864	GAS STRUT	17·00	8237	0 0																										
1100	30S94134	ELEV. MOT. BRACKET	62·30	8237				0																					0		
210	130P90307	SENSOR	"	8237				0						0																	
230	140S91354	STK SENSOR PWB	"	8237																	0			0					0		
250	127P91103	DISC DRIVE MOTOR	"	8237				0						0										0					0		
260	121S90607	DISC CLUTCH	"	8237				0																							
1400	101S91216	CHASSIS ELEC ASSY	"	8237																	0										
570	5P90486	DISC STACKER	"	8235			0	0									0					0									

FIGURE 7–4 Critical component register, a form of criticality spreadsheet
Courtesy: Rank Xerox Limited, Mitcheldean Plant

COMPONENT / ASSEMBLY CRITICALITY ANALYSIS

RME: M.E Payne	MODEL: Printer	PART NO: 2593816
* Delete as applic.	SS:	DESCR: Platen Cover

	MED AFFECTED	QUALITY AFFECT	COMM OPS AFFECT	REF	ITEM	
	•	•	•	1	PROBLEM HISTORY	
	•	•	•	2	NEW TECHNOLOGY	
CRITICAL PROCESS MAKE/ASSY/VENDOR*	•	•	•	3	TIGHT TOLERANCES	
	•	•	•	4	CRITICAL PARAMETERS	
	•	•	•	5	RIGID STANDARDS	
	•			6	OPERATOR CERT.	
		•		7	INSPECTOR CERT.	
	•	•	•	8	COMPLEX	
SAFETY	•	•	•	9	MECH SAFETY	
	•	•	•	10	ELEC SAFETY	
	•	•	•	11	ENVIRONMENTAL SAFETY	
	•	•		12	SPEC CLOTHING/APPAR	
CRITICAL TOOLING	•	•		13	HIGH COST	✓
	•	•	•	14	LONG LEAD	✓
	•	•		15	REQUIRES CALIBRATION	
CRITICAL HANDLING	•	•	•	16	HANDLING SENSITIVITY	✓
	•	•	•	17	SPECIAL TOTING	
	•		•	18	SPEC VENDOR PACKING	✓
CRITICAL INVENTORY	•		•	19	HIGH UNIT MANUF COST	✓
	•		•	20	LONG LEAD	✓
	•	•	•	21	SHELF LIFE	
			•	22	STORAGE BULK	✓
	•		•	23	WEIGHT	
CRITICAL SOURCING		•	•	24	NEW VENDOR	✓
			•	25	S.P.P.S.	
			•	26	I.P.O.	
			•	27	PROPIETARY PART	

REF	MED PLANNED ACTIONS
16	Process Instructions To Indicate Handling Sensitivity And Plant Damage
18	Monitor Packaging For Sufficient Protection
REF	**QUALITY PLANNED ACTIONS**
16	Planned Inspection For Damage
24	Ensure Vendor is Fully Conversant With Rx Procedures i.e. 88P9.
REF	**COMM OPS PLANNED ACTIONS**
13	Monitor Tool Schedule For Progress
18	Special Toting Must Be Stipulated With Purchase Order
19, 20	Delivery Date And Price Critical. Need Close Monitoring
24	Ensure Vendor Has All Relevant Specifications
22	Bulk Storage Must Be Considered

FIGURE 7–5 Component/assembly criticality analysis
Courtesy: Rank Xerox Limited, Mitcheldean Plant

COMPETITIVE ANALYSIS

Competitive analysis is essential in a market-based society and is applicable to all aspects of business operation. We shall limit our examination to those aspects which are of special importance to product development. They include product features and process features. However, the methodology is applicable to all aspects of business operation.

Product Features

Evaluation of competitiveness of product features is essential, because clients make such evaluations when deciding which products to buy.

It is quite common for companies to tabulate their product features alongside those of competitors. The resulting comparison identifies the *presence or absence* of specific features and is an essential first step in competitive analysis.

For many product features, the competitive analysis should go further. It should evaluate *performance,* e.g., fuel consumption, comfort, millions of instructions per second. Making such evaluations can be done in part in the laboratory, but some must be done from data based on actual performance under operating conditions.

In some product lines the competitors are so numerous that full-scale competitive analysis can become very costly. Companies solve this problem by use of the Pareto principle—they concentrate on the key product features, on the key competitors, or on both.

> One electronics company conducts competitive analysis with respect to its three principal competitors in each product line. "Principal" is based on share of market.
>
> In the case of the Taurus-Sable automobiles (page 108), the competitive analysis concentrated on about four hundred key features.

What about competitive analysis when the company is a monopoly, e.g., the local school district or electric power company? In such cases the comparison should be made with similar monopolies. In most of such "industries" there are professional societies, industry associations, and other agencies that have established systems for pooling, analyzing, and publishing data on performance, including performance as to quality.

Aside from objective determinations of competitive quality there is also the need to determine customer *perceptions* of competitive quality. Where those perceptions differ significantly from reality, steps must be taken to bring the two into closer agreement, whether by product changes or by education aimed at changing perceptions.

Process Features

A second level of evaluation of competitors' quality is the features of the *process* used by competitors to produce their products. Generally, analysis of the product also tells a good deal about the process used to make that product. (Additional information is sometimes volunteered by suppliers of equipment, tools, consumables, and so forth.) The respective process capabilities can then be estimated, as well as the process costs, leading to an estimate of the unit costs.

There is a further, though subtle, aspect of competitive process features which is quite useful if it can be learned. It relates to the competitive *process yields.* There have been numerous instances in which two companies using "the same" process facilities have nevertheless differed remarkably in yields. The differences have usually been traced to the respective rates of quality improvement. The superior competitors have tackled the most quality improvement projects and thereby have learned the most about the relationship between process variables and product results.

SALABILITY ANALYSIS

Salability of product is the resultant of numerous forces. Some of them do not seem to be closely related to quality. An obvious example is the demographic pattern—the makeup and trend of the age pattern of the population. Study of such forces is certainly a part of business planning. The business interpretation of such forces then finds its way into quality planning, especially during product development.

Broad Application

Note that the term "salability" applies beyond the clients who provide our income. Salability also applies to internal customers.

> A training director concludes that a certain training program would benefit some of the company personnel. His efforts to convince his colleagues are often called "selling" his program.

Note also that salability can apply to "product features" that do not seem to be a part of the sales contract.

> For large buyers of telephone service the monthly telephone bill is also large. Some of those clients insist that the invoices provide details and summaries, which facilitate analysis and internal cost control.

Evaluation of Salability—A Contrast

For many decades, marketing managers have studied how to evaluate, quantify, and predict salability. A great deal has been learned about how to interpret economic indicators so as to provide predictions of purchasing power and affluence.

In contrast, there has been only limited progress in understanding the relation between product quality and product salability. Some of the needed tools have already been invented, as we shall see shortly. However, to apply those tools (and to invent others) requires a new level of collaboration between the marketing and quality functions. This opportunity should not be missed.

The Tools of Analysis

There are many tools of analysis, so we shall limit ourselves to the several that seem to be the vital few. Each involves analysis of some combination of the following phenomena:

Customer behavior
Customer perceptions
Customer opinions
Product differences

Customer Behavior

Customer behavior is a factual phenomenon. It consists of deeds: what customers did or did not do. The behavior is exhibited in these forms:

Products purchased or not purchased This form of customer behavior is widely evaluated in terms of "share of market." It is a most important measure of company performance.

Demands for options Some product lines are marketed on the basis of a standard product supplemented by options. Analysis of the purchase of options then leads to decisions as to which options to offer as standard equipment in future models.

Demands for "specials" In like manner, customer demands for products that differ from the standard can lead to changes in what is regarded as standard.

A company in the health industry was processing seven hundred special orders annually, with delivery intervals averaging three months. Analysis showed that a relative few part numbers accounted for 95 percent of the special orders. The remedy was to convert those frequent specials into standard products. The delivery interval dropped dramatically—85 percent of the orders were now delivered within two days. The number of special orders dropped from seven hundred to two hundred per year. All that was done at a substantial cost reduction.[2]

Bids: successful and unsuccessful In some industries the unsuccessful bids dominate the successful bids by a wide margin. It is useful to analyze the results retrospectively in an effort to discover what features of the bids dominated in success or failure.

Figure 7–6 shows the results of such an analysis involving twenty unsuccessful bids to sell and install heavy industrial equipment.

The analysis identified installation price as a leading reason. Further analysis then disclosed a weakness in the cost estimating process. That weakness required a revision in the factors used to convert work estimates into money.

[2]David L. Ball and David S. Engle, "Improving Customer Service for Special Orders," IMPRO 85.

Contract proposal	Bid not accepted due to				
	Quality of design	Product price	Installation price•	Reciprocal buying	Other
A 1	. . .	X	X	. . .	X
A 2	. . .	. . .	XX	. . .	. . .
A 3	XX	X	. . .	. . .	. . .
A 4	XX	. . .	X	. . .	. . .
A 5	XX	. . .	. . .	. . .	. . .
A 6	XX	. . .	. . .	. . .	. . .
A 7	. . .	XX	. . .	. . .	. . .
A 8	. . .	XX	. . .	. . .	. . .
A 9	. . .	. . .	XX	. . .	. . .
A 10	. . .	. . .	XX	. . .	. . .
B 1	X	. . .	X	. . .	. . .
B 2	. . .	. . .	. . .	XX	. . .
B 3	. . .	. . .	. . .	XX	. . .
B 4	. . .	. . .	. . .	XX	. . .
B 5	. . .	X	X	. . .	. . .
B 6	. . .	X	XX	. . .	. . .
B 7	XX	. . .	. . .	. . .	. . .
B 8	. . .	X	X	. . .	. . .
B 9	. . .	. . .	. . .	X	. . .
B 10	X	X	X	. . .	. . .
Totals	7	8	10 (of 14)	4	1

X = Contributing reason
XX = Main reason
•Only 14 bids were made for installation.

FIGURE 7–6 Analysis of unsuccessful bids

Products used or not used We saw an example in the case of the Marriott Hotel guests not using the bath crystals (page 46). In such a case, the existence of the behavior is an adequate basis for decision-making even if we don't know the reasons for the behavior.

Customer Perceptions

In many cases, knowledge of customer behavior is not an adequate basis for decision-making; it is necessary to know in addition the reasons behind that behavior. Those reasons can come from supplementary information such as customer perceptions and customer opinions. In the discussion that follows,

Customer *perceptions* are conclusions derived mainly from use of the product.

Customer *opinions* are assertions based mainly on judgment.

(These definitions are not mutually exclusive; there is some overlap.)

A common example of securing customer perceptions is the study of consumer preferences. Consumers are offered samples of competing products. After use of the products, the consumers state their preference.

A classic case involved shaving systems: Some years ago the Schick Company marketed a new design featuring easy blade changing. The Gillette Company then conducted a defensive market research study to determine the impact of the new design on consumers. Samples of the competing shaving systems were given to each of several hundred consumers. Each was asked to use each of the systems for an entire month. Then each consumer was asked to (1) rank the various qualities as to their order of importance and (2) rank the competing systems as to each of the qualities (see Figure 7–7). The study showed that:

1. Ease of blade changing was the least important quality.
2. The competing systems were equal with respect to ease of blade changing.
3. The Gillette system was inferior with respect to a different and very important quality.

Customer Opinions

Suppliers are understandably hungry for information as to the reasons behind customer behavior and perceptions. Why do customers buy or not buy product X? Why do customers prefer product X over Y?

To secure such information, suppliers ask customers for their opinions, using various channels: the sales force, the customer service personnel, marketing research studies. An example of the latter was the study made by Qantas Airways to learn about customer priorities (pages 49–50).

QUALITIES	USERS' RANKINGS: ORDER OF IMPORTANCE	GILLETTE	GEM	SCHICK
A Remove beard				
B Safety				
C Ease of cleaning				
D Ease of blade changing				
E - - - - -				
F - - - - -				
G - - - - -				

FIGURE 7–7 Field study: the shaving system case

The hope is that the customers will be able to identify those quality-related features which explain their behavior. Sometimes that hope is realized. More usually the answers are blurred by the numerous variables that enter into the customers' decision-making processes.

The situation is at its worst when we ask for predictions: Would you buy this product, at this price? We can obtain answers, but the reality is missing, since the customers are not faced with making an actual choice and outlay.

Product Differences

Yet another approach to sales analysis is through study of product differences. It is an approach of great promise.

Competitive products can differ in quality along a spectrum that runs from the obvious to no difference. The location of products along the spectrum tends to determine the strategies that can be employed for salability. At the "obvious" end of the spectrum the quality differences can be decisive in product salability. At the "no difference" end, it is the marketing skills that become decisive.

Quality Differences Translatable into User Economics

The spectrum includes cases in which there is a real quality difference, but the difference is not known to, or understood by, the customers. In such cases the technologists and marketers should join forces to demonstrate the quality differences in terms that can be understood by customers.

The power tool case: A maker of power tools succeeded in improving their reliability to a level well beyond that of competing tools. A team was then sent to secure field data from users on the costs of using those high-reliability tools versus those of competitors. Based on those data the differences in reliability were converted into differences in operating costs. The cost data were then propagandized, and it became feasible to secure a premium price.

That case and similar ones are found on analysis to exhibit the following commonalities:

There is in fact a quality difference among competing products.

The difference is technological in nature so that its significance is not understood by many users.

It is possible, by appropriate data collection in the field, to translate the technological difference into the language of money or into other meaningful forms.

To stimulate action by users the results must be presented in terms of the users' system of values, not the manufacturer's.

Quality Differences Minor but Demonstrable

A manufacturer of ball bearings carried out an in-depth study of the process capabilities of his machines. He succeeded in making bearings much more precise than those made by competitors using similar machinery. The superior precision was in most cases not really needed by the (industrial) clients. Nevertheless, they preferred to buy the more precise product since there was no price differential.

A company making sugar-coated chocolate candies came under the control of a knowledgeable marketer. He used television commercial messages to dramatize a small difference: The sugar-coated chocolates were less likely to smear the clothes and hands of children than uncoated chocolates. His share of market soared.

In those and similar cases the quality differences might be dismissed by some as minor. Yet the engineers and purchasing managers who could get greater (though unneeded) precision at the same price were strongly influenced. In like manner the television propaganda was so successful in dramatizing a relatively rare occurrence that consumers remembered it and acted accordingly.

Quality Difference Not Verifiable but Accepted on Faith

Some years ago Schick, a manufacturer of electric razors, published the results of tests conducted by an independent test laboratory. During the test, users shaved themselves twice, using two electric razors one after the other. On one day the Schick razor was used first and a competing razor immediately after. On the next day the sequence was reversed. In all tests the contents of the second razor were weighed precisely. The data assertedly showed that when the Schick was second its weighed contents were more than those of competitors. The implication was that Schick gave a cleaner shave. Within a few months the Schick share of market rose from 8.3 to 16.4 percent.

The most striking feature of the above case is the fact that the consumers had *no way to verify* the validity of the published account. They had the choice of accepting it on faith or not. Many accepted it on faith.

Interaction: Product Development and Marketing

That same spectrum of product difference has a profound impact on the source of salability, that is, whether salability is due mainly to the tools of product development or to the tools of marketing. An interesting study of the interplay between those two sources of salability is seen in Figure 7–8.

Each point on the diagram represents some food product: corn flakes, frozen potatoes, chocolate, and so on. The horizontal scale is consumer preference for the product of one company over the leading competitive product. The vertical scale is share of market.

The absence of points in the right-hand and left-hand zones of the diagram is mainly the results of quality differences created by product development. A high degree of consumer preference for

CONSUMER PREFERENCE FOR COMPETITOR'S PRODUCT, %

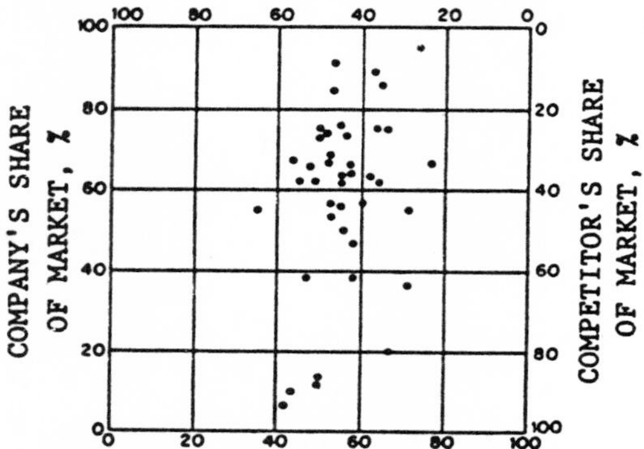

CONSUMER PREFERENCE FOR COMPANY'S PRODUCT, %

FIGURE 7–8 Study of consumer preference versus share of market

one product soon becomes widely known and drives the competing product out of the market.

The vertical spectrum contains surprises. Some products hold more than 80 percent share of market despite being neutral as to consumer preference. On analysis those surprises were mainly the result of marketing skills: getting to market first ("prior franchise"), attractive packaging, persuasive propaganda, and the like.

The diagram also contains some investment implications. An investment in product development to raise consumer preference for some product from (say) 47 to 53 percent would not be likely to create a significant change in salability. That investment might better be put into the marketing effort.

ANALYSIS TO AVOID PRODUCT FAILURES

While the top priority in product development is a salable product, the product features should also be such as to minimize product failures, both external and internal. Such product failures add to our costs to an extent that can be shocking. The external failures also add to our clients' costs and are thereby a threat to continued salability of the product.

The planned approach to product development makes specific provision for guarding against external failures. The approach does so by establishing "features" such as reliability, uptime, and so on as targets to be met during product development. Despite such provisions, a good deal of costly failure continues. Mostly it results from:

Carryover of failure-prone features of prior products

High internal failures

Carryover of Failure-Prone Features

The product features that result from product development are a mixture of:

1. Features carried over from prior products
2. Features carried over but modified to correct prior weaknesses, or to adapt to new needs
3. Features newly developed

Within this mixture the carryover usually dominates the newly created by a considerable margin. The extensive carryover makes it important for the product developer to understand what results came out of those predecessor features, both as to performance and as to failures. Carryover of failure-prone features is a form of cancer that has destroyed many well-established product lines.

> The original producer of dry copiers enjoyed a remarkable growth in sales and profits during the years when its patents gave it a monopoly. However, its products were quite failure-prone. Then, as the business grew, it was necessary to bring out a procession of new models to perform added functions, serve new applications, and so forth. To a considerable degree the new models, carried over the failure-prone features of the old. In due course, competitors found ways around the patents, came out with products of distinctly lower failure rates, and took over much of the market.

Carryover of failure-prone features is widespread. The subtle reason is that in most companies the responsibility for diagnosis and remedy of chronic problems is so vague that such problems just go on and on. Moreover, the prime responsibility of the product developers has been not to remedy long-standing chronic quality problems; their prime responsibility has been to develop new product features that can create new sales. The vagueness of responsibility, along with the need to meet the (tight) schedules for new products, has contributed to much carryover of failure-prone features.

Avoiding Internal Failures

Internal failures are in part traceable to product development. A frequent example has been that the normal operating processes are unable to produce the new product features without excessive costs.

For the most part the excess costs are traceable to lack of early warning. Product developers are generally experts in their specialty, but seldom experts in other specialties, such as operating economics. The need is to establish an early warning system to enable the product developers to draw on the expertise of other specialists. One such early warning system is "design review." Under this concept, selected specialists from internal customer organizations meet with the product developer to provide such inputs as: "If you develop the product this way, here will be the consequences in my department."

The most subtle form of carryover of costly wastes has been to include them in the budgets (or cost standards). The resulting inflated budgets hide the wastes—they disconnect the alarm signals. Whoever meets such budgets is "doing things right but not doing the right things."

In some companies the stated quality policies require that new models of products be put on the market only if their reliability (the opposite of failure-proneness) is at least equal to that of the models they replace, and of competitors' models as well. Those policies are then enforced by requiring the product developers to prove, through laboratory and field test data, that the policies have been met. Such policies are obviously constructive with respect to quality, but they do not directly address the problem of carryover of failure-prone features. The solution seems to lie elsewhere, such as:

> Bring the extent of failure-proneness out into the open by requiring the product developers to quantify the extent of failure-proneness as part of the planning process. Such disclosure then requires the business managers to face up to the decision of whether to carry over or not.

Carryover of failure-proneness is clearly not limited to development of goods and services. It extends to development of processes of all sorts: factory, clerical, transportation, storage, services in general.

A NOTE ON NOMENCLATURE. The term "failure rate" is widely used to quantify the frequency of failures in manufactured products. In *service industries* and nonmanufacturing processes the term "failure rate" is seldom used. Instead, terms like "errors," "defects," "discrepancies," or "outages" are used. The summarized measures become "error rate," "percent downtime," "defect rate," and so on.

VALUE ANALYSIS

Value analysis is a process for evaluating the interrelationships among the functions performed by product features and the associated costs.

The aim of value analysis is to help supply the functions needed by customers and to do so at minimal cost. The inputs to the value analysis process consist largely of:

The list of customers' needs and the associated order of importance

The corresponding list of product features

The estimates of the costs of providing the product features

Information on competing product features and their costs

Starting with such inputs, the value analysis process undertakes several activities:

Define the product functions with precision. Express each function in terms of a verb and a noun.

Break the primary product functions down into subfunctions: secondary, tertiary, and so on.

For each subfunction estimate the cost of carrying it out.

Use the resulting cost estimates as an aid to judging the merits of the respective product development alternatives.

Practitioners have evolved a number of methods of analysis to aid in carrying out the above activities. Generally those methods are all built around a matrix or spreadsheet, which establishes relationships between product functions and the costs of providing those functions. An example of such a spreadsheet[3] is shown in Figure 7–9.

In the spreadsheet each vertical column represents some function performed by a product feature. Each horizontal row represents some cost associated with the product feature: a component, an operation, a test, and so on.

In this analysis the left-hand column lists the various elements that generate costs. Next, the "Cost" column shows:

1. The total cost for each element (shown above the diagonal)
2. The ratio of that cost to the grand total cost for all elements (shown below the diagonal).

For example, in the top horizontal row the total cost of the comb elements is £11.58, which is 13.14 percent of the total of all costs (£88.15) for all functions.

The remaining columns then show the estimates of the extent to which the elements of cost are allocatable to the various functions.

Once the matrix has been filled in, the totals for the columns show the estimated total cost for each function.

The estimated costs can then be compared to (1) the estimates of the value (salability) of the associated product features, and (2) the estimated costs and values of competing product features.

The comparisons become a useful input to the planning and business decisions relative to meeting customer needs.

The matrix also provides useful detail on the cost buildups. There are twenty-eight "active" cost-value combinations within the matrix, adding up to a total of 88.15 pounds. However, these follow the Pareto principle, so that several of the combinations collectively account for the bulk of the costs. Any significant reduction in costs will obviously have to come from those "vital few."

Note: No one should be fooled by the seeming precision of the

[3]Derived from Sonia Withers, *Functional Cost Analysis: An Interdisciplinary Analytical Language,* paper presented at Royal Aeronautical Society's Spring Convention, May 1983. Centre for Extension Studies, University of Technology, Loughborough, Leicestershire.

DEPARTMENTS, OPERATIONS, ASSEMBLIES, PARTS, ETC.	COST	FUNCTIONS (VERB + NOUN)									
		PROVIDE LANDING	ACCEPTS STEPS	PROVIDE SAFETY	BE DURABLE	BE INTER-CHANGE-ABLE	PROVIDE RIGIDITY	BE SERVICE-ABLE	PROVIDE IDENTITY	BE ADJUST-ABLE	ASSEMBLY
COMB (4)	£11.58 / 13.14%	0.58	2.90	4.05	0.23	1.16		1.40		1.27	
SAFETY SWITCH	£13.14 / 14.90%			5.26		4.60		1.31		1.97	
COMB BEARER	£28.94 / 32.83%	11.57					14.47			2.89	
TREAD PLATE	£ 3.22 / 3.65%	0.64		0.64	1.28	0.32			0.32		
ENTRY GUIDE	£15.26 / 17.31%		5.34	3.81	1.53	1.53		1.53		1.53	
LOGO	£ 1.01 / 1.15%				0.51				0.51		
ASSEMBLY	£15.00 / 17.02%										15.00
TOTAL COST (£)	88.15	12.79	8.23	13.76	3.54	7.61	14.47	4.23	0.82	7.66	15.00
% OF TOTAL COST	100%	14.51	9.33	15.61	4.01	8.63	16.41	4.80	0.93	8.69	17.02

FIGURE 7–9 Value analysis spreadsheet

numbers in the spreadsheet. They are carried out to the second decimal place, but the real precision of the figures depends heavily on the validity of the estimates. The estimates are usually made to the nearest 10 percent, and they have a range of error beyond that.

SPREADSHEETS: MERITS AND LIMITATIONS

During our journey on the quality planning road map we have been evolving a rather extensive interrelationship between customer needs and product features. In the language of spreadsheets what we have been doing is:

Listing customer needs in the horizontal rows

Using the vertical columns to evolve the product features

As we have seen, the vertical columns can also become numerous. We have already encountered the following:

Translation into our language, unit of measure, sensor, criticality (customers' view), criticality (our view), safety, government mandate, competitive status, salability, investment, failure rate, performance, and so on.

The spreadsheet assembles a great deal of information into condensed, convenient form and is clearly an aid to a systematic approach. Through judicious use of symbols, a great deal of information can be compressed into a small space. The spreadsheet can also grow to unwieldy size and complexity through sheer volume of entries, like the cockpit of a large aircraft. To avoid such complexity we can and do break the spreadsheet up into "bite-size" segments.

It is also easy to be carried away by the elegance and convenience of the spreadsheet. The spreadsheet *does not provide answers;* it is mostly a depository for answers. For example, a column in a spreadsheet can easily be headed "salability." However, to evaluate salability can require extensive data collection and analysis. The quality of that data collection and analysis is then decisive as to the validity of the salability entry in the spreadsheet.

SUMMARY

Each customer need must be met by a product feature.

Each product feature should:

- Meet customers' needs
- Meet our needs (as suppliers)
- Meet competition
- Optimize the combined costs of our company and our customers

A complex product contains numerous product features to satisfy the numerous customer needs.

The more numerous the product features, the greater is the need for formality in quality planning.

An important tool for dealing with numerous product features is the quality planning spreadsheet.

Other tools that provide formal structure to the quality planning process are:

- The phase system
- Product subdivision
- Criticality analysis
- Competitive analysis
- Salability analysis
- Analysis to avoid failures
- Value analysis

The spreadsheet compresses much information into a small space. However, it does not give answers; it stores them.

] 8 [

Optimize Product Design

THE MISSION FOR THIS CHAPTER

The mission is to arrive at an optimum for product design. Figure 8–1 shows the input–output diagram.

The *input* is the product features resulting from product development.

The *process* is one of optimizing product designs.

The *output* is optimum product goals.

We define the optimum as that result which will:

Meet customers' needs and our needs

Minimize our combined costs

PRODUCT GOALS: THE TERMINOLOGY

The end result of optimizing is goals for the product features that collectively define the product. Before we get into the optimizing process, it is useful first to

Redefine the word "product"

Define the word "goal"

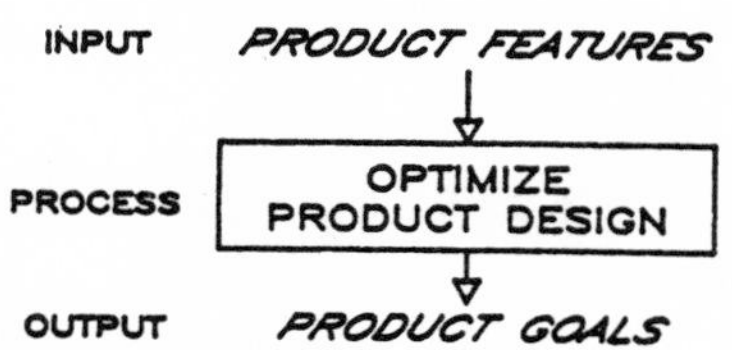

FIGURE 8–1 The input–output diagram for "Optimize product design"

Products

We are using the word product in its broad sense as the end result of *any* process.

A systems analyst works up a plan for preparing invoices. His product is the *plan.*

An office department then uses that plan to prepare invoices. Its product is *invoices.*

An engineer prepares a design for a gear box. His product is a *design.*

A factory department then makes gear boxes to that design. Its product is *gear boxes.*

A family prepares a checklist as a guide to planning future vacations. The product is a *checklist.*

Subsequently the family uses the checklist to plan vacations. Now the product is *vacations.*

A company prepares next year's quality plan—a list of quality-related objectives to be met. The product is a *quality plan.*

During the following year the company carries out the quality plan and meets most of the objectives. Here the product is quality *performance.*

A departmental supervisor undertakes a review of his triple quality-related roles: as a customer for inputs, as a processor, and as a supplier to his customers. Based on his review he prepares a proposal for revision. His product is a *proposal.*

The supervisor then receives approval to carry out his proposal. When he does so, his product is a *revision.*

Quality Goals

As used here, a goal is an aimed-at target, an achievement toward which effort is expended. A quality goal is an aimed-at quality target.

In the examples just given, efforts were expended to reach a wide variety of targets. Some were technological in nature, others were managerial. Each was a kind of goal.

The fact that a quality goal is set does not prove that it will be met; to meet it may require a significant improvement over past performance. The process for establishing quality goals usually includes a degree of voluntarism and negotiation. Quality goals are neither uniform nor static. They vary from one organization to another, and from one year to the next.

Quality Standards

A quality standard (as used here) is a mandated model to be followed. The standard is often mandated by external sources.

For example, the Fair Packaging and Labeling Act (administered by the Federal Trade Commission) requires that packaged products contain minimally the amount of product claimed on the label. Other familiar examples of mandated standards include:

Quality Program Requirements MIL-Q-9858 (Department of Defense)

Building construction codes (various municipalities)

Such quality standards are mandates to which all suppliers are subject. Generally they have been proved; it has been demonstrated that they can be met. They are not just a wish or a hope. Such standards also tend to remain stable for long periods of time.

Other quality standards are originally established by common consent. Widespread examples are the codes published by industry associations relative to product safety, interchangeability, and so on. Once established, such standards tend to have the force of mandates. A departure from the standards reduces the marketability of the product.

A Blurred Distinction

The distinction between quality standards and quality goals is clear in theory but blurred in practice. In part the blurring is due to looseness in use of the terminology. However, there are also cases in which the two concepts overlap.

A common example is the technological specification for new products. It contains tolerances that possess some of the features of goals, e.g., not yet proved, and subject to negotiation. To the operating areas those tolerances possess some of the features of standards, e.g., they are mandated by "external" forces; the mandate applies to everyone; and the tolerances tend to remain stable for long periods of time. In fact, as experience is acquired and the tolerances are met regularly, they do acquire the status of standards and are usually called standards, not goals.

The quality planning process must provide the means for meeting quality standards and goals alike. In the case of standards, the first need is to identify those which are pertinent, along with the applicable provisions. In the case of quality goals, the planning process itself is the means for establishing some of the goals.

Doing Things Right Versus Doing the Right Things

Once established, any goal or standard becomes the focal center for supplemental quality planning. The ultimate purpose of such supplemental planning is to assist the operating forces in reaching the quality goals. If the goals are poorly chosen, the planning will be done to reach the wrong goals. We shall then be successful in conformance but not as to fitness for use. We shall be "doing things right, but not doing the right things."

HIERARCHIES OF GOALS

During quality planning we regularly encounter hierarchical or pyramidal structures. We saw such structures in customer needs, units of measure, sensors, and product features. Similar structures apply to quality goals. In addition, the quality goals interact with each other.

> For example, we have the primary goal of collecting the money clients owe us. To reach that goal requires a product—an invoice—to be delivered to clients. To produce those invoices requires multiple activities or subprocesses. Those multiple activities are directed at multiple secondary goals and require process inputs in the form of data of various sorts. Producing those data requires tertiary processes with tertiary goals, and so on.

Applied to Organization Performance

The hierarchical structure also applies to the quality goals used to judge organization performance and the associated worker and manager performance. For those purposes, quality goals are established for groupings of product features.

The groupings are done in ways that parallel the organization structure and the associated responsibilities assigned to the human beings at all levels of the organizational hierarchy.

At the nonsupervisory level of the organization, the quality goals may be expressed in such terms as error rates in clerical operations or percent defective in factory operations.

In the supervisory levels the groupings of quality features may be based on product families. The resulting quality goals are expressed in such terms as error rates in Type X insurance policies or assembly repair rates for Type Y color television sets.

As we continue up the organization hierarchy the groupings of quality features become broader. The associated quality goals also become broader. At middle management levels the goals are stated in such terms as:

Cost of poor quality related to operating costs

Error rates for an entire function relative to error rates (for the same function) in other companies

In many cases the functions and the organization units that perform the functions are coextensive. For example, the function of filling customer orders may be carried out by a Customer Order Department, which has no other function. In such cases the quality goal for the function can also serve as a goal for the organization unit, and thereby as a goal for the manager of that unit.

In other cases function and organization unit are not coextensive. Some organization units carry out multiple functions; some functions are carried out by multiple organization units. Where function and organization are not coextensive it is common to evolve goals for the organization units as well as for the functions.

Applied to Corporate Levels

At the highest level are the strategic corporate goals for quality. Those goals are properly an extension of the business goals of the corporation. Here are some examples:

On-time arrivals must attain a level of 80 percent by the end of the next year (an airline).

Our product performance must at least be equal to that of our three principal competitors.

Any new model of product must have a level of reliability at least as high as the model it replaces.

During the next five years our objective is to bring the cost of poor quality down to 6 percent of sales.

During the next five years we should cut by a third the time required to bring new products to market.

During the next five years we should extend training in quality matters to managers and specialists in all departments.

During the next calendar year we should create opportunities for workers to participate actively in quality matters.

A GOAL SHOULD BE . . .

From long experience, we have evolved a list of criteria to be met by those who establish goals. A goal should be:

Optimal as to overall results Goals that "suboptimize" performance of various activities can easily damage overall performance.

All-inclusive Activities for which goals have been set tend to have high priority, but at the expense of the remaining activities.

Maintainable Goals should be designed in modular fashion so that elements can be revised without extensive teardown.

Economic The value of meeting the goals should be clearly greater than the cost of setting and administering them.

No less important is the list of criteria as perceived by those who are faced with meeting the goals. To those operating forces, goals should be:

Legitimate Goals should have undoubted official status.

Understandable They should be stated in clear, simple language, ideally in the language of those who are faced with meeting the goals.

Applicable The goals should fit the conditions of use or should include the flexibility to adapt to conditions of use.

Worthwhile Meeting the goal should be regarded as benefiting those who do the added work as well as benefiting the organization that established the goal.

Attainable It should be possible for "ordinary" people to meet the goals by applying reasonable effort.

Equitable Since performance against goals is frequently used for merit rating of individuals, the goals should be reasonably alike as to difficulty of attainment.

THE BASES FOR ESTABLISHING QUALITY GOALS

There are various bases for setting quality goals: history, engineering study, the market, mandates. Each of those (and others) has its merits and deficiencies. Let us look at the bases most commonly used.

History as a Basis

Historical performance is widely used as a basis for quality goals. In manufacturing areas we make use of historical data (on scrap, rework, and so on) for planning the amount of material to order, how much machinery to provide, how many workers, and so forth. In the field service department we make similar use of historical field failure data for planning the size of the field service force and the inventories of spare parts. In the functional departments we use historical data on error rates as an input to next year's planning. In preparing the annual budget, we take notice of historical levels of performance such as cost of poor quality.

The historical basis for a goal has much appeal for the operating forces who face the problem of meeting that goal in the future. A key reason is that such a goal meets the criterion of attainability. It has already been attained, hence it is attainable. Historical bases are also a source of stability and predictability since they demand no departure from established practice. In addition they are also economical: The data base is largely in existence.

All those benefits of historical bases can easily hide a serious weakness: We may be perpetuating a poor level of performance. That has in fact taken place on a huge scale. Many companies have lost their quality leadership by perpetuating failure-prone product designs, incapable manufacturing processes, error-prone clerical processes, and high costs of poor quality. The quality leadership was taken over by companies that moved aggressively into planning to improve on historical performance. The amazing Japanese revolution in quality featured just such an aggressive movement.

Engineering Study as a Basis

By engineering study we mean scientific collection and analysis of data. This approach has long been used for such activities as design of technological products and processes. The resulting quality goals (often called standards) are expressed in technological units of measure and take the form of limiting tolerances: maxima, minima, ranges. Products and processes based on such engineering studies have in general greatly outperformed those that are empirically based.

Despite the inherent superiority of the scientific approach, we continue to encounter severe problems when we try to meet the quality goals established by engineering study. Some of the problems are traceable to weaknesses in our use of the scientific approach. However, the bulk of them seem to be traceable to weaknesses in our organizational and managerial structure.

The organizational and managerial weaknesses usually arise from the fact that two categories of people are often involved ("two worlds"):

Those who establish the quality goals: systems analysts, researchers, product developers, designers, and so on

Those who are impacted by the resulting quality goals: the end users, the intermediate users, the operating forces who have the responsibility of meeting the goals

Where there is a strict organizational separation between those categories it is easy to end up with quality goals that are:

Not applicable—the goals were evolved under "laboratory" conditions, not under operating conditions

Not attainable—for the same reason

Here are several examples of designs for which we make wide use of engineering study to set quality goals:

1. *Physical end products,* such as automobile or computers. The end users (external "customers") include industrial compa-

nies and consumers. Other users include internal customers such as those who are faced with meeting the quality goals: process designers, production workers, maintenance workers.

2. *Manufacturing processes,* such as machine tools or oil refineries. Those faced with meeting the quality goals include the builders (toolmakers, construction workers, installers) and the operating forces—the workers in the production facilities.

3. *Data processing systems,* for which the end users ("customers") of the data are largely company managers. Those faced with meeting the quality goals are largely the office workers.

In these and other examples the quality goals are typically developed in a "laboratory" world characterized by distinct features:

Conditions of use are simulated, not real.

Many environmental conditions are deliberately controlled in order to keep out extraneous variables.

The personnel are trained in the associated technology.

The basic mission is to attain "structural integrity."

The main emphasis is on external customers and end use. Other customers, including "those faced with meeting the quality goals," receive lower priority.

In contrast, the "real" world of the customers exhibits a different set of features:

The conditions of use are "actual," including misuse.

The environment is subject to entry of extraneous variations.

The personnel are not necessarily trained in the associated technology. (In the case of consumers, there is extensive ignorance of the technology.)

There are multiple users, many of whom are not end users.

The basic mission is to meet operating goals and/or fitness for end use.

Many of our quality problems have their origin in the separation between those two worlds. To minimize the problems we must provide connecting bridges. Chief among those is the participation concept. Under that concept the operating forces and other customers are brought into the process of establishing the quality goals. We shall shortly look more closely at the concept of participation since it is applicable to all methods of setting quality goals.

The Market as a Basis

Another important basis for setting quality goals is "the market." We define the market as the composite of performances in a competitive society. As shoppers we make price comparisons and thereby use the market price as a basis for buying. Industrial companies and other organs of society for centuries have similarly done comparison shopping by getting competitive quotations or bids as a basis for buying. More recently they have evolved market information on such matters as automobile repair rates, energy consumption of appliances, and accident rates, again as a basis for setting goals. The present emphasis on quality has stimulated a search for market information on quality as an aid to setting quality goals.

There are some persuasive reasons for using the market as one of the bases for setting quality goals:

The market goal is *attainable under operating conditions*. The proof is that others are already attaining it.

If we are not meeting the market level of quality, our clients in due course will discover that fact. (We may already be in trouble.)

We should have early warning of lack of competitiveness so we'll have time to take remedial action.

It can be a lot of work to discover the level of market quality. We must acquire information on competitive products in a variety of ways. The more usual ways include:

PHYSICAL INSPECTION AND TEST. It may be necessary for us to buy or borrow competitors' products and to conduct the necessary programs of inspection and test.

ACQUISITION OF FIELD PERFORMANCE DATA. We may need to put competing products into service to secure such data. Alternatively we can buy the data from ultimate users, maintenance shops, and so on. We can even contract to do maintenance service for ultimate users with a view to securing the performance data as a by-product.

MARKETING RESEARCH TO DISCOVER CUSTOMERS' PERCEPTIONS. Beyond the technological data from laboratory tests and field use, we need also to discover the perceptions of customers. Some of those perceptions relate to features not measureable through laboratory tests or field use: responses to customers' inquiries; satisfaction in the event of complaints; courtesy of service personnel. Other perceptions relate to values placed by customers on various quality characteristics; customers' biases; and actions taken by customers under various circumstances.

The concept of market-based quality goals applies to all levels in the company, from the general manager to the nonsupervisors. In our final chapters we shall have a look at applying such goals to all those levels.

DECREED QUALITY STANDARDS: INTERNAL MONOPOLIES

A decreed quality standard is one imposed on us by forces that are largely beyond our control. Either we comply with the decree or we will be "out." If the decree comes from a client, we must comply or we will lose the contract. If the decree comes from government regulators, we must comply or we may face criminal penalties. If the decree comes from the boss, we must comply or we may be guilty of insubordination.

The more subtle forms of decreed standards are self-imposed within the company. Any of the activities around The Spiral is a supplier who can create problems for various internal customers. For example, Product Development may unilaterally publish tolerances that Operations is unable to meet at competitive costs. Those tolerances are engineered standards, but they are also decreed, since they are imposed by a department that has a sort of monopoly with respect to setting tolerances. *Such monopolies abound in our companies.* Many departments are given responsibility for making specific types of decisions. To illustrate:

DEPARTMENT	JURISDICTION
Marketing	Sign sales contracts
Purchasing	Sign purchase contracts
Staff departments	Establish schedules, issue procedures manuals, interpret regulations

These and other decisions can and do impact quality. Yet the associated jurisdictions are generally interpreted as having a degree of exclusivity or monopoly over the respective areas of decision-making. Let us look closely at the nature of that monopoly. It involves several rights with respect to decision-making on quality standards, including the right to:

Participate in the decision-making process

Have the last word (make the final decision)

Publish the final decision

It is easy to agree that the right of publication should be a monopoly. Multiple sources of publication inevitably result in conflicting standards and associated confusion. Such confusion is avoided by designating one and only one department as the official publisher. That form of monopoly is widely used for such documents as product specifications, sales contracts, purchase orders, and budgets.

While a monopoly on publication has much merit, it can easily be allowed to grow to include two additional monopolies:

A monopoly on the choice of the input and criteria, which then become the basis for decision-making

A monopoly on decision-making

To illustrate, virtually all companies give their product design departments a clear monopoly on publication of product designs. No product design has official status until it is published by that department. However, in many of those same companies the product design department has over the years acquired a monopoly on choice of input and criteria, and on decision-making. The latter two monopolies have been a source of much discord and damage. They have often resulted in designs of products that are uneconomic to produce, difficult to test, unreliable in service, and difficult to maintain. In terms of The Spiral, one activity (product development) has used its monopoly unilaterally to create problems for other activities. The key to avoidance of such damage and discord is *participation* in setting quality goals.

ZERO DEFECTS AS A GOAL

A flood of confusion arises from the two principal meanings of the term "zero defects":

1. Defect-free product, which is the literal meaning
2. A slogan to be used during "drives" to improve quality

Defect-free product has value as a long-range goal, since it implies the need for never-ending improvement. The concept rejects the idea that we can relax our efforts short of perfection.

In contrast, if we decree defect-free product as a short range goal, such a goal is in the great majority of cases not attainable. In such cases the risk is that the decree will be counterproductive by shutting off efforts to reach attainable goals.

Zero defects as a slogan means the term is adopted as a kind of banner to fly during a company "drive" to improve quality. In its best usage this is comparable to adopting an appealing brand name to help sell a product. In such cases much depends on the substance behind the drive. If the drive is well-conceived (a "good" product), then a good brand name is an aid to selling it to the internal customers. If the drive is ill-conceived (e.g., an attempt to solve the company's quality problems by exhorting the workforce), then it will fail no matter how clever the slogan.

SUMMARY (Interim)

A goal is an aimed-at target.

A quality goal is an aimed-at quality target.

A quality standard is a mandated model to be followed.

Quality goals vary from organization to organization and from one year to the next.

Once established, any goal or standard becomes the focal center for subsequent quality planning.

Quality goals exhibit hierarchical forms.

Quality goals are applicable to goods, services, processes, organization functions, and organization units.

A goal should be:

Optimal as to overall results
All-inclusive
Maintainable
Economic
Legitimate
Understandable
Applicable
Worthwhile
Attainable
Equitable

There are various bases for setting quality goals, including:

History
Engineering study
The market place
Decreed quality standards

Goals based on history are attainable but can lead us to perpetuate a poor performance.

Goals based on engineering study have generally produced better results than empirically based goals.

Market-based goals are essential in a competitive society.

Internal monopolies on goal setting lead to unilateral creation of problems for other functional departments. The remedy is participation.

Internal monopolies on goal setting require clear distinction to be made among the various "rights" with respect to decision-making:

Participation in the decision-making process

Having the last word (make the final decision)

Publishing the final decision

CONCEPT OF THE OPTIMUM

The optimum quality goal is to:

Meet the needs of customer and supplier alike

Minimize their combined costs

Knowledge of the customers' needs is often sufficient to enable the suppliers to meet those needs forthwith. Most of society's activities consist of transactions in highly standardized goods and services. Many stated needs of customers specifically call for such standardized products. Many other needs can be met by suppliers who have designed their processes to provide a range of products corresponding to the usual range of customer needs.

However, we also have many cases in which despite knowledge of customers' needs we do not proceed forthwith to meet them. Our processes may simply be unable to meet those needs. We may be able to meet the needs, but at a price that customers would be unwilling to pay. We may be able to meet the customers' real needs but not the stated needs. Reconciling those and other cases of incompatibility requires a search for the optimum.

From the standpoint of the benefit to society, the optimum is clearly the ideal goal. Reaching that goal requires overcoming several obstacles, mainly:

The traditional urge of customers and suppliers to *suboptimize*—to meet their separate goals

Creating the participation needed to secure the necessary inputs and discover the optimum

Securing the needed inputs and determining the conditions that provide an optimum result

Resolving differences

SUBOPTIMIZING

An important cause of failure to reach the optimum is the pursuit of local goals. Suboptimization takes place between companies and also within companies.

Suboptimization Between Companies

In market-based societies, the dominant tradition has been for each company to look out for its own interests—to meet its own quality needs and to minimize its own costs. The competitive society does contain forces that favor arriving at the optimum, but the pace can be agonizingly slow.

> The concept of life cycle costing has been known for many years. It offers a key opportunity to improve our national quality and productivity. Yet application of the concept is still in its infancy.

Joint Planning

The main remedy for suboptimization is joint planning. Such joint planning is already going on in many forms.

> Some service companies prepare and publish information to help customers analyze their needs. A widespread example has been in the area of energy conservation.

> Many manufacturing companies offer a service of "Technical Representatives" to visit with customers, analyze their needs, and provide consulting assistance.

> The "just in time" concept of manufacture requires extensive joint planning between customer and supplier.

In some instances, joint planning has resulted in extensive shift of work between independent organizations.

> A major activity in the Postal Service is sorting the mail based on destination. It was determined by joint studies that companies who send out large volumes of mail were in a position to presort such mail with less effort than the Postal Service, and with resulting speedier delivery. In turn, the Postal Service established a discounted price for presorted mail.

Suboptimization Within Companies

Suboptimization is also a widespread problem within companies. A contributing cause is the practice of establishing departmental goals and then judging the performance of managers based on departmental performance against those goals.

That practice is inherently sound. People get more done when they do have goals and are judged by their performance against goals. However, it is all too easy for a department to improve its performance and in doing so to damage company performance.

> A purchasing department reduced the cost of purchased materials by buying a year's supply rather than one month's at a time. However, the net result was a loss to the company. The material deteriorated gradually during storage. The effect over a month or two had been tolerable. Over a period of many months it was not tolerable.

As with the problem of suboptimization between companies, the chief remedy is joint planning. In turn, this requires carrying out several activities noted previously: creating participation, securing the needed inputs, and resolving differences. We shall now look at each of those more closely.

PARTICIPATION

Finding the optimum involves balancing of needs, whether multicompany needs or multidepartmental needs. Ideally the search for the optimum should be done through the *participation* of suppliers and customers alike. (A well-known case in point is the design review concept.) All have experience and expertise to share. They use their experience and expertise to make such contributions as:

EARLY WARNING OF UPCOMING PROBLEMS. "If you plan it this way, here is the problem I will face."

DATA TO AID IN FINDING THE OPTIMUM. The various customers are frequently in a position to provide data in the form of costs that will be incurred, process capability of facilities, and so on. Such data are of obvious help for optimizing overall performance.

CHALLENGE TO THEORIES. Specialist departments are typically masters of their own specialty but seldom masters of the specialties of other departments. In the absence of participation by those other departments the risk is that unproved theories or unwarranted beliefs will prevail. Participation by the customers provides an informed challenge.

Collectively those and other contributions make the whole greater than the sum of the parts. The equation takes the form $1 + 1 = 3$.

Creating such participation goes beyond scheduling phone calls and meetings. It requires creation of an atmosphere of mutual trust. In turn, this requires face-to-face meetings, mutual visits to see and understand operations, sharing of experiences and feedback, and exchanging critiques and ideas.

All that communication and sharing must be done with sincerity. Any "secret" holding back is soon sensed and resented. The resulting mutual suspicion is an obstacle to the free flow of communication, and thereby to finding the optimum. (In some cases there are logical reasons for restrictions on sharing information or on areas open to visits. For example, some suppliers compete with their clients for sales in the same market. In any such case the need is to make the restriction in the open rather than in secret—to make clear that it is a justified exception to the rule.)

ORGANIZING FOR PARTICIPATION

To organize for participation, it helps to look at the main activities involved in the process of goal setting:

Assemble the inputs
Find the optimum
Resolve differences
Decide on the goal
Publish the goal

This list of activities is common to all bases for setting goals: historical, engineered, market-based, or decreed. Obviously, there should be clear definition of responsibility with respect to each of those activities.

Alternatives for Organization

The two most common forms of organization for participation are (1) the coordinator and (2) the interdepartmental team.

The *coordinator* may be a member of the same specialist department that plays the leading role in planning the product or process to which the goal is to apply, e.g., Systems and Procedures or Product Development. Alternatively, the coordinator may be a member of some department whose chief role is coordination, e.g., Program Management. Either way, the process of participation is essentially the same, namely:

The coordinator "makes the rounds," that is, visits each customer to secure input.

Based on that input, the coordinator prepares a draft proposal, which is sent to all customers for comment.

The comments are then talked out, after which the draft is revised and published as a quality goal.

The use of a departmental specialist as coordinator has an obvious risk of bias: The specialist may resolve doubts in ways that pursue departmental goals, avoid departmental blame, and so on. The risk can be reduced by providing clear policy guidelines, clear definition of responsibility, channels for upper management reviews, and so forth. Use of a coordinating *department* reduces the inherent biases but increases the "front end" costs. (Those costs often earn a high return on investment in the form of fewer crises, shorter time cycles, and other benefits.)

The main alternative to the coordinator concept is the *interdepartmental team* (also called committee or task force). The team may be created for a specific limited purpose—an *ad hoc* committee. Or it may have a continuing existence, e.g., a design review committee.

In contrast to the coordinator concept and its associated "making the rounds," the team convenes for multidirectional discussion. All members provide input and contribute ideas. The job of drafting proposals may be delegated to some individual member, but the review will again be conducted at a team meeting.

RESOLVING DIFFERENCES

The validity of the concept of an optimum is absolute. Nevertheless, customers and suppliers are tugged by powerful local forces to an extent that can easily lead to a result other than the optimum. Avoiding such a result requires an understanding of the interplay among those local forces. In the case of external customers the forces are mainly technological and economic. In the case of internal customers some additional forces of a behavioral nature can intervene.

Essential Inputs

In some cases the main obstacle to resolving differences is lack of essential information. Each of the participants does have pertinent information, but it is usually limited to his local area of responsibility. In turn his defined area of responsibility impels him to optimize his departmental performance, which often means suboptimizing the overall performance. The missing "essential inputs" are usually those which cut across departmental lines. We looked at some of them in earlier chapters: competitive analysis, salability analysis, value analysis, life cycle costing.

For those who have the responsibility to find the real optimum, it is tempting to "make do" with such information as is already available. That temptation should be resisted. A part of the job of finding the optimum is to identify the essential inputs. Once those have been identified, each poses questions of this sort:

Is this information now available?

If not, is it worthwhile to create it?

A further input to goal setting is derived from the processes needed to produce the product features. (The next two chapters are titled "Process Development" and "Optimizing, Proof of Process Capability, and Transfer to Operations.") The optimal process design interacts with the optimal product design, which makes each an input to the other.

Technological Analysis

For complex products the analysis of essential inputs can also become complex. "Criticality Analysis" (page 115) was an example.

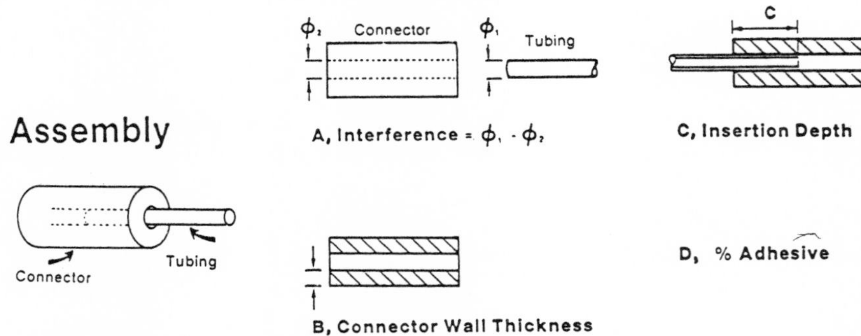

FIGURE 8–2 Connector assembly: Controllable variables A,B,C and D

While such analyses can be complex, there are now available some tools to deal with their complexity. An example is "orthogonal arrays"—a form of design of experiment used to find the optimum combination of values of variables during product design and/or process design.

An example was an assembly of an elastomeric connector to a nylon tube.[1] The objective was to minimize assembly effort and to maximize pull-off force.

Figure 8–2 is a sketch of the components and the method of assembly, indicating the controllable variables.

Study of the pertinent product and process variables showed that there were four controllable variables or "factors," and three uncontrollable factors. They are listed in Figure 8–3.

Controllable Factors	Levels		
A. Interference	Low	Med.	High
B. Connector Wall Thickness	Thin	Med.	Thick
C. Insertion Depth	Shallow	Med.	Deep
D. % Adhesive	Low	Med.	High

Noise Factors	Levels	
E. Conditioning Time	24h	120h
F. Conditioning Temperature	72°F	150°F
G. Conditioning Relative Humidity	25%	75%

FIGURE 8–3 Factors and levels

[1]Diane M. Byrne and Shin Taguchi, "The Taguchi Approach to Parameter Design," 1986 ASQC Quality Congress Transaction, pp. 168–177. Example taken from Baylock Manufacturing Company.

Test Condition	Int. A	Thick. B	Depth C	Adhes. D
1	1	1	1	1
2	1	2	2	2
3	1	3	3	3
4	2	1	2	3
5	2	2	3	1
6	2	3	1	2
7	3	1	3	2
8	3	2	1	3
9	3	3	2	1

FIGURE 8–4 Test combinations: Controllable factors

The researchers decided to conduct experiments at three levels of values for each of the controllable factors, and at two levels for each of the noise (uncontrollable) factors. The values chosen for those levels are also listed in Figure 8–3.

To minimize the amount of experimentation, use was made of combinations into "orthogonal arrays." Figure 8–4 shows that nine such combinations were created for the controllable factors.

For the uncontrollable factors, eight combinations were created, as shown in Figure 8–5.

The design required 8 × 9, or seventy-two experiments to be conducted. Figure 8–6 shows the overall data plan and results. Analysis of the data then determined the optimum product and process conditions needed to reach the objectives of minimum assembly effort and maximum pull-off force.

Test Condition	Time E	Temp. F	Humidity G
1	1	1	1
2	1	1	2
3	1	2	1
4	1	2	2
5	2	1	1
6	2	1	2
7	2	2	1
8	2	2	2

FIGURE 8–5 Test combinations: Uncontrollable factors

					2	2	2	2	1	1	1	1	E Time
Test	Int.	Thick.	Depth	Adhes.	2	2	1	1	2	2	1	1	F Temp.
Condition	A	B	C	D	2	1	2	1	2	1	2	1	G Humid.
1	1	1	1	1	19.1	20.0	19.6	19.6	19.9	16.9	9.5	15.6	
2	1	2	2	2	21.9	24.2	19.8	19.7	19.6	19.4	16.2	15.0	
3	1	3	3	3	20.4	23.3	18.2	22.6	15.6	19.1	16.7	16.3	
4	2	1	2	3	24.7	23.2	18.9	21.0	18.6	18.9	17.4	18.3	
5	2	2	3	1	25.3	27.5	21.4	25.6	25.1	19.4	18.6	19.7	
6	2	3	1	2	24.7	22.5	19.6	14.7	19.8	20.0	16.3	16.2	
7	3	1	3	2	21.6	24.3	18.6	16.8	23.6	18.4	19.1	16.4	
8	3	2	1	3	24.4	23.2	19.6	17.8	16.8	15.1	15.6	14.2	
9	3	3	2	1	28.6	22.6	22.7	23.1	17.3	19.3	19.9	16.1	

FIGURE 8–6 Overall data plan and results

Economic Analysis

The goal in economic terms is to minimize the combined costs of customers and suppliers. Arriving at the optimum obviously requires that we determine:

What are the alternative ways for meeting (or revising) customers' needs

What are the associated costs, for customers and for suppliers

Preparation of such inputs requires digging well below the surface. A widespread example is life cycle costing for long-life goods. Design of those goods requires a decision of whether to:

1. Design for low original cost so as to permit a low selling price. Such designs often result in a high "cost of ownership"—a high cost of operating and maintaining the product over its lifetime. The high cost is in turn due to maintenance costs, downtime, high energy consumption, and other factors resulting from design emphasis on low original cost.
2. Design for low cost of ownership over the life of the product. Such designs often result in a high original price, with associated selling problems.

The life cycle cost concept is sound and can contribute importantly to improving national productivity. The chief obstacle is cultural resistance. For most of human history, the main determinant in purchasing has been the original price.

Behavioral Obstacles

The technological and economic considerations spelled out above apply to internal as well as external customers. In addition, internal customers erect other obstacles to attaining the optimum. Those obstacles have their origin in the mysteries of human behavior. However, they are very real obstacles, and they must be overcome if we are to attain the optimum.

The Claim of Exclusive Jurisdiction

In planning meetings it is common to hear claims like this: *We* are "responsible" for quality (or for cost, safety, design). Those are claims to a vague monopoly on some phenomenon that is in fact multidepartmental: Many departments are impacted by decisions and actions which affect quality (or cost, safety, design). Dealing with such claims requires an analysis to identify the *specific decisions and actions* that are at issue. We can usually agree on who should have responsibility for making specific decisions or taking specific actions. We can seldom agree on who should have responsibility for broad abstractions.

A case in point is the question: Who is "responsible for quality" on the work floor? No answer is possible until we break that vague question up into answerable pieces—decisions and actions. It is fairly easy to answer such questions as: Who should make this decision? Who should take this action?

> For example, the managers in one factory had for years debated the question, "Who is responsible for quality on the factory floor?" There had never been an agreement. Then, during a meeting convened for resolving that question, the participants "voted" on who should have responsibility for the critical decisions and actions. Figure 8–7 shows their conclusions. It became evident that they could reach a consensus once they restated the question in terms of decisions and actions.

Authority of Expertise

In some types of problems we rely on the judgment of the acknowledged experts. Here are two examples:

> Our planning requires preparation of a new form of product warranty. The wording of the warranty is critical. If poorly

Who Should Make These Decisions and Take These Actions?

	PRODUCTION			INSPECTORS	
DECISIONS AND ACTIONS NEEDED	SETUP SPECIALIST	WORKER	SUPER-VISOR	BENCH	PATROL
Set up the process	16	7			
Verify the setup	8	3	10	1	4
Run the process		23			
Verify the running (two hours later)		19	3		5
Judge the conformance of the resulting product	1		5	1	18

FIGURE 8–7 **Views on responsibility for decisions and actions**

worded, it may expose us to extensive costs in the form of unjustified claims. We rely on the lawyer's opinion as to how the wording would be interpreted by the courts.

A new product involves potential safety hazards for ultimate users. What is critical is the factor of safety to be used in the design. We rely on the design engineer's opinion as to the factors of safety needed to ensure the structural integrity of the design.

In each case the reliance is on expertise derived from special training and experience. In their areas of expertise, we give the experts the benefit of the doubt and the last word.

Specialties and Broad Planning

While we rely on the experts as to their area of expertise, we should distinguish carefully between areas of expertise and the broad planning of which those areas are a part.

We look to the lawyer to provide the legal interpretation of the wording of the warranty. We do not look to the lawyer to determine what should be the features covered by the warranty, or what should be the duration of the warranty. Those are business questions to be answered by the managers who collectively run the business.

We look to the product designer to provide expertise relative to using the laws of nature to attain structural integrity. We do not give the designer the last word on whether we should go to market with the product. That is a business decision.

RESOLVING DIFFERENCES: SOME METHODOLOGIES

Practicing managers and behavioral scientists have given much thought to ways to resolve differences. We shall look at an example from each group.

The Coonley–Agnew Process

A process for resolving differences was set out in a paper published in 1941. It related to an attempt to establish national quality standards for cast iron pipe. The climate for agreement was decidedly unfavorable; the manufacturers and the ultimate users had for years been unhappy with each other. When a joint committee was set up to develop the quality standards, the chairman stipulated three conditions:

1. They must identify their areas of agreement and their areas of disagreement. "That is, they must first agree upon the exact point at which the road began to fork." When that was done, it was found that a major point of disagreement concerned the validity of a certain formula.
2. "They must agree on why they disagreed." They concluded that the known facts were inadequate to decide whether the formula was valid or not.
3. "They must decide what they were going to do about it." The decision was to raise a fund to conduct the research needed to establish the necessary facts. "With the facts at hand, the controversies disappeared."[2]

[2]Howard Coonley and P. G. Agnew, "The Role of Standards in the System of Free Enterprise," American National Standards Institute, 1941.

The Alternatives of Follett

Mary Parker Follett's writings included an analysis[3] of resolving differences through:

Dominance

Compromise

Constructive conflict

Dominance

Dominance is exemplified in some types of purchase contract negotiation. When supplies are plentiful, large customers may impose their financial terms on suppliers. Quality needs are mandated—the suppliers' offers to work jointly for an optimum are brushed aside. Contracts include voluminous fine print to plug potential loopholes.

The economic power of such customers begets compliance; the supplier who short-cuts full compliance risks losing an important client. But suppliers resent such autocratic behavior. The result is an adversary relationship with associated suspicion and mistrust. In times of shortage, the suppliers retaliate. Each party works to optimize its own results, not to find ways to improve results for both. The adversary relationship effectively shrinks the communication and teamwork needed to find the common optimum.

Dominance is also widely practiced between internal suppliers and internal customers. Most of that has its origin in monopolies granted by top management to various process teams. To illustrate:

> The Budget Office is given responsibility for preparing the budget. To simplify its work it imposes elaborate forms and procedures on all other departments. The end result is higher overall cost to the company.
>
> In like manner, Management Information Systems may impose unwarranted burdens on other departments. Marketing may demand perfectionism in quality with little effect on sales volume but with costly consequences. Product Development

[3]Reported in H. C. Metcalf and L. Urwick (eds.), *Dynamic Administration* (New York: Harper & Row, 1941).

may come up with new product designs that are uneconomic to make.

As to internal customers the rule must be: No process team has the right, unilaterally, to make trouble for a customer.

Compromise

Wide use of the concept of compromise is found in the political process. Legislators have divergent goals, yet they need the votes of a majority to get action. A common practice is "logrolling": "You vote for my bill and I'll vote for yours." Each meets some desired goals but at the price of taking some unwanted and even unpleasant actions.

The atmosphere of compromise is less abrasive than that of dominance. But compromise still falls short of arriving at the optimum. It satisfies no one in a fundamental way. It also lacks the basic spirit of teamwork, which is essential to create the communication and joint effort needed to discover the optimum.

Constructive Conflict

"Constructive conflict" is Follett's term for a teamwork approach to discover the optimum.

> A supplier shipped bulk materials to clients, using packages each containing 100 kilos. One client made products in batches, which required weighing out specific amounts of material in accordance with the batch formula. A teamwork approach resulted in the supplier shipping the materials in containers whose contents were even fractions of the quantities called for by the batch formula.
>
> In this case one product feature was weight of package contents. The supplier was in any case required to fill containers to some specified weight, and to do enough weighing to ensure conformance to specification. A way was found to eliminate the need for the customer to repackage, reweigh, relabel, and so forth. That was done without adding significantly to the work of the supplier.

PUBLICATION OF STANDARDS AND GOALS

Publication of standards is a natural monopoly. If there is more than one publisher for the same standard, there will inevitably be confusion as to which is the official standard.

Publication actually involves two separable functions:

1. *Authentication* is the job of certifying that the standard is ready to be issued. The authenticator may be that specialist department which has "the benefit of the doubt and the last word." The authenticator may also be some coordinating department, which secures a consensus and then in effect certifies: "Here is the consensus that was reached."

2. *Issuance* is the administrative job of preparing duplicate copies of the official standard and distributing them to the customers. Here again, the issuing department may be the same as the authenticator, or it may be a separate service.

There is nothing trivial or demeaning about the job of publishing quality standards. A great deal of damage can be done and has been done because of publication errors in product design specifications, operating instruction manuals, maintenance manuals, and so on. The publication job should be in the hands of people whose training and experience qualify them to carry out such exacting work.

Publication of goals is also a natural monopoly, although it is not always as well structured as is the case with publication of standards. Nevertheless, some aspects of publication of goals are influential in meeting the criteria for what "a goal should be."

Goals should be written out. This discipline helps to ensure that the goals are *understandable.*

Goals should be approved by the appropriate authority. This helps to ensure their *legitimacy.*

The process of optimizing concludes with a list of product goals for the various product features. Figure 8–8 is an example showing a number of product features and associated product goals.

The establishment of goals also completes the quality planning spreadsheet we have been filling up, starting with the list of customer needs. (See Figures 3–4 and 3–5, pages 42 and 43.) In the

PRODUCT FEATURE	GOAL
Vehicle weight	
Total vehicle weight	1,500 kg. maximum
Body weight	1,000 kg. maximum
Combined engine/transaxle weight	2,500 kg. maximum
Training for service personnel	
Service manuals	Cleared by cognizant departments and in dealer hands one month prior to product introduction
Video training	Same as above
Owner's manual	Cleared by cognizant departments and at assembly plant in quantity in time for assembly pilot run
Warranty documents	
Vehicle warranty document	Cleared by cognizant departments and ready for printing in owner's manual
Emissions system warranty document	Cleared by cognizant departments and at assembly plant in quantity in time for assembly pilot run
Tire warranty document	Available from tire manufacturer in quantity in time for assembly pilot run

FIGURE 8–8 **Tabulation of product features and goals (the automobile example)**

remaining chapters we shall be making use of two additional, related spreadsheets:

The process design spreadsheet. It is an aid to establishing the process features needed to meet the product goals.

The process control spreadsheet. It is an aid to establishing the controls needed to keep the process running at its planned level.

SUMMARY (Concluded)

The optimum quality goal is to:

Meet the needs of customers and suppliers alike

Minimize their combined costs

A serious obstacle to reaching the optimum is suboptimization.

The chief remedy for suboptimization is joint planning.

Suboptimization is an obstacle within companies as well as between companies.

Participation is a further remedy for suboptimization.

To provide participation requires special design of organization.

Participation may be organized through use of:

Coordinators

Interdepartmental teams

Participants are able to provide several kinds of input to goal setting:

Early warning of upcoming problems

Data to aid in optimizing

Challenge to theories

Resolving differences between companies is aided by providing needed inputs, especially analysis of the technology and the economics.

Resolving differences within companies is aided by looking for the behavioral obstacles.

To resolve differences it is advantageous to identify the specific decisions and actions that are at issue.

The Coonley–Agnew process for resolving differences stipulates three conditions:

The parties in the negotiation must identify their areas of agreement and their areas of disagreement ("the exact point at which the road began to fork").

The parties must agree on why they disagree.

They must then decide what they are going to do about it.

Follett's alternatives for resolving differences are:

- Dominance
- Compromise
- Constructive conflict

] 9 [

Process Development

THE MISSION OF THIS CHAPTER

The mission is to develop a process for producing products that meet product goals. Figure 9–1 shows the input–output diagram.

The *input* is product goals.

The *process* is process development.

The *output* is a process capable of producing products that meet product goals.

The product quality goals have already been defined through study of who the customers are and what their needs are. The definitions are in the form of product specifications, mission statements, objectives, and so on. The job now is to create a process that can, under operating conditions, produce those products or meet those goals and objectives.

Process development as used here includes process planning and process design. The ingredients of process planning are set out in this chapter (page 171). The term "process design" is also defined in this chapter (page 195).

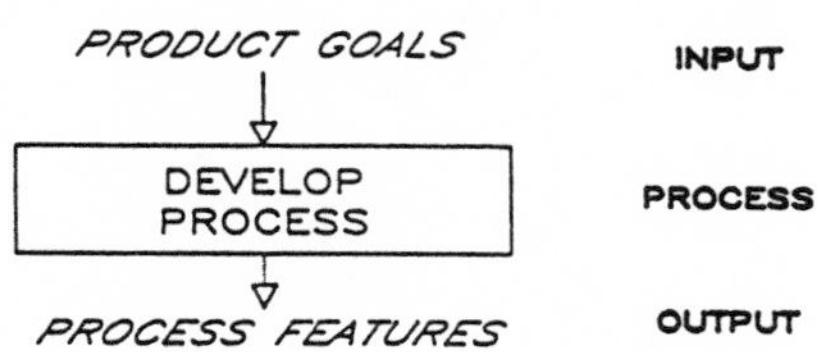

FIGURE 9–1 The input–output diagram for "Process development"

WHAT IS A PROCESS?

We define a process as "a systematic series of actions directed to the achievement of a goal." To comply with the terms of that definition, a process should be:

Goal oriented We cannot plan in the abstract. We can plan only if we know what the goal is. This means that to plan for quality we must first establish the quality goals and standards we are trying to reach.

Systematic The "actions" that make up a process are all interconnected and interdependent. They are also progressive—they follow a designated sequence.

Capable The proper end result of the planning is a process capable of meeting the goals under operating conditions.

Legitimate The process is evolved through authorized channels. It bears the approval of those to whom the associated responsibility has been delegated.

Process: What Does It Include?

Much of the literature on quality has used the word "process" in the special sense of a manufacturing process or, even more specifically, the physical facilities of a manufacturing process: the machine tools, conveyors, instruments, computers, and so forth.

We have defined "process" as a systematic series of actions directed to the achievement of a goal. That generic definition applies to processes in all functions, nonmanufacturing as well as manufacturing. It also includes the human forces as well as the physical facilities.

VARIETIES OF PROCESSES

Our definition of a process (along with the associated criteria) is applicable to processes of all sorts—processes for:

Launching new products

Recruiting new employees

Filling customers' orders

Providing manufacturing facilities
Producing goods
Providing customer service
Performing various tasks and operations
Maintaining control during operations
Etc.

In Chapter Eight we saw that there are many kinds of quality goals: companywide, divisional, departmental, functional, and so on. This variety of goals gives rise to a corresponding variety of quality-oriented processes, each designed to meet its respective quality goal. Quite often those quality-oriented processes must be fitted into broader company processes. To illustrate:

A process for employee selection, training and motivation for quality must be woven into the broad human relations structure.

A process for qualifying suppliers as to quality must be woven into the broad purchasing process.

A process for administering quality warranties must be woven into the broad customer relations process.

It might seem from those examples that no two processes are alike—each is "different." That is true as to the functions, the technology, and other features. However, the managerial approach to process planning is largely common to all processes.

That same variety of processes gives rise to various titles for those who plan processes or products. To illustrate:

END RESULT OF THE PLANNING	THE PLANNER IS OFTEN CALLED
Physical goods	Product designer Development engineer Product engineer Design engineer
Manufacturing processes	Process engineer Manufacturing engineer Master mechanic
Clerical process	Procedures analyst
Computer program	Systems analyst

RESPONSIBILITY FOR PROCESS PLANNING

(For a discussion of the general problem of separation of planning from execution, see "Who Are the Quality Planners?" page 105.)

The hierarchies of goals and processes creates also a hierarchy of process planners. To simplify our discussion, let's limit the hierarchy of processes to just three levels:

1. *Interdepartmental processes* link together various intradepartmental processes. Planning of an interdepartmental process requires some sort of interdepartmental organization. The forms most widely used are:

   A team of line managers, called a task force, committee, or the like

   A separate planning (or "staff") function, which has responsibility to prepare a plan and then secure approval from the line managers.

2. *Intradepartmental processes* involve multiple departmental tasks or operations. Responsibility for planning of such departmental processes is usually assigned to one or a combination of the following:

   The same process planning office that has responsibility for planning of the interdepartmental process.

   A departmental process planner

   The departmental supervision

3. *Tasks and operations* make up the base of the hierarchy of processes. At this level of the hierarchy the responsibility for process planning is usually assigned to one or a combination of the following:

   A departmental process planner

   A local supervisor

   The work force

INGREDIENTS OF PROCESS PLANNING

Process planning is itself carried out by a process. The aim is to provide the operating forces with the means for meeting operating goals.

The table below sets out the planning activities usually involved in process planning for manufacture, along with the end result of those activities.

ACTIVITIES	RESULTS
Review product design for clarity and producibility	Producible design
Choose process for manufacture: operations, sequences	Economic, feasible process; process specifications
Provide machines and tools capable of holding tolerances	Capable facilities
Provide instruments of an accuracy adequate for process control	Capable instrumentation
Provide software: methods, procedures, cautions	Operation sheets, etc.

If we broaden the above table to apply to process planning in general, the result looks like this:

ACTIVITIES	RESULTS
Review goals for clarity and attainability	Attainable goals
Choose process for conduct of operations	Economic, feasible process: process definition
Provide physical facilities capable of meeting goals	Capable facilities
Provide methods, procedures, cautions	Information required by operating forces to conduct operations

The final result—the process—consists of one or more of the following:

The "software": the description of a process able to meet the goals under operating conditions

The hardware: the physical facilities needed by the operating forces to carry out operations

The information (sometimes also called software) needed to provide instructions, explanations, and cautions on how to use the software and hardware.

We are now poised to go into the specifics of process planning. We shall begin with the most far-reaching concept in process planning, the concept of process capability.

PROCESS CAPABILITY: THE CONCEPT

All processes have an inherent capability for performance. That capability can be evaluated through data collection and analysis. The resulting evaluation of capability becomes a valuable aid both during quality planning and during subsequent conduct of operations.

The concept of evaluating process capability goes back centuries. In the transportation industry, ancient planners measured the load-carrying capacities of animals (and of human slaves) along with their food consumption. In the mining industry, the early steam engines were used to pump water out of mines. The planners evaluated competing steam engines in terms of "duty," that is, coal consumed per unit of work done. Those measures were influential in managerial decision-making and in stimulating engine development.

The service industries for centuries have used the concept of process capability, but without calling it process capability. A widespread example is "credit rating." Most companies do their selling on credit—they deliver the product before being paid. A fraction of the buyers do not pay up. The resulting risk of losses from bad debts led to a demand for early warning: information that can predict whether prospective debtors will pay their debts. The best-known basis for such prediction is information on (1) whether the prospective debtor currently has the means, and (2) whether he has in the past had the inclination, to pay his debts. In earlier centuries that information was acquired through the grapevine—gossip in the market place and elsewhere. Today in some countries there is a formal data bank (Dun & Bradstreet), which compiles and publishes data on credit worthiness.

There are also data banks that "rate" bonds and other securities as to credit worthiness. All those ratings are expressions of process capability. The companies or securities being rated are regarded as a financial process. The published ratings constitute a process capability data bank. Those data banks are widely used as planning tools by credit managers, purchasing managers, financial managers, and others.

In recent decades, the widest application of the process capability concept has been to manufacturing processes. Many manufacturing processes make units of product for which quality is evaluated on a variables basis, e.g., length in millimeters, resistance in ohms. For such manufacturing processes, a standardized method of evaluating process capability in terms of the inherent variability of the process has evolved. (Measures of variability are discussed later in this chapter.) Other manufacturing processes make units of product for which quality is evaluated on an attributes basis, e.g., presence or absence of electrical continuity. For such processes, process capability is expressed in such forms as percent yield or percent defective.

THE URGE TO QUANTIFY

It has always been a key requirement that a process be capable of producing products that meet goals. Historically, evaluation of process capability was done by empirical means: rule of thumb, cut and try. The cases of the draft animals and the steam engines were the exceptions.

In recent decades there has evolved a strong trend to *quantify* process capability and to *standardize the quantitative evaluation methods* so that they can be used to express the capability of a wide variety of processes. The term "process capability" is now generally used as a nonmathematical name for a standard evaluation. The mathematical expressions vary, depending on the nature of the process.

Life Without Quantification

Quantification of process capability requires doing added work in the form of data collection and analysis. Yet the great majority of quality planning has been done empirically, without quantitative evaluation of process capability, and certainly without standardized methods of quantifying. Why do we now need to go to all that extra work? The reason is that *organizations that have adopted such methods of quantification have significantly outperformed those which have not.*

To illustrate, in the U.S. automotive industry the activities of manufacturing planning had for decades been carried out without quantifying the capability of manufacturing processes. During those same decades a notorious situation existed where manufacturing processes were unable to hold the product design tolerances. The planners of those processes were intelligent, competent engineers. They certainly had training in the technology of the processes. In addition, they had practical experience derived from having engaged in prior cycles of quality planning. Their training and experience made them competitive with other planners who relied on similar training and experience.

In due course those quality planners found that they were being outperformed by a new level of competition. The superiority in planning was found to be due, in part, to the use of quantification of process capability. It then became imperative to adopt quantification as a tool for competition in quality planning. The U.S. automobile companies did so under such names as "Statistical Process Control."

Another way of describing the situation is in terms of the resulting percent defective. Empirical ways of quality planning resulted in processes that yielded 80 to 90 percent good product; the defects were in terms of parts per hundred. The scrap, rework, detailed inspection, and so on were a price paid for the deficiencies in planning. It worked for as long as competitors conducted their affairs in the same way. It could not work when competitors came up with ways to drive defect levels down to parts per million.

EVALUATING PROCESS CAPABILITY: THE METHODS

The principal method for evaluating process capability is through data collection and analysis under operating conditions. (Other methods include simulation and mathematical models.)

The term "under operating conditions" means:

The process is already in existence.

Operations are being conducted under "regular" conditions, not "laboratory" conditions.

The personnel conducting operations are the regular operating forces.

Process capability for such an existing process may be evaluated by collecting data on:

The quality features of the *product* turned out by the process

The quality features of the *process* itself

In the case of manufacturing processes, a recent development has been to evaluate process capability by analysis of the *variability* of the process. We shall look at this development later in this chapter.

Evaluating Process Capability from Operating Data

Let's start with a clerical process, the preparation of insurance policies. The process consists of a "policy writer" armed with a keyboard. The inputs are mainly the customer's order, a blank policy form, the company manuals, and the training of the workers. The output is insurance contracts ready for signature.

During operations the policy writers fill in the blank policy forms with data from the various inputs. The policies then go to a checker, who reviews them for errors. During a certain time period the checker reported 80 errors, as shown in Figure 9–2.

On the face of it we seem to have arrived at an evaluation of process capability. Six workers made a total of 80 errors among them, or an average of 13.3 per worker. However, as we analyze the data we soon see that the workers varied widely in their error-

Error type	Policy writer A	B	C	D	E	F	Total
1	0	0	1	0	2	1	4
2	1	0	0	0	1	0	2
3	0	(16)	1	0	2	0	(19)
4	0	0	0	0	1	0	1
5	2	1	3	1	4	2	(13)
6	0	0	0	0	3	0	3
27							
28							
29							
Totals	6	(20)	8	3	(36)	7	80

FIGURE 9–2 Matrix of errors by insurance policy writers

proneness. Four were well below the average—their errors numbered 6, 8, 3 and 7 respectively. Two (workers B and E) were well above the averages—20 and 36 respectively. None was close to the average.

In the case of Worker B, her total of 20 errors is inflated by 16 errors of a single error type. That was found to be due to her misunderstanding of a part of the procedure. In consequence, her error rate is properly measured by her four scattered errors. In contrast, Worker E made 36 errors, and made them in virtually all error categories. So the number 36 does reflect the error-proneness of Worker E on this type of work.

That simple table of data on the policy writers has brought out two important added concepts relative to process capability:

1. The difference between process performance and process capability
2. The concept of variability

Every planner should have a firm grasp of each of those concepts.

Process Performance and Process Capability

Process performance is what a process *actually does.*

Process capability is what a process *could do* if we removed the significant causes of poor performance.

In the case of the policy writers, Worker B's *performance* was represented by 20 errors. Her *capability* was represented by 4 errors. For Worker E, the number 36 seemed to reflect both performance and capability. However, that number was so high compared to the rest that it suggested Worker E was misassigned to this type of work.

If we now put the data on the basis of capability (omitting Worker E) the numbers of errors become 6, 4, 8, 3 and 7 respectively. The average becomes 5.6, and each worker is close to the average. The number 5.6 would then represent our best estimate of the capability of the process.

Note that the definition of process capability (what a process *could do*) is qualified. There is a proviso: "If we removed the *significant* causes of poor performance." In some cases it becomes important to define how big is "significant."

In the case of the insurance policies, we had no trouble. For Worker B the performance of 20 was obviously significantly different from the capability of 4. For Worker E the number 36 was significantly greater than the number for any of her colleagues.

However, in many cases the differences are not so obvious. In addition there are cases where smaller gaps between performance and capability are nevertheless important. Statistical tools are available to quantify significance with precision.

The distinction between process performance and process capability has wide application to all functions. Ideally, goals should be set based on process capabilities. Projects should be undertaken to upgrade processes so that their performance matches their capability. Actually, most goals are based on past performance, not on process capability.

Process Capability: Effect on Quality Planning

The concept of process capability is much more than an interesting managerial curiosity; it is one of the most fundamental elements in quality planning.

Planners usually have a range of choice among alternative processes. Those alternatives differ from each other with respect to multiple features: productivity, capital investment, operating cost, and so forth, including quality. The ability of the planners to choose the optimal process depends largely on the extent to which they have information on the comparative capabilities of the competing processes.

PROCESS VARIABILITY

All processes exhibit variability. The extent of this variability is a critical input to process planning.

We saw that the insurance policy writers differed in their performance. The respective numbers of errors were 6, 4, 8, 3, and 7. Had the study been repeated, the numbers for the respective workers would almost certainly not have repeated themselves precisely.

Other human beings, e.g., athletes, similarly vary among each other as well as from time to time.

Nonhuman processes also exhibit variability. Input materials vary as to their properties. Variations in the paper supply can affect the performance of the copying machine. Variations in reagents can affect the performance of the chemical process. Similarly, the equipments used in processes are affected by variability. Changes in environmental conditions affect the performance of equipments. So do progressive changes due to depletion, wear, and age.

All those and other sources of variation are a fact of life for the operating forces. Their responsibility is to meet the product goals, but the reality is that they must do so under operating conditions.

In consequence, the planners have the responsibility of determining, in advance, what the operating conditions are, including the nature and extent of those variations. The key to such advance knowledge is in the concepts of process capability and process variability. Planners who lack such information may nevertheless be able to develop a process that works under "laboratory conditions" but not necessarily under operating conditions.

FIGURE 9–3 The bead bowl

The Bead Bowl Demonstration

We can demonstrate variability by use of a bowl of beads (Figure 9–3). In our example the bowl contains 1,000 beads. Of these, 900 are white and 100 are red. Suppose now we go through a series of cycles of (1) taking out a random sample of 50 beads, (2) counting the red ones, (3) returning the sample to the bowl, and (4) mixing thoroughly. We will find that the number of red beads varies from sample to sample despite the fact that the process remains unchanged, that is, when any cycle begins, there are always the same contents in the bowl: 900 white and 100 red.

ATTRIBUTES AND VARIABLES DATA

So far our discussion of process capability has dealt with cases involving "attributes" data. The insurance policy error was there or it was not. The bead drawn out of the bowl was red or it was not. The product possesses a particular attribute (feature) or it does not. For those and myriad other such cases, process capability is commonly expressed in terms of the proportion of product that possesses or lacks the attribute in question.

There is a second world of data: variables data. In this world the data consist of numbers along a scale of measurement: 110 volts; 182 grams; 23.2 seconds. For such data the methods of quantifying process capability have become more sophisticated and also more rewarding. So let us have a look at that second world.

The New Development: Process Capability Based on Variability

During the last few decades many manufacturing industries have gone heavily into evaluating process capability through analysis of process variability. That approach has considerable merit; it is here to stay. Also, it is very likely to spread to other industries. So it is worthwhile for planners to understand the concept of variability and its application to process planning and process capability.

The Measurement of Variability

A relaxed way of getting into this subject is to study some process in action. We can conduct such a study right in the training room with the help of a pinball machine. The scientific name is "Quincunx" (Figure 9–4).

The Quincunx simulates an operating process. The inputs (data, materials, and so on) consist of the beads in the magazine at the top. The beads can be released one at a time through the funnel. The funnel can be moved horizontally so as to change the "setting" or aimed-at value of the process.

Each row of pins is like a "variable" in the process. In a manufacturing process the variables would be things like temperature, cycle time, or acidity. In a sales process the variables would be things like product type, price, credit terms, or delivery terms.

As any bead works its way past any row of pins, it is bounced one way or the other. The final result of going through all those rows of pins is the composite of all bounces. In like manner, in an operating process, the final result for any unit of product is the composite effect of all process variables.

FIGURE 9–4 The Quincunx
Courtesy: Lightning Calculator, Troy, Michigan.

When using the Quincunx for demonstration, we first set up the process; we move the funnel horizontally so that it will discharge at some aimed-at value. Then we release the beads one at a time. Each bead is "processed" by all those rows of pins and finally falls into one of the channels.

The channels are numbered with the appropriate unit of measure. The numbered channels also serve as a sensor—they measure each unit of product as it is made.

As the beads are processed one by one, it is soon obvious that they do not all end up in the same channel. *The exhibit variability in spite of the fact that the process remains unchanged.*

Frequency Distribution

As more and more beads accumulate in the channels, a *frequency distribution* is built up. That frequency distribution shows us how many units of product there are at each value of measurement.

Figure 9–5 shows an actual example of a frequency distribution, a tally of the electrical resistance of 100 coils.

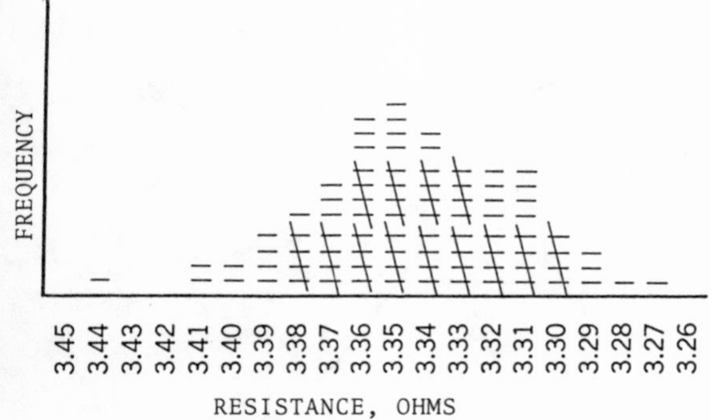

FIGURE 9–5 Frequency distribution data

This frequency distribution exhibits two distinct features:

1. The data are bunched in the middle—they exhibit a *central tendency.* We usually measure the central tendency by calculating the average of all those measurements.

2. The data exhibit a scatter or *dispersion.* That dispersion is the *variability* we are talking about.

In Figure 9–5 the data also exhibit *symmetry* around the average. As we collect more and more data from processes that exhibit such symmetry, the irregularities in the frequency distribution tend to smooth out. The final result is often a smooth curve, which we call a "normal" distribution. It has a characteristic bell shape (Figure 9–6).

Frequency distributions are not alike as to their extent of variability. In some the data are tightly bunched. In others the data disperse widely. The corresponding normal distribution curves would look like Figure 9–7.

(Some frequency distributions are not symmetrical. They have different shapes and are governed by different rules. In the interest of simplicity, we shall not examine them.)

UNIT OF MEASURE FOR VARIABILITY

Variability is universal. It affects every quality feature of every product or process. While each quality feature has its own unit of measure, it would be most convenient to have one universal unit

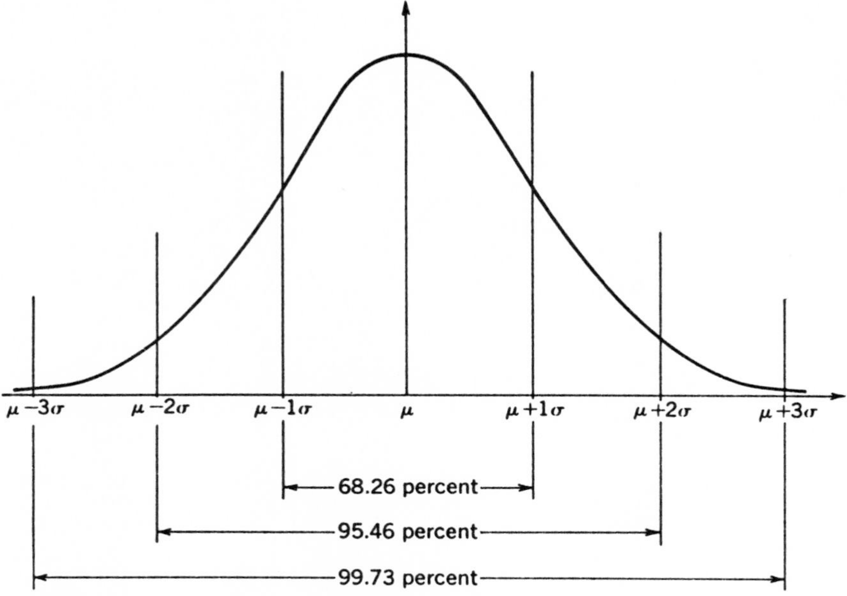

FIGURE 9–6 The normal distribution curve

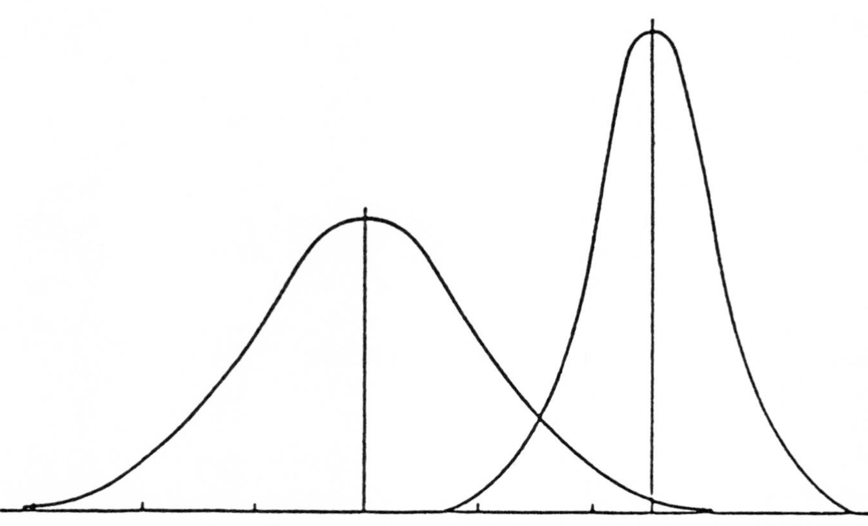

FIGURE 9–7 Two distribution curves of different variability

of measure for variability—some unit that expresses the extent to which *any* frequency distribution is bunched or dispersed. We do have such a unit of measure—in fact, we have several of them. The most widely used is something we call the "standard deviation." We represent it by the lowercase Greek letter sigma: σ.

The standard deviation is usually determined as follows:

For each item of data in the frequency distribution, we determine its distance from the average. That distance is the deviation (d).

We square each of the deviations.

We then add up all the squares, giving us the sum of the squared deviations.

We next divide that sum by the number of items (n) in the frequency distribution. The result is the "mean squared deviation."

Finally, we extract the square root of the mean squared deviation. This final result is the "root mean squared deviation" and is the standard deviation.

That series of steps can be expressed in abbreviated form by a mathematical equation:

$$\sigma = \sqrt{\frac{\Sigma d^2}{n}}, \text{ where}$$

d = the deviation of any unit from the average
n = the number of units in the sample
Σ means "the sum of"

The standard deviation becomes a standardized measure of variability. Our quality features have numerous units of measure: grams, meters, minutes, amperes. Despite those numerous units of measure it is possible to express all variability in terms of a single unit of measure—in terms of standard deviations. Suppose, for example, that we make measurements on certain quality features and calculate the standard deviation for each. The results might be like this:

σ = 37.2 grams
σ = 11.4 millimeters
σ = 3.8 minutes
σ = 1.1 amperes
etc.

Despite the assortment of technological units of measure, we would know from Figure 9–6 that for every one of those normal frequency distributions:

$\pm$ 1 σ contains 68% of the data

$\pm$ 2 σ contains 95% of the data

$\pm$ 3 σ contains 99.73% of the data

Some Refinements

Keeping things simple for managers requires that we avoid getting into refinements that affect mathematical precision but do not significantly affect managerial decision-making. Let us, in passing, note several such refinements.

When we compute the mean squared deviation of a sample, we should divide not by n, but by $n-1$. This statistical correction is obviously unimportant for large samples but grows in importance as the sample size shrinks.

There are two mathematical symbols for standard deviation. The standard deviation of a *sample* of units is symbolized by the English letter s. The known standard deviation of a *population* from which a sample is drawn is symbolized by the Greek letter σ. A process can be regarded as a population, since in theory an infinite number of units can be made by the process.

Our approach in computing standard deviation was based on the frequency distribution. It is a comparatively simple analysis and is often valid. However, it is not valid under certain conditions, mainly when:

The process has a significant time to time variation

The process is subject to sporadic changes due to "significant," findable causes

The frequency distribution is not symmetrical about the average

Under such conditions the "control chart" method should be used to calculate standard deviation. (We regularly encounter instances in which the significant variations are so big that the word "refinements" no longer applies. The more rigorous method becomes essential.)

APPLICATION TO MANUFACTURING PROCESSES

Having a universal unit of measure for variability greatly simplifies the problem of quantifying and applying the concept of process capability. In recent years the concept has in fact been widely applied to manufacturing processes.

A usual form of application is to measure units of product at regular time intervals during the course of production. The variations in the product data are commonly the result of variations in the process that made the product. Hence we use data on product variation as an indirect measure of process performance. "The product tells on the process."

Once the standard deviation has been calculated, it is readily possible to determine process capability. Some manufacturing industries, notably the automotive industry, have arbitrarily adopted the rule:

Process capability = 6 standard deviations

Process Capability Index

Adoption of such a universal unit of measure has greatly simplified communication and goal setting. To illustrate, in the automotive industry it is common to require that process capability (six standard deviations) should be no greater than 0.75 of the tolerance width. Stated in reverse, the rule requires that the ratio of tolerance width to process capability should be at the minimum 1.33. This latter ratio is sometimes called Process Capability Index, or Capability Index.

Establishment of such quantified criteria for Process Capability

Index provides quantitative goals for planners. As data on process capability are worked up for various processes, the planners can use the data in multiple ways. The principal use has been to determine whether a process will be able to meet the goals.

> For example, a specification requires maximum 4.320, minimum 4.290 for some quality feature. The tolerance width is the difference of 0.030 (millimeters, amperes, or whatever.) If six standard deviations of the prospective process is equal to 0.035 (millimeters, amperes, or whatever) then we have an early warning: choice of that process means perpetual trouble for the operating forces.

While the widest use of quantified process capability has been to evaluate the ability of a manufacturing process to hold tolerances, there are other uses, such as:

To judge the relative merits of alternative processes

To communicate our needs for precision to suppliers of processes

Note that the term "process capability" can be misleading in some respects:

> Process capability is different from process performance: "Could do" differs from "does do." A manufacturing process that is easily able to hold tolerances may fail to do so because the input materials are substandard, the process is set to aim at the wrong average, the process is not receiving adequate maintenance, or some other reason.

Process capability, when expressed in such terms as six standard deviations, tells us a good deal about the inherent uniformity of the process. However, it does not tell us whether the process is *able to meet goals.* We learn that only when we compare process capability with the goal. In the case of manufacturing processes, we can compare process capability with the tolerances and estimate what will be the resulting fraction defective under optimum operating conditions. (The process doesn't know what the human goal is.)

A simple way of comparing process capability to goals is by use of the frequency "histogram." A histogram is an envelope drawn around a frequency distribution. Figure 9–8 shows the histogram for the data on electrical resistance of coils (Figure 9–5).

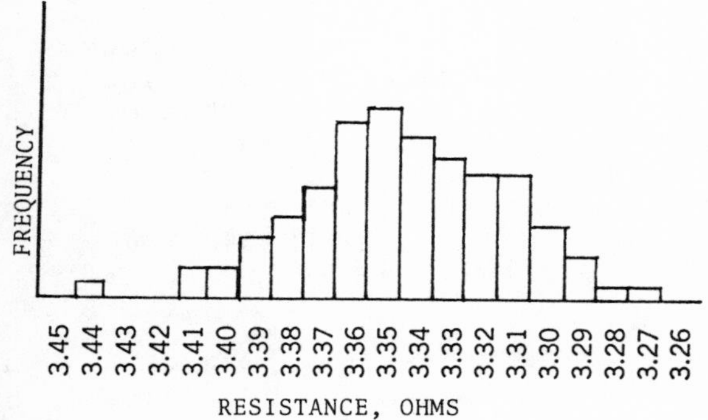

FIGURE 9–8 Frequency histogram

Figures 9–9A to 9–9E are simple examples of comparison of process capability to goals. The goals are shown as tolerance limits from some engineering specification.

APPLICATION TO NONMANUFACTURING PROCESSES

We have seen that for many manufacturing processes we have evolved a standardized means of quantifying process capability, based on six standard deviations of variability. As yet we have no such standardized approach to most nonmanufacturing processes (and to many manufacturing processes as well.)

It is theoretically possible to extend the concept of six standard deviations to any process, provided we are able to acquire an adequate data base. However, that has not yet been widely tested in practice. Moreover, such tests as have been made have not been encouraging; they have not been very successful in readily separating process performance as between:

What the process did do, and

What the process could do

Lacking such separation, the planners do not readily know what is the inherent capability of the process. If they do their planning on the basis of historical performance, they run the risk of perpetuating poor performance—carryover of poor yields, carryover of failure-prone features, and so on. Of course, there are ways to analyze past performance in order to separate inherent capability

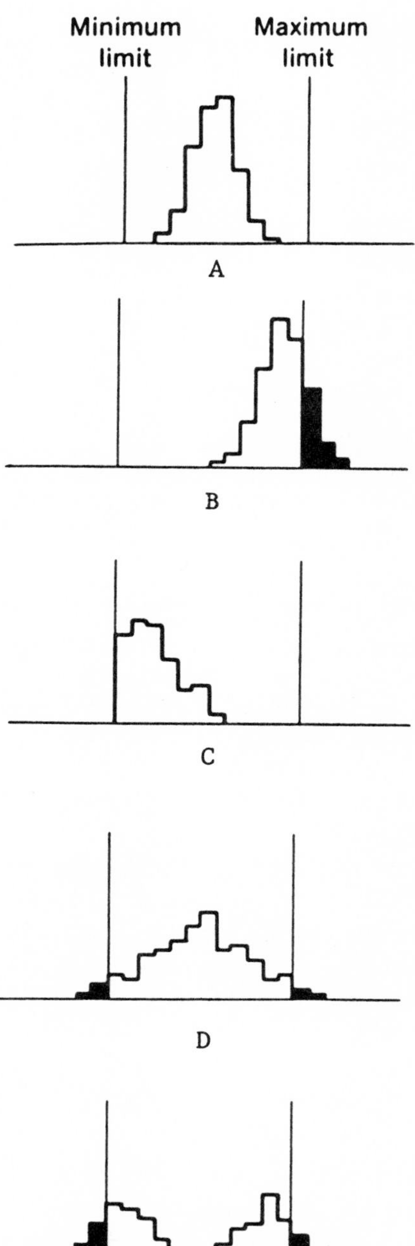

Histogram A shows an ideal condition. The proce[s] is clearly capable of holdi[n] the tolerances and is actually doing so--the cent[e] of the histogram is virtual[l] at the midpoint of the tolerances.

Histogram B also shows process which is capable of holding its tolerances. However, an off-center setting has resulted in manufacture of a high percen[t] of oversized product.

Histogram C is similar to B. Off-centering of a capable process has resulted in a high percent of defective product (undersize in this case). However, the defectives have been removed by sorting.

Histogram D shows a wel[l] centered process which is nevertheless producing defectives, both oversized and undersized. Seemingly, the inherent dispersion is too wide for these tolerances. The "process capability" is inadequate.

Histogram E exhibits a high percent of defectives, both undersized and oversized. However, the product is a mixture of work from two off-center settings of the same capable process.

FIGURE 9–9 Frequency histograms compared to product tolerances

from extraneous factors. But those ways are as yet not as neatly standardized as the study of manufacturing processes based on six standard deviations derived from frequency distributions and control charts.

A good deal remains to be done to study a spectrum of nonmanufacturing processes and to evolve a method of quantifying process capability that is widely applicable.

DATA BANKS ON PROCESS CAPABILITY

Use of Data Banks

A data bank on process capability is an organized collection of evaluations of process capabilities. Once such a data bank has been prepared, process planners can use the information in various ways, such as:

Predict results in advance of conducting operations

Secure early warning of deficiencies

Choose the best from the available alternatives

Outside of the Company

Data banks on process capability abound. They are found in all company functions and in the outside world as well.

> In the world of sports there are extensive records of past performance of teams and individual athletes. Those records are widely used to assign teams to various league classifications, determine handicaps and seedings for individuals, predict future performance, and establish pay scales.

Within the Company

Within the company, data banks on process capability are found in all functions. To illustrate:

FUNCTION	DATA BANKS
Product design	Tables of properties of materials Lists of approved components (those which may be specified without further qualification testing.)

FUNCTION	DATA BANKS
Purchasing	Credit worthiness of suppliers
Manufacture	Tables of inherent uniformity of production processes
Marketing	Sales potential of various territories Credit worthiness of potential clients
Industrial engineering	Work standards for tasks and operations
Human relations	List of workers certified as qualified to perform various tasks

Units of Measure

Creation of data banks requires also the creation of units of measure. The units of measure vary among company functions. Here are some examples:

FUNCTIONS	EXAMPLES OF UNITS OF MEASURE
Product design	Percent of designs that require change
Bidding for business	Percent of bids that result in contracts
Manufacture	Standard deviation
Marketing	Percent of sales calls that result in contracts Percent of contracts subsequently canceled
Customer service	Time required to provide service Percent of service calls that resulted in service complaints
Human relations	Time required to recruit new employees Extent of labor turnover
Clerical	Extent of documents requiring correction
General management	Length of new product launching cycle

As Seen by Ultimate Users

Many products sold by manufacturers become processes in the hands of ultimate users. Examples of such products include office copiers, machine tools, trucks, and computers. To users of such products, process capabilities may be expressed in positive terms, e.g., percent uptime, copies per minute. Alternatively the expression may be in negative terms: percent downtime, failure rate, spare parts usage.

Such evaluations are the modern equivalent of the "duty" of the early steam engines. As in those early days, the modern evaluations are influential in deciding whose products will be bought. It is obviously useful for manufacturers to acquire the information in those data banks.

Procedure for Creating Data Banks

Establishing data banks on process capability requires an organized approach such as is used for improvement projects. A team is appointed to guide the project. The team is given the responsibility to:

Determine the scope of the data banks—what processes should be included

Define and standardize the basic terminology

Establish the conceptual approach, including definition of process capability, essential input data, units of measure, method of evaluation

Prepare the instruction manual for evaluating process capability: forms for data collection and analysis, criteria for precision of measurement, sample sizes

Provide a training course to guide those who will collect and analyze process capability data

Establish a procedure for publishing the data bank: format, distribution list, and so on

Provide for audit to ensure adherence to the plan

SUMMARY (Interim)

A process is a systematic series of actions directed to the achievement of a goal.

A process should be goal-oriented, systematic, capable, and legitimate.

Process includes nonmanufacturing as well as manufacturing activities, human forces as well as physical facilities.

The aim of process planning is to provide the operating forces with the means for meeting operating goals.

The final result of process planning consists of:

The software, or process description

The hardware, or physical facilities

The instructions for use

Process capability is the inherent ability of a process to deliver performance.

Process capability is an ancient concept. What is new is the trend to standardize the quantitative evaluation methods.

The process capability concept applies to nonmanufacturing processes as well as to manufacturing processes.

Processes can be planned without evaluation of process capability, but such processes cannot compete with those planned through evaluation of process capability.

Process capability is most usually evaluated from operating data.

Process performance is what a process actually does; process capability is what a process could do.

Process performance is often below inherent process capability because of the influence of significant causes of variation.

Some statistically significant differences in performance are economically important; others are not.

All processes—human and nonhuman—exhibit variability. This variability is measurable.

A frequency distribution is a graphic method for depicting the extent of variability.

The most widely used measure of variability is the standard deviation.

Many manufacturing companies have adopted the arbitrary definition:

$$\text{Process capability} = 6 \text{ standard deviations}$$

Many manufacturing companies use a process capability index of the form:

$$\text{Index} = \frac{\text{Product tolerance}}{6 \text{ standard deviations}}$$

A widely preferred minimum for the process capability index is 1.33.

Quantification of process capability serves multiple purposes, such as:

Evaluate ability to meet tolerances

Judge relative merits of alternative processes

Communicate needs to suppliers of processes

Data banks can be compiled to tabulate process capability for various processes.

Such data banks can be of aid to operating managers as well as to planners.

Process capability can be quantified for nonmanufacturing processes as well as for manufacturing processes.

In the case of nonmanufacturing processes, we lack a standardized measure of process capability.

PROCESS DESIGN

The term "process design" as used here is the activity of defining the specific means to be used by the operating forces for meeting the product goals. The resulting definition covers:

The physical equipment to be provided

The associated software (the brain and nervous system of the equipment)

Information on how to operate, control, and maintain the equipment

To arrive at that definition requires such inputs as:

Knowledge of the goals

Knowledge of the operating conditions

Knowledge of the capability of alternative processes

The inputs needed by process planners exhibit a good deal of commonality despite wide variation in technology. Additional commonality exists in the skills and tools associated with the planning process. Those include understanding of: the anatomy of processes, the concept of dominance, the concept of process capability, and the nature and use of flow diagrams and spreadsheets. Of those skills and tools the most powerful is probably the concept of process capability.

REVIEW OF GOALS

Ideally, quality goals are established with the prior participation of those who will be impacted. They include:

The planners who have the job of establishing the processes needed to meet the goals

The operating forces who will have the job of meeting the goals

(The methodology for such participation has been discussed in earlier chapters.)

In many situations, prior participation is incomplete. In such cases, review of goals should be the first step in the planning process. Sometimes the review is simple.

A Middle East manager ordered steel from a Japanese supplier. The purchase order referenced a standard specification number. Back came a cable: "What use will you make of this steel?"

If review of goals is delayed until late in the game, there is a corresponding reduction in the available options:

Alternatives that could have been readily adopted in earlier stages become more expensive, or even prohibitive.

Those who have set the goals develop a vested interest in

their decisions and exhibit cultural resistance to proposals for change.

Despite those complications, the reviews should be undertaken. Some of the findings will turn out to be usable. Other findings will turn out to be academic—it is too late to use them.

The author recalls his early experiences as a member of a New Product Review Committee. The reviews took place much too late in the day. The designs had been frozen, the tools had been built, the schedules had been fixed. The reviews were largely an exercise in futility.

OPERATING CONDITIONS: USERS' UNDERSTANDING OF THE PROCESS

By users we mean those who will be employing the processes to meet goals. Those users consist in part of internal customers (processor teams or persons) of the kind we identified in Chapter Two. They have the responsibility of running the processes to meet operating goals. The users also include external customers who run the processes to meet *their* goals.

Users vary greatly in their capability for unaided use of the process. Some users have the training and skills needed to use sophisticated technological processes. Other users may be able to acquire supplemental training to bridge any deficiency. Still other users, e.g., the general public, occupy a wide spectrum of technological literacy. The process design, along with the software (manuals and the rest) should ideally be such that the entire spectrum of users can use the process successfully.

Consumers are a class of users who present special problems resulting from their wide range of knowledge and ignorance about technological goods and services. Some appliance makers report that more than 25 percent of consumer complaints involve cases in which there is nothing wrong with the product. Many consumers fail to follow the instructions or lose or discard the owner's manual. Increasingly, manufacturing and service companies are placing higher priority on foolproofing the use of products and services, providing self-maintaining designs, and so on.

OPERATING CONDITIONS: HOW WILL THE PROCESS BE USED?

The prime question is: Shall we plan based on intended use or actual use (and misuse)? The planner always knows the intended use, but not necessarily the actual use. If we decide on the latter course, there are ways for the planner to find out about actual use:

Personally acquire firsthand experience in actual use (Some training courses are designed to provide such experience.)

Make the rounds, that is, observe users in action and secure their comments

Secure knowledge indirectly, e.g., through design review by those who are familiar with actual use

In some respects the choice of whether to plan for intended use or actual use is a policy decision, not purely a technological decision. An obvious example is a case involving human safety or health. In such a case the decision (plan for intended use versus plan for actual use) involves legal, marketing, and other business expertise as well as technological expertise.

OPERATING CONDITIONS: WHAT WILL BE THE ENVIRONMENTS OF USE?

Planners can learn about environments of use in the same way they learn about how the process is actually used:

Firsthand experience

Make the rounds

Secure knowledge indirectly

Planners are well aware that their plans must take account of environments that can influence technological performance. Planners of physical processes or products usually do take account of such environmental factors as temperature, vibration, and dirt, among others.

Planners of processes that depend heavily on human responses must similarly take into account the way in which the environment can affect human performance. A remarkable example involved the loss of an important football game played on December 26, 1982, between the New York Giants and the St. Louis Cardinals.

The Giants were leading by a score of 21 to 17, with twenty-seven seconds remaining to be played. The Cardinals were in possession of the ball, and the Giants were in a defensive huddle, anticipating a forward pass. The Giants' process for defense against a forward pass included:

A "man-to-man" defense. For this type of defense the official signal was the phrase "five green," but actually only the word "green" was used.

A "zone" defense. For this type of defense the official signal was the phrase "stack three," but actually only the word "three" was used.

The Giants' defensive quarterback called out the signal "green," but one of the players thought he heard "three." As a result, in the words of the Giants' defensive coach, "At the snap, we had three guys playing man-to-man like they were supposed to, and another guy playing zone."

The journalist who reported the event tended to assign blame to the player who "misunderstood" the call. However, neither the journalist nor the coach discussed the design of the signaling system or the associated environmental factors.

The most audible portion of the two signals ("green" and "three") consists of the identical letters "ree." The two signals are close to "sound-alikes." The environment in a football stadium is inherently hostile to oral communication. The spectators are in any case a noisy lot. In this case, circumstances combined to raise the noise level to a deafening pitch: It was an important game, with tens of thousands in attendance; it was a close game, with the ultimate winner still in doubt; the game had reached its climax, with only twenty-seven seconds remaining. It is understandable that the noise tended to drown out the signal. (The Cardinals won, 24–21.)

Environment is not simply a matter of the physical conditions that impact on the operating forces. Environment also includes such factors as:

Job stresses: multiple goals to be met, the boss, peer pressure

Outside stresses: personal health, family problems, the social community

Those and other nonphysical aspects of "environment" abound. They have plagued human beings throughout history. That is why one of the criteria of a good process is that it be capable of meeting the goals under operating conditions.

THE PROCESS DESIGN SPREADSHEET

For process design the spreadsheet takes the form shown in Figure 9–10. In this spreadsheet the product goals are listed in the horizontal rows. The vertical columns are used for entering the various process features needed to produce the product features and meet the product goals. The process features in the vertical columns consist of such things as processing equipment, instruments, and process conditions.

The intersections of rows and columns are then coded to identify the areas of impact: which process features are pertinent to which product features. The codes also indicate the nature and extent of the impact, e.g., critical or noncritical. That coded information in the intersections then becomes an input to subsequent spreadsheets.

PRODUCT FEATURE	PRODUCT GOAL	PROCESS FEATURES					
		PARTS BIN ARRANGEMENT	WAVE SOLDER CONDITIONS				
			SOLDER TEMP.	CONTACT TIME	ALLOY PURITY	...	
Identity of components	100% correct part numbers inserted	**				...	
Component polarity	100% correct orientation	*				...	
Continuity of solder joints	100% continuity		**	**	**	...	
:	:	:	:	:	:		

KEY: ** Strong relationship
* Weak relationship

FIGURE 9–10 The process design spreadsheet

PROCESS DESIGN: MACRO-LEVEL

Process design usually starts at the broad macro-level. It then progresses down to lower levels and details. An office "procedure" consists of a series of specific "steps." A chemical process consists of a series of "unit processes." Factory assembly consists of a series of specific "operations."

At the macro-level the process designer faces some important decisions as to which of several broad alternatives to adopt. Should he "carry over" existing processes or adopt new processes? If the latter, which new process? What about new, state-of-the-art features?

Let us examine some of those alternatives, starting with the question of carryover of existing process designs.

CARRYOVER OF EXISTING PROCESS DESIGNS

Virtually all processes are made up of a mixture of:

Features carried over from existing processes

Features carried over but modified to correct weaknesses or to adapt to new needs

Features newly developed

The advantages of carryover are considerable. The cost of process development is minimal. The performance is predictable: The prior performance can be evaluated. The operating forces are already on familiar ground. Such advantages make carryover the dominant ingredient in most process designs.

Carryover also includes a potential uninvited, unwelcome guest. The process feature may include chronic quality problems that have never been solved.

> In the early days of computer installations it was common practice to design the new data processing systems to do electronically what had previously been done manually by clerks and paperwork. Often that approach carried over into the electronic data system the deficiencies of the prior manual system. The "manual mess" became locked into an "automated mess."

To defend against such uninvited guests, process designers should inform themselves as to the prior performance of the potential carryover. Once informed, they face a new alternative: reject, revise, or adopt as is.

THE ANATOMY OF PROCESSES

A second important choice of alternatives relates to the "anatomy" of processes. There are several broad species of processes, of which the most popular include:

THE AUTONOMOUS DEPARTMENT. One process receives basic "materials" and converts them into finished goods and services, all within a single self-contained department. A schematic diagram is shown in Figure 9–11.

A widespread example is the self-employed professional (e.g., physician) or artisan (e.g., Coop, the cooper of Chapter Two). In the factory, a well-known example is a tool room. It starts with tool steel and ends up with punches, dies, fixtures, gauges, and so on.

For such autonomous departments much of the planning is done by the departmental supervision and by the workers. Additional planning is acquired from outside sources. For example, the physician may purchase equipment and other planned processes from supply houses and pharmaceutical companies.

THE ASSEMBLY "TREE." The assembly tree is a familiar process widely used by the great mechanical and electronic industries,

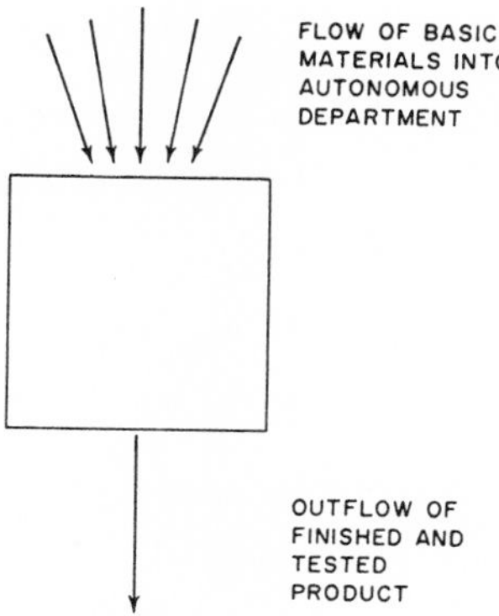

FIGURE 9–11 The autonomous department

which build automotive vehicles, household appliances, electronic apparatus, and so forth. The roots (or leaves) of the tree are numerous suppliers or in-house departments making parts and components. Those elements are assembled by still other departments. Figure 9–12 shows this process schematically.

In the office, certain processes of data collection and summary also exhibit features of the assembly tree. Preparation of accounting reports (e.g., balance sheet, profit statement) requires assembly of myriad bits of data into progressively broader summaries, which finally converge into the consolidated reports.

The assembly tree requires planning of two very different kinds: interdepartmental and intradepartmental. In large operations, it becomes mandatory to use staff planners for the interdepartmental planning. However, it is not mandatory to use staff planners for intradepartmental planning as well, though it is sometimes done.

THE PROCESSION. In the procession form, there are again numerous in-house departments (with occasional supplier departments). However, all the product progresses sequentially through all departments, each performing some operation that contributes

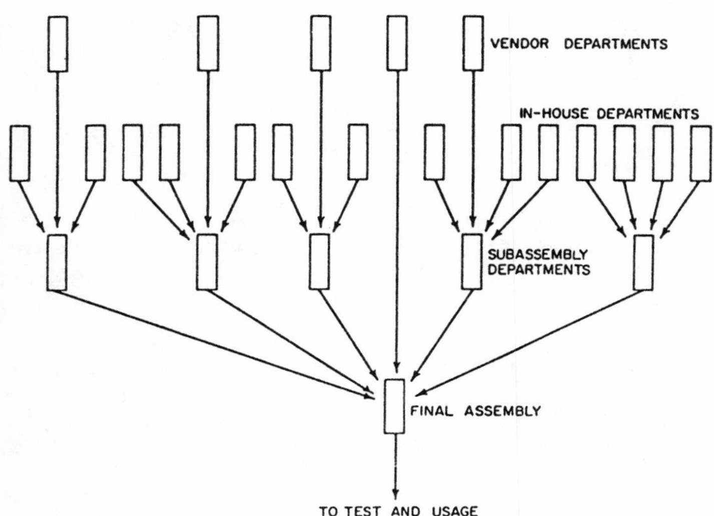

FIGURE 9–12 The assembly tree

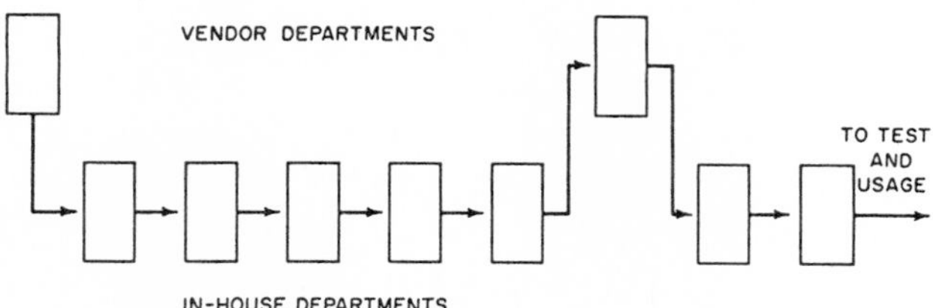

FIGURE 9–13 The procession

to the final result. This form is exhibited by the bulk of the "process" industries. It is also exhibited by many clerical processes in which documents move sequentially from desk to desk. Figure 9–13 shows the schematic.

As in the assembly tree form, an extensive procession requires both interdepartmental and intradepartmental planning. For the former, it is usually mandatory to make use of staff planners. For intradepartmental planning, it may be feasible to use departmental planners, departmental supervisors, or the workforce.

THE BIOLOGICAL PROCESS. A cell divides into multiple cells, which differentiate to create an organism with multiple organs, all coordinated by a nervous system. An enterprise created by a single founder and then "franchised" follows a similar process of growth.

Figure 9–14 shows some examples of the processes listed so far in various industries.

CONVERSIONS. Some processes are convertible into each other. An example is the "job enlargment case" involving telephone directories.

> Every telephone company produces numerous telephone directories, one for each city served. In one telephone company the directories were prepared for publication using a procession of twenty-one clerical steps, each step being performed by a separate employee. (Some steps required more than one person's full time, so the total department consisted of thirty-three employees.) The reorganization gave each employee the job of preparing a complete telephone directory, that is, each

INDUSTRY	AUTONOMOUS DEPARTMENT	ASSEMBLY TREE	PROCESSION	BIOLOGICAL
HOTEL	Bar	Assembling buffet	Assembling kitchen meal	
MILITARY	Ranger/unit	Invasion	Basic training	Insurrection
PUBLISHING	Pamphleteer	Handbook	Printing and binding	Experimental newsletter
TRANSPORT	Independent taxi	Assembling a freight train	Guided Tour	
COMPUTER	Personal computer	Complex computer installation		Building an unmanaged user system
TRAINING	Plato plus a student	Training for an astronaut mission	College curriculum	Training in an emerging "discipline"
CONSTRUCTION	Henry Thoreau at Walden Pond	Building construction	Laying pavement	Shanty town
COMMUNICATION	Ham operator	Network election returns	Relay repeaters	
HEALTH CARE	Dr. Schweitzer	Heart surgery	Physical examination at army camp	Home remedies
FOOD SERVICE	Family kitchen	Restaurant table service	Cafeteria	Franchised chain

FIGURE **9–14 Anatomy of various processes**

person performed all the twenty-one clerical steps needed to do the job. The results of the change were stunning:

	BEFORE	AFTER
Annual turnover of employees	28	0
Absenteeism rate	2.8%	0.6%
Errors per 1,000 lines	3.9	1.1

In our dialect, the anatomy of the process was changed from a procession to an autonomous unit.

THE EMERGING PROCESS FEATURES

As process design progresses from the macro-level down into details, a long list of very specific process features emerges. Each of those features is directly aimed at producing one or more product features. For example:

Product feature X (for an invoice) requires a process feature that can perform calculations in arithmetic.

Product feature Y (for a gear wheel) requires a process feature that can bore precise holes in metal.

Such process features are entered into the vertical columns of the process design spreadsheet (Figure 9–10). In due course each of those process features becomes the focal point of a system of process control (see page 211).

MAKING USE OF PROCESS CAPABILITY DATA

The work of process designers is greatly simplified if they have access to data on process capability of alternative processes.

For example, some processes require purchases to be made from external suppliers. One criterion for choice of supplier is financial stability—a sort of financial process capability. Process planners who have access to data banks on financial stability of prospective suppliers can use such data as inputs to decisions on choice of suppliers. Similarly, credit managers can use data banks on credit worthiness of prospective clients; investment managers can use data banks on merits of listed securities to improve investment decisions.

The concept of competition based on process capability is of long standing. Honors were awarded to ancient Greek athletes and Chinese scholars based on comparative testing of the respective human capabilities. In our century, the same concept is widely applied to evaluation of competitive process inputs: facilities, materials. Employee performance is evaluated as a prerequisite to job assignment. Most recently, companies have discovered that precise evaluation of process capability is a key aid to quality planning—far more so than had been generally realized.

The widest application of this precise evaluation has been to manufacturing processes. By quantifying process capability in standardized terms (such as six standard deviations), manufacturing planners have markedly increased their ability to:

Judge the adequacy of a process relative to product tolerances

Compare competing processes in terms of their inherent precision

Predict process yields

Judge the effectiveness of steps taken to improve quality

Of course, the manufacturing planners have been helped by the fact that many of their processes are measurable by precise technological instruments. Quality planners for other processes cannot as yet attain similar levels of precision. Nevertheless, those same planners do have considerable opportunity to make use of the concept of process capability despite the limitations in precision.

PROCESS CAPABILITY DATA NOT AVAILABLE

In many cases the process designer lacks information on process capability. The data may be nonexistent; the data may exist, but not in usable form. In such cases the quality planners can nevertheless create sources of usable information. They can:

1. Assemble information on prior performance of like or similar facilities or materials and estimate process capability from that

information. Such information is a form of "lessons learned" (see Chapter Thirteen)

2. Conduct competitive tests of alternatives
3. Acquire or buy data from other users or data banks
4. Use simulation to estimate process capability (see Chapter Ten)

CONCEPT OF DOMINANCE

Operating processes are influenced by numerous variables: input materials, physical facilities, human skills, environmental conditions, and so on. Those variables are not equally important. Often one variable is more important than all the rest combined. Such a variable is said to be the dominant variable.

The prevalence of such dominance is an important aid to process planners. Once planners know which variable is dominant, they can confidently assign top priority to acquiring mastery over that variable. The more usual forms of process dominance include:

1. *Setup-dominant.* Such processes exhibit high stability and reproducibility of results, over many cycles of operation. The planning should provide means for precise setup and validation before operations proceed. A common example is the printing process.

2. *Time-dominant.* Here the process is known to change progressively with time, e.g., depletion of consumable supplies, heating up, wear of tools. The planning emphasizes means for periodic evaluation of the effect of change and provision for convenient readjustment.

3. *Component-dominant.* Here the main variable is the quality of the input materials and components. For the short run it may be necessary to resort to incoming inspection. For the long run, the planning should be directed at supplier relations, including joint planning with suppliers to upgrade the inputs.

4. *Worker-dominant.* In these processes, quality depends mainly on the skill and knack possessed by the workers. The planning emphasizes aptitude testing of workers, training and certification, quality rating of workers, and foolproofing to reduce worker errors.

5. *Information-dominant.* Here the processes are of a "job-

shop'' nature, where the job information changes frequently. The planning should concentrate on providing an information system that can deliver accurate, up-to-date information to all who are impacted.

TASKS FOR PROCESS DESIGNERS

Some of the tasks for process designers consist of acquiring the necessary inputs. We have already discussed some of those tasks earlier in this chapter under the headings:

Review of goals

Users' understanding of the process

How will the process be used?

What will be the environments of use?

Carryover of existing process designs

From those and other inputs the process designers proceed from the macro-level into details with the aid of spreadsheets. Use is made of various concepts and tools: anatomy of the process, concept of dominance, process capability.

The process designers have additional tasks. Their nature can be deduced from the contents of the ''package'' they are expected to deliver to the operating forces. Those contents of course vary with the customer needs and the associated product features. However, some contents are common to most of the delivered packages.[1]

Establish the Relation of Process Variables to Product Results

For simple processes the simple process capability study goes a long way toward establishing the relationship between variables and results. The histograms of Figure 9–9 illustrate how helpful such simple studies can be.

[1]Much of what follows is derived from an excellent article: John L. Bemesderfer, ''Approving a Process for Production,'' *Journal of Quality Technology,* 11, no. 1 (January 1979): 1–12.

For complex processes, the simple process capability study, though still useful, is not sufficient. The process designers in addition should evolve an understanding of the relationships between the multiple variables of the complex process and the associated product results. That understanding is needed not only during process development in the laboratory; it is needed also by the operating forces who, in due course, must deal with those same variables.

To establish those relationships requires designed experiments. We saw an example of a designed experiment in Chapter Eight (Figures 8–2 to 8–6 and associated discussion.) That experiment involved a combination of product features and process features. The specific methodology was "orthogonal arrays." There are other methods as well: evolutionary operations, response surface methodology. What they all have in common is a planned, systematic collection of data on multiple process variables and the associated product results. The data are then systematically analyzed to establish the relationships. The resulting relationships provide multiple benefits: Operations can be conducted at optimum yields and costs; process controls can be designed for optimum effectiveness; and the workforce can be provided with a deeper understanding of the variables it is to keep under control.

Provide Measurement Capability

The task of providing measurement capability is actually a part of the broader tasks of "establish process capability" and "design process controls." Measurement is a vital part of the feedback loop.

Measurement capability depends mainly on precision of measurement—the ability of the sensor to reproduce its results on repeat test. For technological instruments such repeatability is relatively easy to quantify. Instrument designers have made astonishing progress in improving precision of measurement.

For other types of sensors, notably the use of human beings as sensors, progress in precision has been less than astonishing. (See the shave test case, pages 86–88; see also the discussion on "Planning to Reduce Human Error" in Chapter Ten.) The comparative lack of progress requires that the process designer establish measurement capability through designed experiments.

Establish Adjustment Capability

From the viewpoint of the operating forces, the ideal system of process control includes the following provisions:

Each product feature should be linked to a single process variable.

Means should be provided for convenient adjustment of the process setting for that variable.

There should be a predictable, precise relationship between the amount of change in the process setting and the amount of effect on the product feature.

For complex processes those ideal provisions can be difficult and even forbidding. However, the process designers are making visible progress. Think of the adjustments available today compared to several decades ago, for products such as office copiers or automobiles. Similar changes have evolved in the control panels for power plants, municipal fire stations, machine tools, county jails, and other facilities.

Transfer to Operations

The transfer of responsibility from planners to the operating forces is a critical step along the quality planning road map. We shall take it up as a part of Chapter Ten.

PLANNING FOR PROCESS CONTROL

"Process control" as used here is the activity of keeping the operating process in a state that continues to be able to meet product goals. "Control" consists of several activities:

Evaluate the actual performance of the process

Compare actual performance with goals

Take action on the difference

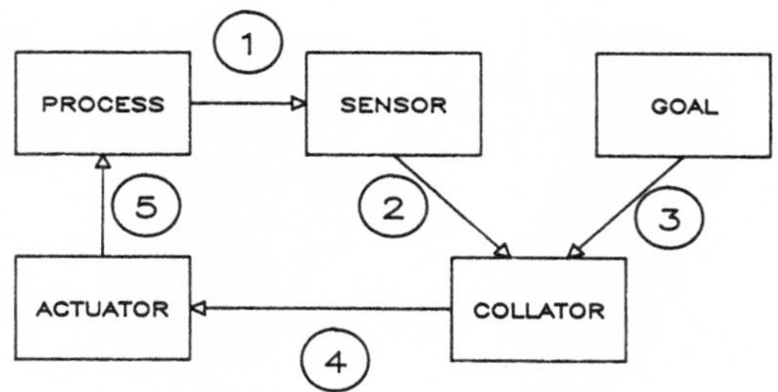

FIGURE 9–15 The feedback loop

THE FEEDBACK LOOP

The control activities take place in a systematic sequence called a feedback loop. In its simplest form the loop can be diagrammed as in Figure 9–15. The flow of information proceeds as follows:

1. The sensor (which is "plugged into the process") evaluates actual performance.
2. The sensor reports on performance to a collator.
3. The collator also receives information on what is the goal or standard.
4. The collator compares actual performance to goal. If the difference warrants action, the collator energizes an actuator.
5. The actuator changes the process conditions so as to bring performance into line with goals.

SELF-CONTROL: THE CRITERIA

The purpose of planning for process control is to provide the operating forces with the means of carrying out process control, that is, evaluation, comparison, and action. The ideal outcome of such planning is to place the operating forces in a state of self-control.

To create a state of self-control the planners must meet three essential criteria. They must provide the operating forces with:

1. The means of knowing what is their actual performance. This criterion is met by establishing the system of measurement.

2. The means of knowing what is their target performance. This criterion is met by establishing and publishing goals and standards.
3. The means for changing their performance in the event that performance does not conform to goals and standards. To meet this criterion requires an operating process that:
   a. Is inherently capable of meeting the goals
   b. Is provided with features that make it possible for the operating forces to change the performance as needed to bring it into conformance with the goals

CONTROL SUBJECTS

All control is centered on specific things to be controlled. We shall call those things "control subjects." Each control subject is the focal point of a feedback loop. Control subjects are a mixture of:

Product features Some control is carried out by evaluating features of the product itself (the invoice, the gear wheel, the research report).

Process features Much control consists of checking those process features which directly impact the product features, e.g., the state of the ribbon in the printer, the temperature of the annealing furnace, the validity of the formulas used in the researcher's report.

Side effect features These features do not impact the product but may create troublesome side effects, such as irritations to employees, offense to the neighborhood, threats to the environment.

RESPONSIBILITY FOR PLANNING PROCESS CONTROLS

Assignment of responsibility for planning process controls varies with (1) the nature of the process, (2) the traditions in the industry, and (3) the organization structure in the company. The actual assignment consists of determining who is to carry out the following specific activities:

1. Identify the control subjects
2. Identify the process control features needed to carry out process control for the control subjects (Typically these features relate to units of measure and type of sensor.)
3. Establish the criteria to be met, e.g., rules for data collection and analysis or rules for decision-making (In critical processes these may extend to include criteria for selection, training and qualification of operating personnel; use of specific managerial tools—design review, Shewhart control charts.)
4. Establish the procedures needed to meet the criteria, e.g., tasks or operations to be performed, sequence of operations, data to be recorded
5. Execute the control plan: carry out the tasks, follow the procedures, meet the criteria
6. Audit to make sure that the execution follows the control plan

That array of specific responsibilities gives rise to many possible combinations of assignment of responsibility. In the case of very critical processes, e.g., nuclear reactors, the responsibility pattern tends to be as follows:

SPECIFIC	ASSIGNMENT IS TO	
RESPONSIBILITY	PROCESS DESIGN	OPERATING FORCES
A	X	
B	X	
C	X	
D	X	
E		X
F	X	

For more conventional processes some of the planning for process control is joint, and some is delegated to the operating forces. A typical pattern might be:

SPECIFIC RESPONSIBILITY	ASSIGNMENT IS TO PROCESS DESIGN	ASSIGNMENT IS TO OPERATING FORCES
A	X	X
B	X	X
C	X	X
D	X	X
E		X
F	X	

For well-standardized processes it is quite common for much or most of the planning for process control to be delegated to the operating forces. The process planners may retain a responsibility to review the process control plan as well as an audit responsibility.

THE PROCESS CONTROL SPREADSHEET

To plan process controls involves a great deal of detail. The process control subjects are numerous. Each requires a feedback loop made up of multiple process control features. To keep track of all that detail, planners make use of a process control spreadsheet, as set out in Figure 9–16.[2]

In this spreadsheet the horizontal rows are the various process control subjects. The vertical columns consist of the elements of the feedback loop plus other features needed by the operating forces to run the process so as to meet the product goals.

Some of the contents of the vertical columns may be unique to specific process features. However, certain vertical columns apply widely to many process features, such as:

Unit of measure

Type of sensor

Goal (aimed-at value)

[2]The author is indebted to Harry Betker and Curt Gustafson of GTE Communication Systems Corporation for providing the precise and complete information concerning the wave solder process from which this simplified example was extracted for purpose of illustration.

PROCESS CONTROL SUBJECT	UNIT OF MEASURE	TYPE OF SENSOR	GOAL	FREQUENCY OF MEASUREMENT	SAMPLE SIZE	CRITERIA FOR DECISION-MAKING	RESPONSIBILITY FOR DECISION-MAKING	. . .
Wave solder conditions:								
Solder temperature	Degree F	Thermo-couple	505 Deg.F	Continuous	N/A	510 Deg.F reduce heat 500 Deg.F increase heat	Operator	. . .
Conveyor speed	Feet per minute(fpm)	fpm meter	4.5 fpm	1/hour	N/A	5 fpm reduce speed 4 fpm increase speed	Operator	. . .
Alloy purity	% Total contam-inants	Lab chemical analysis	1.5% max.	1/month	15 grams	At 1.5%, drain bath, replace solder	Process engineer	. . .
. . .	. . .	. . .	. . .	. . .	. . .	. . .	. . .	

FIGURE 9–16 The process control spreadsheet

Goal for uniformity (tolerance)
Frequency of measurement
Sample size
Criteria for decision-making
Responsibility for decision-making

STAGES OF PROCESS CONTROL

Process controls can take place at several stages of progression. The following are the most frequent.

Setup (Startup) Control

The end result of the setup form of control is the decision whether or not to "push the start button." Typically this control involves:

A *countdown* listing the preparatory steps needed to get the process ready to produce

Measurement of process and/or product features to determine whether, if started, the resulting product will meet product goals

Criteria to be met by the measurements

Verification that the criteria have been met

Assignment of responsibility, which varies, depending largely on the criticality of the process features (The higher the criticality, the greater the tendency to assign the setup tasks to specialists, supervisors, and "independent" verifiers rather than to the workforce.)

(Note that in addition, the more the criticality, the greater is the need for clear definition of responsibility. It is more important for responsibility to be clear than to be logical.)

Running Control

Running control takes place periodically during the operation of the process. The purpose is to make the decision of "run or stop"—whether the process should continue to produce product or whether it should be stopped.

Running control consists of closing the feedback loop, over and over again. The process performance is evaluated and compared with goals. In the absence of a significant difference, the decision is "continue to run." If the difference is too great, some sort of corrective action is in order.

At this point much depends on how well the process design provided for such corrective action. In some cases the restart has been made simple: Turn this calibrated knob until the green light comes on; remove this cartridge and insert a replacement. In such cases the workforce can be trained to carry out the corrective actions and restart the process. In other cases the process planning may not have provided simple ways to make process adjustments. In such cases the workforce may be forced to shut down the process and call for assistance from some designated source (the supervisor, the setup specialist, the maintenance department).

Product Control

Product control takes place after some amount of product has been produced. The purpose of the control is to decide whether or not the product conforms to product goals.

The control features associated with product control parallel those needed for setup control and running control: measurement, criteria for decision-making, and so on. However, since the product has already been produced, product control is a sort of after-the-fact determination. (If the product fails to conform to the product goals, the damage has already been done.)

Being a factual determination, product control can be assigned to anyone who is able to:

Understand the goals

Make the measurements

Determine the difference

In theory, "anyone" includes the workforce and even the automated instruments. In practice, the determination of conformance to product goals is not delegated to those workers whose responsibilities might bias their judgment.

Facilities Control

The "process" includes the physical facilities: equipment, tools, instruments. The trend has increasingly been to use automated processes, computers, robots, and the like. That same trend makes product quality more and more dependent on maintenance of the facilities.

The elements of planning for facilities control are well known:

Establish a schedule for conducting facilities maintenance

Establish a checklist—a list of tasks to be performed during maintenance

Assign clear responsibility for adherence to schedule

The weak link in that listing has been adherence to schedule. Until the operating forces acquire the habit of strict adherence to schedule, the management should maintain an independent audit as a form of assurance.

SUMMARY (Concluded)

Process design is the activity of defining the specific means to be used by the operating forces for meeting the product goals.

Prior to process planning, the goals should have been reviewed by those impacted. Failing such prior review, the first step in process planning is review of goals.

The process planner should understand and take into account:

Users' understanding of the process

How will the process be used (and misused)?

What will be the environments of use?

The process design spreadsheet permits an orderly accounting of product goals and the related process features needed to meet the product goals.

A process feature carried over from prior processes has many advantages. A potential disadvantage is the carryover of unsolved chronic problems.

Planners should evaluate process capability of prior process features before carrying them over into the new process.

The choice of process "anatomy" includes:

Autonomous department

Assembly "tree"

Procession

Biological replication

Process design is aided by the use of process capability data.

In the absence of data on process capability, planners may resort to:

Use of information from similar processes

Tests of alternatives

Acquisition or purchase of data from other users or data banks

Simulation

Planners should seek out the dominant process variable and assign top priority to mastery of that variable, whether setup, time, component, worker, information, or other.

Tasks for process designers include:

Establish the relation of process variables to product results

Provide measurement capability

Establish adjustment capability

Transfer to operations

Control activities follow a systematic sequence called a feedback loop.

To put workers into a state of self-control requires providing them with:

The means of knowing what their actual performance is

The means of knowing the target performance

The means of adjusting the process to meet the target performance

Assignment of responsibility for planning process controls varies depending on process criticality.

The process control spreadsheet is an aid to planning for process control.

Process controls can take place at several stages of progression, including setup (startup) control, running control, product control, facilities control.

] 10 [

Optimizing, Proof of Process Capability, and Transfer to Operations

THE MISSION OF THIS CHAPTER

The mission is to transfer the process plan to the operating forces so that they can commence operations. The input–output diagrams are shown in Figure 10–1.

The *input* is the process features as developed so far.

The *process* consists of:

Optimizing the process features

Proving process capability

Transferring the process to the operating forces

The *output* is a process ready to produce.

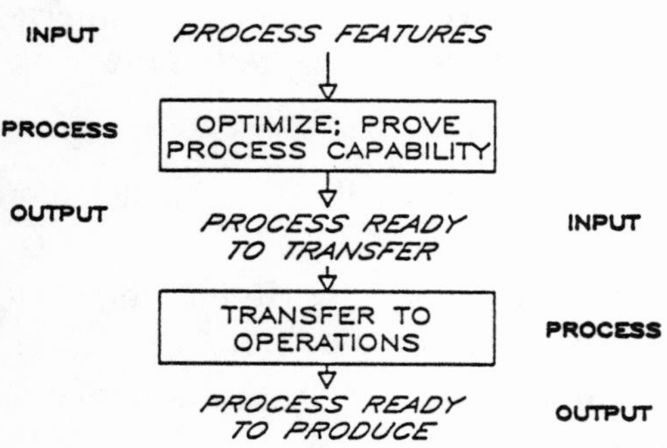

FIGURE 10–1 The input–output diagram for "Optimizing, proof of process capability, and transfer to operations"

OPTIMIZATION: A LOOK BACK

Our travels along the quality planning road map have already included a good deal of optimizing:

In developing product goals, we tried to meet our needs as well as customers' needs.

We looked at value analysis as a means of providing needed functions at minimal cost.

We looked at life cycle costing as a means of optimizing cost of ownership of long-life products.

We noted the use of designed experiments to optimize product and process performance.

Most of our optimization to date has involved our relationship to our external customers. There are other areas which also require optimization. Two of the most important are:

Our relationship to our external suppliers

The planners' relationship to the operating forces

OPTIMIZATION RELATIVE TO EXTERNAL SUPPLIERS

Each external supplier is an extension of our operating forces. Viewed in this way, everything we have said about our "operating forces" applies to the external suppliers as well. However, some things are different:

The external supplier is a separate legal entity; there is no common boss.

The external supplier seldom has a monopoly. He has competitors, and there is wide use of competitive bidding.

The external supplier may supply product design and process design as part of his services.

A widespread adversary relationship has stimulated an urge to suboptimize. External suppliers exhibit this urge more strongly than internal suppliers.

Generally those differences are inherently divisive. Nevertheless, the potential gains from optimizing are considerable:

The assignment of work can be based on who is best qualified to perform the tasks.

Quality improvement by suppliers can lead to lower costs as well as to further improvements, e.g., "just in time" operations.

An emerging teamwork spirit can lead to joint planning.

An emerging mutual trust can lead to reduced duplication of facilities, instruments, tests, reports, and so forth.

The key to achieving such gains is teamwork, which takes such forms as design review and joint planning. (See below under those headings.) Creating such teamwork is a delicate task if the prior history has included an adversary relationship between external suppliers and customers. Such a prior history leads to suspicion and mistrust, the worst possible climate for optimization.

One way to break out of the adversary relationship is to experiment. All organizations have multiple external suppliers. Invariably they include some with whom there has existed a long-standing, comfortable relationship. Such suppliers become the testing ground for optimization. The results of those tests then provide an experience base for extending the concept.

OPTIMIZATION INTERNALLY

Here the main problem is to strike the optimum balance between the work of planning and the subsequent work of operations—carrying out the plan. Planners are always under pressure to meet their schedules and budgets. Yet shortcuts in planning usually result in far greater burdens on operations, in such forms as: failure-prone products, incapable processes, frequent fire-fighting, high maintenance costs. The key to internal optimization is the team approach.

Suppose we ask an audience of upper managers: Do you favor teamwork within your organization? The answer is an obvious, unanimous: Of course! Yet many of those same upper managers act otherwise.

They establish structured departmental goals and structured merit rating systems to reward departmental managers for meeting departmental goals. Such reward systems *inherently tend to result in suboptimization* unless well coordinated.

Those same upper managers fail to establish the structured means needed for coordination.

The point is that exhortations to work as a team are not enough; there is also a need to provide coordinating structures that *inherently result in optimization.* Two such structures—design review and joint planning—are in wide use.

Design Review

Design review was originally evolved as an early warning device during product development. The method is to create a *design review team,* which includes specialists from those classes of customers who are heavily impacted by the design—those who are to develop the manufacturing process, produce the product, test the product, use the product, maintain the product, and so on.

Those specialists have no responsibility for design of the product. Their responsibility is to provide early warning to the designer: "If you design it this way, here are the consequences in my area."

The design review concept has application well beyond review of product designs. It is applicable to any kind of quality planning in which there is a wide separation of responsibility for planning from responsibility for execution.

No matter what kind of product or process is undergoing planning, the design review concept involves:

- Identification of the areas that will be impacted
- Creation of a design review team that includes members from those areas
- Reviews by the team, at various stages of the planning
- Early warning identification of problems ahead
- Appropriate action to revise the plans or to provide for dealing with the problems during subsequent operations

In the design review concept, the responsibility for decision on what enters the plan remains with the planner, e.g., the product designer. The other members of the design review team are there to provide input and early warnings to the planner, not to make decisions. The warnings are often heeded. Where they are not, the team members have a channel for appeal to higher authority through the regular chain of command.

Joint Planning

Yet another form of optimizing internally is joint planning. In some elaborate undertakings, e.g., a major new product development program, there are even migratory teams that remain with the program as it progresses through its phases.

Those joint planning approaches tend to establish team responsibility for the final plan. Such team responsibility stimulates good communication and full participation among team members and thereby contributes to proof of process capability.

PLANNING TO REDUCE HUMAN ERROR

The concept of optimization need not be limited to instances in which the planners try to avoid creating problems for the operating forces. The concept can be extended to cases in which the planners undertake to solve long-standing problems of the operating forces. A case in point is planning to reduce human error.

Human beings are by nature error-prone. They are unable to maintain attention 100 percent of the time, to continue muscular exertion 100 percent of the time, to recall all past events, to make 100 percent good decisions. Beyond that error-proneness, human beings vary in their capabilities. Some develop a knack that enables them to outperform those who lack the knack. In addition, we must contend with conscious errors committed by human beings. Some consciously violate company rules, e.g., they fail to report errors because they feel that a prevailing atmosphere of blame will assign guilt to the messenger who brings bad news. Some are not aware that innocent-looking violations can do a lot of damage to users, so they take unauthorized short cuts for personal convenience, or to avoid disagreeable work. Some are rebels who deliberately violate the rules in order to take revenge on society for real or imagined grievances.

To a degree, the operating managers can reduce those errors. However, the residue is large enough to require that the planning process itself provide for means to reduce human error. Many planners have recognized the need, and we have numerous examples of planning specifically for reducing human error.

The starting point is to analyze the data on human errors and to apply the Pareto principle. The vital few error types are normally candidates for special planning on an individualized basis. For example, some workers persisently outperform others on specific quality features. The likely reason is possession of a special knack. In such cases the need is to study the methods used by the respective workers in order to discover the differences in methods. The differences usually include the knack—a small difference in methods that produces a big difference in performance. Once the knack is discovered, the planners can arrange to include the knack in the technology or in the workers' training program so that all workers are brought up to the level of the best.

A useful principle in planning human tasks is to provide instant feedback to the worker so that the *performance of the work conveys a message to the worker.* For example, a worker at a control panel pushes a switch and receives three feedbacks: the *feel* of the shape of the switch handle; the *sound* of an audible click, signaling that the switch went all the way; the *sight* of a visual illumination of a specific color and shape.

Another useful principle is that of designing human work in ways that require human attention as a prerequisite, that is, the task cannot be performed unless the person doing it devotes attention to it and to nothing else. A widespread case in point is "checking" or inspection of documents, products, or whatever.

Human checking is done in two very different ways:

1. By *passive* deeds: listening, looking, reading. Such deeds are notoriously subject to lapses in human attention. Also, such deeds leave no trail behind them; we have no way of knowing when the human being in question is really paying attention or is in a state of inattention.

2. By *active* deeds: operating a keyboard, writing, speaking. Such deeds cannot be performed at all without paying attention to the task at hand, to the exclusion of all else. Those active deeds do leave a trail behind them.

To illustrate, telephone companies have the problem of assuring that subscribers' listings in the telephone directory correspond to the original copy approved by the subscriber. The conventional approach for providing such assurance was passive checking: a clerk visually compared the printer's proof with the approved original. The current approach, using the active principle, is as follows:

1. Working from the basic subscriber data, a data entry clerk uses a keyboard to put this information on magnetic tape.
2. Subsequently the proofreader, also working from the basic subscriber data, uses a keyboard to put this information into a computer.
3. The computer compares the two inputs to see if they are alike. If so, the verified tape is used to produce the directory.

(The assumption behind the concept is that it is most unlikely that two clerks will independently make identical errors on the same listing.)

It is also possible to plan the reduction of human errors at the low end of the Pareto distribution—the numerous error types each of which is comparatively rare. Here the planners look for some generic remedy that applies to a wide assortment of error types.

For example, office work has long had the annoying problem of misspelled words. Most misspellings are inadvertent errors scattered over a wide assortment of different words. Now, some word processing programs include a dictionary in their memory as a means of detecting misspelled words. The planners found a way to deal with numerous error types, each of which is comparatively rare.

Similar planning approaches can be found in the factories.

In conveyor assembly line planning, each work station is designed to give the worker enough time to perform the operation under normal operating conditions. Occasionally an abnormality arises—any of a wide variety of abnormalities: an input component doesn't fit; the worker fumbles; a passerby creates a distraction. In such cases the worker may be unable to complete the operation before the conveyor has taken the unit out of reach. Some assembly conveyors now provide means for the workers to detach the product from the conveyor in order to complete the operation. Here again the planners have found a way to deal with numerous error types each of which is comparatively rare.

Inadvertent human errors can also be reduced, but the means involve "foolproofing"—building safeguards into the technology: fail-safe designs, automation, robotics. Nonhuman processes do not have lapses in attention, do not become weary, do not lose their memory (so long as they are properly maintained). It is also helpful to provide self-checking systems to secure prompt detection of errors.

The accountants' spread sheet has long involved a built-in self-check: The grand totals of the columns and the grand totals of the horizontal lines must agree.

Some utility companies (electricity, gas) send out millions of invoices annually. A key input to the computerized invoicing process is the meter readings showing the amount of service used. Where the meters are read by human beings, they are subject to human error. To guard against incorrect invoices going to customers, the computerized system is programmed to reject invoices that show abnormal charges—charges out of line with the predicted range. (The rates of usage of the service, and hence the size of the bill, are quite predictable within rather narrow limits.) Rejected invoices are then checked out by human means.

In like manner, some factory operations are provided with instruments that check the product and/or the process, and sound alarms when things go out of control.

PRINCIPLES OF FOOLPROOFING

Two Japanese authors[1] have recently generalized the principles of foolproofing. They reviewed nearly 1,000 case examples of foolproofing—steps taken to guard against the effects of human error.

[1]Takeshi Nakajo and Hitoshi Kume, "The Principles of Foolproofing and their Application in Manufacturing," *Reports of Statistical Application Research,* Japanese Union of Scientists and Engineers, 32, no. 2 (June 1985): 10–29. Also presented (in abbreviated form) at the EOQC Annual Conference, Stockholm, June 1986. *Proceedings,* pp. 221–28.

From those cases they established a classification of foolproofing methods as set out below.

Elimination

Elimination means changing the technology so as to eliminate operations that are error-prone. For example, in some materials handling operations the worker should insert a protective pad between the lifting wire and the product so that the wire will not damage the product. Elimination could consist of using nylon bands to do the lifting.

Replacement

The replacement method retains the error-prone operation but replaces the human worker with a nonhuman operator. For example, a human worker may install the wrong component into an assembly. A robot avoids such errors.

Facilitation

Under the facilitation method the error-prone operation is retained and so is the human worker. However, the human worker is provided with means to reduce error-proneness. Color coding of parts is an example.

The authors use the term "prevention of occurrence" as a generic expression of the above three methods (elimination, replacement, and facilitation). The two additional methods (detection and mitigation) are classed under "minimization of effects."

Detection

The detection method does nothing to prevent the human error from happening. Instead, it aims to find the error at the earliest opportunity in order to minimize the damage done. A widespread example is automated testing between processes.

Mitigation

Here again, the method does nothing to prevent the human error from happening. However, means are provided to avoid the damage done. A common example is providing a fuse to avoid damage to electrical equipment.

Classes of Errors

The authors have also classified human errors, as follows:

Errors of memory

Errors of perception

Errors of motion

Having provided bases for classifying human errors and methods of foolproofing, the remainder of the paper goes into detail to show how the various foolproofing methods are applied to the various categories of human error. A great many case examples are presented to illustrate those applications.

The case examples will be quite familiar to the experienced practitioner. However, the organization of the subject of foolproofing is mostly new, and entirely enlightening. It is a useful research, and it should become a classic in its field.

PLANNING FOR CRITICAL PROCESSES

Of all processes requiring freedom from human error, the most critical are those which present serious dangers to human life, health, and the environment, or risk the loss of very large sums of money. Such processes must obviously be planned with ample margins of safety as to structural integrity, fail-safe provisions, redundancy, multiple alarms, and all other safeguards of modern technology. However, it is necessary to go further in the planning. *The basic planning must also include planning of the operating quality control system.* This is quite different from what is done in less critical processes. There the planning of the control system is largely left to the operating forces.

Critical processes usually require numerous safety features to be built into the operational quality control system. However, a vital few of those features seem to have figured predominantly in the history of disasters and near disasters.

Time to Respond to a Crisis

Timing may well be the prime consideration. When a crisis develops, the operating forces need adequate time to recognize the symptoms, discover the causes, and take remedial action.

> The Bhopal, India, gas poisoning disaster took 2,000 lives and injured 200,000 others. The Three Mile Island nuclear power plant near-disaster terrified hundreds of thousands of people. The Chernobyl nuclear power plant disaster took some lives, shortened others, and made a large area uninhabitable. In all cases the developing crisis seemingly demanded that the operating forces diagnose and remedy the burgeoning hazard promptly—in a matter of minutes, or hours at the most.

The basic design of such critical processes should provide the operating forces with ample time—enough hours or days—to head off a disaster.

Criteria for Qualification of Operating Forces

Selection and training of the operating personnel is always a responsibility of the operating managers. In critical processes, something else is needed—the planners must provide those selection and training criteria which are required as a part of the security system. The most obvious expression of those criteria is the licensing requirement: Those who are to conduct the key control activities must first pass a qualifying examination.

> In the pharmaceutical industry a key operation is weighing out the ingredients for the batch. The mandated standard requires that there be two independent weighings, each by a graduate pharmacist.

Rehearsal, Simulation

For critical processes the operating forces must be qualified by experience as well as by training. This poses a dilemma: how to provide the key operating personnel with the needed experience *before* the process goes into operation.

In some cases the personnel can be assigned to acquire familiarity and experience on *existing* processes before being assigned to the process undergoing planning. Such assignments include drills—*rehearsals* to acquire experience in dealing with crises.

In other cases the planners resort to *simulation*. Small scale models are built, equipped with means for creating many combinations of operating conditions and crises. A good deal of pertinent experience can be acquired from such models.

Maintenance

In conventional processes the planning of maintenance (frequency of check, countdown during check) is done by the operating forces. In critical processes the need for maintenance becomes absolute; such processes are planned to rely absolutely on the proper functioning of the technological equipment and safeguards. That reliance in turn demands that the basic system planning include setting out the maintenance criteria to be met in order to ensure the integrity of the system.

Systematic Feedback

In these critical processes provision is usually made for progressive replanning based on feedback of information from operations.

For example, investigations of "critical incidents" sometimes disclose a disturbing degree of nonconformance to authorized practice: short cuts, actions for local convenience, and so on. Of course, the operating managers are responsible for establishing a level of discipline that will result in compliance with the rules. However, the highest integrity is achieved through replanning so as to put the safeguards into the technology.

PROOF OF PROCESS CAPABILITY

"Transfer to operations" includes a transfer of responsibility from the planners to the operating managers. Those managers understandably do not want to accept responsibility for results if the process cannot do its intended job—in our dialect, if the process lacks process capability or lacks controllability. In earlier chapters we discussed direct methods for quantifying and proving process capability. What about the cases where such direct methods are not feasible?

Dry Runs

The dry run is a test of the process under operating conditions. The purpose is to test the process. The resulting product is not sent on to customers.

> A bank data processing manager purchased computer software designed to replace manual processing of a complex data

system. She tested the software by running the same input data through both systems—manual and computer—and then comparing the results.

In manufacturing processes it is common practice to conduct "tool tryouts." The aim is to produce enough units of product to demonstrate that the tool can meet quality standards under operating conditions.

Pilot Testing

Another approach is to introduce an intermediate scaling up between the planning phase and full-scale operations. The approach goes by various names:

A "test town" for trying out a new marketing plan

A "pilot lot" for testing out a manufacturing process

A "test department" for trying a new managerial concept, e.g., QC Circles.

The results of such pilot tests are often decisive on whether to go to full scale operation or not. For that reason it is necessary to define in advance the questions to which answers are needed and to design the data collection plan accordingly.

Process Validation

In some industries "process capability" is used in the sense of conformance to specifications rather than ability to meet the needs of customers or fitness for use. Typical examples are those in which:

The client is a government agency, e.g., the Defense Department.

Human safety, health, or the environment is impacted, as in pharmaceutical manufacture.

In such industries the clients and the regulators prepare product and process specifications that are presumed to reflect fitness for use. The supplier is then given the responsibility to:

Provide products that conform to product specifications

Provide processes that conform to process specifications ("Process" here extends to managerial processes as well as technological processes.)

Government clients and regulators tend to stress quality assurance in the form of "process validation." The following is an example of a definition (from a guideline drafted by the Food and Drug Administration):

> Process validation is a documented program which provides a high degree of assurance that a specific process will consistently produce a product meeting its predetermined specifications and quality attributes.

A principle aspect of quality assurance is then a review of all quality-related process features to assure that they do conform to the process specifications. Those specifications take such forms as the Defense Department's MIL-Q-9858 or the FDA's Good Manufacturing Practice.

SIMULATION TO PROVE PROCESS CAPABILITY

New processes normally consist of a mixture of:

Features carried over from predecessor processes for which we have operating experience

New features for which there is no prior operating experience

As to carryover features, it is feasible to prove (or disprove) process capability by direct data collection and analysis. In the case of truly new process features, such an approach is not available. The process features in question have not yet been in service under operating conditions. In consequence, the quality planners must resort to other forms of proving process capability. One of the most widely used of those other forms is simulation.

We are using the word simulation in its literal sense of *an imitation of the real thing.* Our planning may contemplate a new process that involves considerable investment. Since the process is new, such an investment is at risk; we have no proof that it will be able to meet our goals under operating conditions. However, we can reduce our risk by simulation. We can design a scaled-down process and then test it out. We can then use the test results to predict what the results will be under full scale operation.

Examples of Simulation

A well-known form of simulation is that used in product development and design. A model (prototype, mockup, breadboard circuit, pilot plant) is designed, built, and tested. The test results provide a degree of prediction as to what to expect if we scale up to the real thing.

The concept of simulation is not limited to product development and design. It extends to all processes. To illustrate:

> A market survey asks the question: Would you buy this product? The answers are an imitation of the real thing—no money is being spent.

In like manner, the armed forces stage maneuvers to test out operational readiness. The theater troupe conducts rehearsals. The office building holds fire drills. Trainees work out exercises before applying the new tools to their jobs.

Mathematical Models

A special form of simulation is through mathematical models, which deal with symbols rather than with physical things. In design of physical products and systems, use can be made of reliability models to aid in quantifying reliability, predicting reliability, identifying likely weaknesses in the designs, and so on. Numerous special tools have been evolved to enable designers and other planners to understand and use those models.

The designers' acceptance of the mathematical models has been less than enthusiastic. Designers do not want their designs to fail. However, their long-standing method for judging fitness for use has been by test of the hardware, either in the laboratory or in service. A design that failed on test was an alarm signal, which the designer heeded. (He still does.) In contrast, a design that "fails" a mathematical analysis is not regarded as an alarm signal, since no hardware has failed on test.

All that is undergoing change. Increasingly, designers are acquiring training in the use of reliability models as an extension of the simulation process.

LIMITATIONS AND RISKS IN SIMULATION: TWO WORLDS

Simulation is a tool of great value, provided we understand the limitations and risks. We can better understand the limitations and risks by noting that simulation and full-scale operation are carried out in two different "worlds." Let us call those two worlds the "laboratory" and the "real world" respectively. The existence of the two worlds means that we are dealing with two versions of process capability:

Process capability in the laboratory

Process capability in the real world

In a sense we are evaluating process capability in the laboratory and then extrapolating to predict process capability in the real world. Now let us list some of the differences exhibited by the two worlds, as well as some of the methods used to face up to those differences.

Scale of Operations

When we progress from the laboratory to the world of operations, we commonly scale up by orders of magnitude. We are then faced with extrapolating from small numbers in order to predict the effect on the subsequent large numbers.

Small numbers are a treacherous basis for decision-making. They do exhibit the effect of the treatment they received in the laboratory, but they also exhibit considerable variation due to chance. Those chance variations can and should be quantified so that their statistical meaning is evaluated. The technologists should learn how to do this. Until they do learn how, someone else should do it for them.

Technology

In part the two worlds differ because of the demands of technology. In the laboratory we may take pains to exclude the effect of certain variables in order to secure adequate data on relationships between cause and effect. In the real world it may be impractical to exclude those variables.

The Mission

In the laboratory the mission is to produce the plan: the system design, the procedure, the product design, the process design, or whatever. In the real world the mission is to meet the various operating goals: quality; productivity; cost; safety. The difference in mission creates other differences, e.g., in:

The priorities assigned to the various goals

The type and intensity of supervision provided

The integrity of data collection and analysis

Personnel

A further consequence of the difference in mission is various differences in personnel practices, such as:

The educational background of people recruited

The supplemental training and experience

The career concept

The choice of incentives

Those differences require that extrapolation from laboratory findings be based on input from both worlds. The technologists are quite competent to interpret what happened in the laboratory. However, they are not necessarily able to extrapolate—to predict what will happen in the real world—unless they have adequate knowledge of how life is lived in that world. Lacking such knowledge, they must acquire it from inhabitants of the real world through such team efforts as joint planning and design review.

PROCESS NOT CAPABLE

In many cases quality planners evaluate process capability only to discover that the process is not capable of meeting goals. We have plenty of experience with incapable processes. Our former ways of quality planning created a lot of such incapability, often without knowing it. We then learned of the existence of the incapability during operations. Each such case then became a chronic source of quality troubles. By learning about such incapability during the planning stages, we enlarge our range of choice—we create multiple options to avoid burdening the operating forces with an incapable process. The multiple options include:

1. Look closely to see whether "incapability" is really based on inadequate process *capability*, or is due to evaluation based on

process *performance.* If the basis has in fact been process performance, attempt to evaluate process capability.

2. Analyze the extent of incapability. The process may be capable as to some goals but not as to others. Such analysis identifies the incapable residue and thereby narrows the problem.

3. Improve process capability by carrying out a quality improvement project. Such a project requires digging deeper to discover new relationships between process variables and product results. Concentrate on the dominant variables to simplify the analysis. (See "Concept of Dominance," page 208.)

4. Review the product goals associated with the process incapability to see if the optimum is best served by revising the goals.

5. Endure the incapability and the resulting chronic waste. In that event, it is necessary to provide for an adequate level of customer service for both external and internal customers.

The last option (endure the incapability) should always be regarded as a temporary measure. Future planning projects as well as the annual improvement process should keep reviewing such cases to see whether the march of technological and managerial progress has found ways to solve the problem.

PROOF THAT THE PROCESS IS CONTROLLABLE

Transfer from Planning to Operations includes transfer of responsibility for control. The operating forces become responsible not only for producing the product but also for maintaining the process at its planned level of capability. As we have seen, this control is exercised by use of the feedback loop—in essence, by:

Evaluating actual performance

Comparing actual to goals

Taking action on the difference

All this implies that the process is controllable, that the planning has provided the means for carrying out the activities within the feedback loop.

For many processes the planning of the control system is left to the operating forces. In such cases, planning for control should not wait until the transfer has been made. Instead, the planning for control should be done as the process planning proceeds. Failing that, the risk is that the process will lack full controllability and that discovery of this fact will come too late in the day. Our experience has been that such cases involve costly retroactive revisions.

For "critical" processes the planning for control should properly be a part of the basic process planning. (Critical processes are those which involve potential serious risks to human safety and health, to the environment, or to large sums of money.) We saw in the present chapter, under "Planning for Critical Processes," that for certain disasters and near-disasters there seemed to be linkages between the design of the basic process and the design of the control system:

Time to respond to a crisis

Criteria for qualification of the operating forces

Simulation, rehearsal

Maintenance

Generally, the physical facilities have done what they were designed to do. The weaknesses seem to have been centered in the human component of the control system.

Proof of human controllability is best provided by demonstration. In consequence, the planning should include defining the terms of the demonstration, that is, the criteria to be met by the operating forces when faced with crises of the type that might arise during conduct of operations. Those criteria consist of such matters as time of response to alarm signals, accuracy of diagnosis, and adequacy of remedial action.

The same planning may well extend to design of the system of independent audit needed to ensure that the operating forces carry out the control plan and maintain the integrity of the basic process.

TRANSFER OF KNOW-HOW

During process planning, the planners acquire a great deal of know-how about the process. The operating forces can benefit from that know-how, but only if it is transferred. There are various ways of making the transfer.

Process Specifications

Specifications set out the process goals to be met. The information is vital to the operating forces but is the barest minimum.

Procedures

Procedures are a welcome elaboration. They can include instructions, cautions, the why as well as the how. Being written, they become a reference base and an aid to the indoctrination of new employees. A well-written Owner's Manual serves similar purposes.

Briefings

Briefings are meetings specifically set up for transfer of information. When well organized, briefings are most useful. The planners make a presentation built around a written statement and supplemented by visual aids. Questions and discussion are encouraged, so that the transfer goes beyond the surface.

On-the-Job Training

In many cases the planners can usefully participate in the training given to the operating supervisors and the workforce. The merits of this approach go beyond the transfer of know-how; there is an associated valuable feedback to the planners. The supplier learns from the customers.

Formal Training Courses

Courses of training are needed in cases where the new process departs radically from the past. Examples have included introduction of word processors, computer aided design, QC circles, laser drilling, orthogonal arrays. Such formal training courses become essential if the new process is to be applied widely throughout the organization.

Prior Participation

The above forms of transfer of know-how are a mixture of transfer before the fact and transfer after the fact. Both forms are needed, but the greatest damage is done by neglect of transfer before the fact. Such neglect loses the benefits of early warning and of the teamwork that results from participation. Not only is prior participation a form of transfer of know-how; it is the most timely form.

THE FORMALITIES OF TRANSFER

In some companies, transfer of the process from Planning to Operations is structured and formalized. An information package is prepared comprising certain standardized essentials: goals to be met, facilities to be used, procedures to be followed, instructions, cautions, along with supplements unique to the project. The package is accompanied by a formal letter of transfer of responsibility. In some companies the transfer takes place in a near-ceremonial atmosphere. In other companies, formality is minimal.

The structured approach has value. It tends to evolve checklists and countdowns, which help assure that the transfer is orderly and complete. (Formality is useful if it contributes to such orderliness and completeness.)

In companies that already have such a structured approach, the planners need only to adapt the project information package to conform with established practice. If the company has only a loose structure, or none at all, the planners must make their own decision as to what to put into the information package and how far to go with formalities.

QUALITY CHARACTERISTIC

Many quality specialists, especially in manufacturing industries, use the term "quality characteristic" to mean any property of a product or process. In this book we have avoided use of the term "quality characteristic." Instead, we have been using the word "feature" to designate such a product or process property.

The reason for not using the term "quality characteristic" is that it is seldom used within service industries and is used hardly at all by the general public. In contrast, the word "feature" is universally used and understood.

SUMMARY

Optimization includes external relations and requires a teamwork relationship with external suppliers.

Internal optimization requires striking a balance between the work of planning and the subsequent work of operations.

Two principal structures for helping to strike that balance are design review and joint planning.

Quality planning should include provision for reducing human error.

Performance of the work should convey a message to the worker.

Checking for human errors should be planned on an "active" basis, which requires exclusive attention to the checking task.

Foolproofing—guarding against the effects of human error—includes:

Elimination of error-prone operations

Replacement of error-prone human workers with nonhuman operators

Provision of aids to help human workers reduce errors

Detection of errors at the earliest opportunity

Mitigation of the damage otherwise caused by human error

For the processes that are critical to human safety (or that risk large sums of money), the quality planning should provide:

Time for the operating forces to respond to a crisis

Criteria for qualification of operating personnel

Opportunity for rehearsals

Criteria for maintenance

Systematic feedback

Process planning is aided by access to data on process capability.

Transfer to operations should include proof that the process can do its intended job under operating conditions.

In the absence of means to prove process capability by direct measurement, planners may resort to dry runs, pilot tests, process validation, simulation.

Simulation may include the use of mathematical models.

The world of simulation differs extensively from the world of full-scale operation.

Extrapolation from simulated processes into full-scale processes requires inputs from both worlds.

Discovery of process incapability during the planning stages increases the range of options available for dealing with such incapability.

For critical processes, planning should include proof of human controllability.

Proof of human controllability is best provided by demonstration.

"Transfer to operations" includes transfer of know-how gained during the planning process. Means for transferring know-how include:

- Process specifications
- Procedures
- Briefings
- On-the-job training
- Formal training courses
- Prior participation

Transfer from Planning to Operations is best done through a structured approach.

] *11* [

Companywide Quality Management (CWQM)

THE MISSION OF THIS CHAPTER

The mission is to provide upper managers with a structured approach for management of quality at the upper levels of the company. As used here, the term "upper managers" always includes the corporate officers.

In very large companies it is common practice to create "divisions," which are given considerable autonomy over specific sectors of the company's business. In such cases "upper managers" includes the division general managers and their staffs.

Orientation to upper levels is what distinguishes this chapter from all others. Chapters Two through Ten relate to quality planning at intermediate, interdepartmental levels. Chapter Twelve relates to departmental quality planning. The present chapter, while employing some common planning methodology, is oriented to the upper levels.

Note that the term "management" as used here is broader than the term "planning." Management includes conduct of operations, which employs the quality control process of the quality trilogy. Management also includes quality improvement, which employs the quality improvement process of the trilogy. However, the emphasis in the chapter remains on planning for quality, since that is the subject of this book.

WHAT IS COMPANYWIDE QUALITY MANAGEMENT?

CWQM is a systematic approach for setting and meeting quality goals throughout the company. The approach is quite similar to the method long used to set and meet financial goals. The similarity is so striking that it is worthwhile to review briefly the well-known approach to companywide financial management before getting deeply into the corresponding means for CWQM.

The Financial Parallel

In the dialect of finance, the goals are called budgets and the unit of measure is money. When properly done, the budgets (for sales, profits, expenses, capital) are arrived at through extensive participation at all levels. The final result is financial goals at all levels: budgets for the corporation, the divisions, the departments.

Along with setting the goals, plans are established for meeting the goals. For example, to meet the sales budget may require plans to:

Increase the sales force

Strengthen promotion and advertising

Update existing product lines

Launch a new product line

Make acquisitions

Those plans include subplans in the form of schedules, delegation of responsibility, training of personnel, among others.

To carry out the plans then requires resources in such forms as money, facilities, manpower, services, training programs. The planning provides those resources.

The planning also provides for controls (cost controls, expense controls, inventory controls). The controls all involve evaluating actual performance, comparing actual performance to goals, and taking action on the difference.

Finally, the planning provides systematic motivation to urge personnel to meet the goals. The motivation takes such forms as supervisory leadership, merit rating systems, incentives.

The above approach for setting and meeting financial goals has evolved over the centuries. Companies that use the approach outperform companies that do not.

The corresponding approach to CWQM is still in the early stages of evolution. However, there is already a considerable body of evidence to show that companies using the concept of CWQM outperform companies that do not.

The Application to Quality

If we now apply the approach used for finance to managing for quality, the terminology changes, but the concepts remain the same. Now the sequence reads somewhat as follows:

Establish policies and goals for quality

Establish plans for meeting those quality goals

Provide the resources needed to carry out the plans

Establish controls to evaluate progress against goals and to take appropriate action

Provide motivation to stimulate the personnel to meet the quality goals

The analogy of CWQM to financial management is clear enough. However, introducing CWQM into a going company involves a lot of work. It also involves creating a good deal of change in corporate culture and dealing with the associated resistance to change. What justifies going into all that work?

WHY GO INTO CWQM?

The basic reason for taking up CWQM is that companies that have adopted CWQM are outperforming companies that retain the methods of the past. Note, however, that while this assertion is a belief strongly held by some practitioners (including the author), we have no solid research that provides scientific proof of the assertion.

The Methods of the Past

Having already described what CWQM is, let us describe the "methods of the past" for contrast. The most striking feature of our past approach has been:

Every department is responsible for meeting departmental goals

Every department has had responsibility for carrying out its function (marketing, product development, customer service) and doing so properly. Departmental goals were established (schedule, cost, quality). Departmental managers were rewarded for meeting those goals.

There is a good deal of merit in that arrangement, *up to a point.* People who have goals to meet generally get more done and do it better than people who have no goals to meet. Beyond that point lies big trouble. In the case of quality, the departmental quality goals were met, but the goals themselves were grossly in error:

New products were developed to meet the needs of external customers but not the needs of internal customers.

Failure-prone features of prior products were perpetuated by being carried over into new product designs.

Multidepartmental planning projects such as new product launchings suffered perpetual delays because the various phases were carried out consecutively, with inadequate early warning of the damage done to later phases.

A high cost of poor quality was perpetuated by being built into the cost standards.

Such problems being inherently multidepartmental in nature, could be solved only be extensive multidepartmental means: joint planning, project teams, early warning systems, participation. Yet such multidepartmental means tended to interfere with meeting departmental goals.

For example, a planning department is given a schedule to complete a specific planning project in twelve months. If the department were to bring its internal customers into extensive participation, it might benefit the company greatly. However, the department would then miss its schedule by two months.

In addition, the long-standing emphasis on departmental responsibility and departmental goals had tended to create and perpetuate departmental monopolies over the respective departmental functions. Those monopolies were a source of valued benefits: status, careers, power. Such benefits, once attained, are not readily surrendered. Deficiencies like that could go on and on, so long as:

Competitors were operating with similar deficiencies

The market was willing to pay for the deficiencies

The quality crisis of the 1980s was mainly the result of the emergence of new ways of managing for quality—ways that avoided perpetuating those deficiencies. Now the market had no need to keep paying for the deficiencies. The result was drastic shifts in share of market.

To put an end to perpetuating all those deficiencies requires something new. It requires some form of coordination that has enough force to put company performance ahead of departmental goals. All those forms we mentioned (joint planning, project teams, early warning systems, participation) have real value. However, they must compete against powerful traditions: the departmental monopolies, departmental goals, and the rest. What we are learning is that to deal effectively with those powerful traditions requires going after quality on a companywide basis, making quality a part of the company's strategic business planning.

Disadvantages of CWQM

The prime disadvantage is that CWQM adds to the workload of upper managers. As we shall see, upper managers must become personally involved in establishing corporate and divisional quality policies, goals, plans, controls. For upper managers it is time-consuming in several ways. It takes time to:

Undergo training in the nature of quality: how to think about quality, how to plan, control, and improve quality

Create the companywide approach: quality policies, goals, plans, controls, incentives

Review performance against goals thereafter

An understandable reaction of busy upper managers is to avoid adding to their own workload; often they are already fully loaded (and overloaded). One form of such avoidance is delegation to subordinates. In fact, the ability to delegate is an essential qualification of an executive.

Many upper managers have already tried to delegate to subordinates the job of meeting the quality crisis. The delegation process has generally consisted of a drive to exhort subordinates to develop "awareness." Such drives were conducted with the best intentions and with competent promotion: statements of support by top executives, meetings and displays to arouse interest, colorful posters, cleverly worded slogans. The assumption and hope were that such increase in awareness would somehow change behavior and improve results. With some exceptions, nothing of the sort took place.

Those drives were doomed to failure because they did not address the fundamentals. Raising awareness, while having merit, did nothing to change the situation of "each department on its own." The department managers continued to be judged based on meeting departmental goals, and those goals (with exceptions) continued to perpetuate the deficiencies of the past. No provision was made to determine "what should we do different from what we have been doing." The fact that the upper managers' personal involvement (usually) ended with their speeches (made at the launching of the drive) tended to deny the assertions that the upper managers regarded quality as having top priority.

The obstacles to delegation are probably best exemplified by the popular slogan, "Do it right the first time." Advocates of drives on awareness have urged upper managers to adopt that slogan, and many upper managers have done so; it seems a sensible thing to say. It *is* sensible as applied to the company. However, as applied to subordinates the slogan is often divisive. It implies that the subordinates have not been doing "it" right. Yet those same subordinates had for years met the established goals and were rewarded for doing so. Many such subordinates have confided to this author their resentment at the implications of blame. Some have gone further: They have felt that what they are getting from upper management is not leadership but cheerleading.

In the opinion of the author it is a delusion for upper managers to try to meet the quality crisis by exhortation—by somehow saying the right words. The upper managers must personally establish new directions and goals for the company and then personally lead the management team toward those goals.

Effect on Morale

Members of a winning team fight with their competitors. Members of a losing team fight with each other.

The quality crisis has created many losing teams, and the effect on morale has been severe. Upper managers, untrained in the quality function and unsure of which way to take the company, try exhortation and pressure, e.g., "Do it right the first time." However, in the absence of clear goals, plans, and so on, the management team members do not know what they should do different from what they have been doing.

An important by-product of CWQM is the opportunity it provides for raising morale by unifying the efforts of the management team. In some companies this can be a primary reason for going into CWQM.

GETTING STARTED

A company going into CWQM is well advised to create a companywide quality committee (The Committee) of high-level managers to establish and coordinate the approach. (Such committees are widely prevalent in the major Japanese companies.) The chairman is typically the company president or executive vice president. The members are corporate officers. At the division level the chairman is the general manager, and the members are selected members of his staff.

In many companies the recommendation to create a companywide quality committee is initiated by middle managers, not by upper managers. Experience has shown that such recommendations, though coming from middle managers, are well received and often acted on by upper managers at profit center levels, that is, autonomous divisions or business units. However, in very large companies creation of such a committee at the corporate level is still a rarity in the United States (as of the middle 1980s). In Japan such corporate committees are quite common in very large manufacturing companies.

Once CWQM has been organized and running, The Committee's role relative to quality is quite similar to the role of the Finance Committee relative to finance, namely:

Coordinate establishment of quality goals

Coordinate preparation of plans to carry out the goals

Review progress against goals

Coordinate the administration of the reward system

Where CWQM has not yet been put into place, The Committee has the added responsibility of creating the system: establishing quality policy and creating the infrastructure required to run the system.

QUALITY POLICIES

"Policy" as used here is *a guide to managerial action.* Published policy statements are the result of a good deal of deliberation in high places, followed by approval at the highest level.

Many companies have gone through the process of thinking through and publishing corporate quality policies. While the details vary, the published policies have much in common.

Customer Relations

Without exception, all published quality policies declare the intention to meet the needs of customers. The wording often includes identification of specific needs to be met, e.g., the company's products should:

Provide customer satisfaction
Meet customer perceptions of good quality
Be useful, reliable, maintainable
Provide value

Competitiveness

Most published policies include language relative to competitiveness in quality. The various wordings state that the company's products shall:

Equal or exceed competitive quality
Be of the highest quality
Have quality excellence
Be best in class
Provide unmatched value
Attain world leadership

Quality Improvement

A third frequent area of published quality policy relates to quality improvement. The published statements declare the intention to:

Establish a formal process for quality improvement

Conduct continuing improvement (also called never-ending improvement, or regular improvement)

Internal Customers

Some quality policy statements are oriented to internal customers. For example:

Quality should extend to all phases of the business.

Products should be producible.

Processes should be established at high yields and process capability.

Emphasis should be on capable manufacturing processes, not on product inspection.

Use should be made of statistical techniques.

Quality is job number one.

Enforcement

Enforcement of quality policies is a comparatively new problem, because of the relative newness of written quality policies. In some companies provision is made for independent review of adherence to quality policies.

> In one large electronics company there is a quality policy requiring that new models of products must have a reliability at least equal to the reliability of the models they replace, and also at least equal to the reliability of the models of competitors. The product development departments are required to demonstrate that this policy has been met. In addition, the Quality Assurance Department has the responsibility to review the demonstration.

QUALITY GOALS

Our basic definition of a goal (page 137) was as follows:

> A goal is an aimed-at target, an achievement toward which effort is expended. A quality goal is an aimed-at quality target.

The general nature of quality goals is set out in Chapter Eight (pages 136–167). Those pages should be reviewed as a useful input to setting companywide quality goals.

Examples of Corporate Quality Goals

Here are some actual examples of corporate level quality goals as established by industrial companies:

Attain an on-time arrival rate of 90 percent within two years. This goal was established in the late 1970s by a major airline.

Attain world class quality by 1988. This goal was established in 1983 by General Motors Corporation. The term "world class" means quality parity or superiority in all market segments.

Reduce the cost of (poor) quality by 50 percent by 1987. This goal was established in July 1982 by 3M Corporation.

Make the Taurus/Sable models at a level of quality that is best in class. This goal was established by Ford Motor Company.

Cut in two the time to fill customer orders (a health service company)

Reduce billing errors by 90 percent (an electric power company.)

Deployment of Corporate Goals

Corporate goals such as those listed above do not lead to results unless they are deployed. "Deployment" as used here means subdividing the goals and allocating the subgoals to lower levels. Such deployment accomplishes some essential purposes:

The subdivision continues until it identifies specific deeds to be done.

The allocation continues until it assigns specific responsibility for doing the specific deeds.

> Those who are assigned to be responsible respond by determining the resources needed and communicating this to higher levels.

So deployment actually involves communication both up and down the hierarchy. Corporate quality goals may be proposed at the top. The lower levels then identify the deeds that, if done, will collectively meet the goals. The lower levels also submit the bill: To do these deeds, we need the following resources. The subsequent negotiations then arrive at an optimum, which balances the value of meeting the goals against the cost of doing so.

> For example, deployment of the "best in class" goals ended up with four hundred specific deeds to be done—four hundred key product features, each of which was to be designed and built so as to be best in class.

While deployment usually follows the hierarchical organization (corporation to division to functional department), there are many goals that are inherently multidivisional or multifunctional in nature. For such goals, deployment generally must go down to project teams.

> For example, a goal of cutting cost of poor quality in two (over five years) at the outset would be allocated to divisions. However, the chief components of cost of poor quality are invariably multifunctional in nature. Hence the response from the divisions would consist of a list of multifunctional projects, each of which would in due course be assigned to a project team.

Still other goals may inherently be of a project nature, e.g., on-time arrivals for the airline, time to fill customer orders, reduction of billing errors. In many such cases the deployment will involve breaking the project up into subprojects.

> For example, improving on-time airline arrivals may involve such subprojects as: a policy determination—whether to hold up departure of planes until the arrival of late connecting flights; an organization change—appointment of a gate manager for each flight; changes in technology, such as means for loading baggage more quickly.

Corporate goals often originate through nomination from below. Managers at lower levels may identify needs that should be met but require corporate participation because of such features as extensive resources required, multidivisional impact, major precedents that would be set. As experience is acquired in setting and deploying corporate quality goals, the organization becomes progressively more comfortable in upward communication as well.

Infrastructure for Goal Setting

The companywide quality committee (The Committee) is a logical channel for receiving nominations for potential corporate quality goals and for deploying corporate quality goals down to levels below. In some companies, use is made of the concept of sponsors or "champions" for specific goals or projects. One option is to use members of The Committee to carry out that concept. Where such is the practice, the company managers soon learn that their proposals can gain in priority if they can find some member of The Committee to champion the proposal.

Nonfactory Goals

Companies recently have been broadening their concept of quality to include quality of nonfactory activities. That trend has resulted in also broadening the list of corporate quality goals. Examples of nonfactory corporate quality goals are:

- Improvement of sales forecasting
- Establishing teamwork relations with suppliers
- Reduction of sales concellations
- Reduction of time required to recruit new employees
- Improving success in bidding for business
- Reduction in delinquent accounts
- Reduction of errors in office operations

Joint Goals with Clients

All companies strive to establish friendly relations with clients, including good communication and mutual understanding. However, in many cases the need is to go further and to extend the concept of CWQM so that the word "company" includes the client. In effect, the need is to establish joint goals, joint plans, joint controls. To do all that means creation of *joint teams.*

Such arrangements actually exist in some complex projects requiring close relationships among client, designer/architect, contractor, and others. However, in many industries the concept is only in its infancy.

The organization machinery needed is quite similar to that used for internal customers. The techniques and tools are also quite similar. What differs is the state of legal independence and (often) the history of arm's-length dealings.

To break with that tradition, it is useful to start with some pilot project that obviously calls for joint action. If successful, such a project can then become the bellwether to lead into more and more joint projects and finally into the concept of joint CWQM.

Joint Goals with Outside Suppliers

The logic of joint action is also applicable to relations with outside suppliers. However, in many industries the concept is effectively blocked by the long-standing adversary relationship between clients and their suppliers. That adversary relationship has been characterized by competitive bidding, high turnover in suppliers, thin profit margins, deficiencies in quality, mutual blame, mutual mistrust.

Starting in the mid-1980s, some massive changes began to set in: a trend to fewer suppliers and longer supply contracts. More fundamentally, the basic policy of adversary relationships with suppliers became suspect.

In the judgment of the author, the adversary relationship should be replaced by a teamwork relationship, which in due course will lead into the concept of joint CWQM. The approach will have to be through pilot projects that can demonstrate the feasibility of joint action. It will take a long time to dispel all that accumulated suspicion and mistrust.

Goal: The Overlap with Policies

Under our definitions, policies are guides to managerial action, whereas goals are specific results to be achieved. No matter how we may try to define the words with precision, the meanings overlap. For example, it is the published policy in some companies that "Product quality shall be at least equal to that of competitors." As worded, that statement meets the definition of a policy: It is a guide to managerial action.

However, in some industries, market quality has been a rapidly moving target. In such industries, meeting competition requires annual updating. One large electronics company requires each of its divisions to:

Evaluate annually its quality relative to its three principal competitors

Take steps annually to make its products competitive

Now the language comes close to that of goals. It sets out specific results to be achieved and a timetable for doing so. Yet many companies would consider those two mandates part of quality policy.

There is merit to adhering to the meaning of words as defined in the company's glossary. Departures from those meanings are an obstacle to communication. However, in the case of policies and goals the overlap is too great to permit definitions of an absolute nature.

PLANNING TO MEET GOALS

We have previously defined quality planning as a series of steps on the quality planning road map (Figure 1–3, page 15). Those steps were then elaborated in the subsequent chapters Two through Ten. In the present chapter the problem is one of applying that planning process so as to meet the corporate goals and the associated subgoals.

To a considerable extent, the deployment of goals is itself a part of the planning process. It starts with the needs of a class of customers (the corporate officers). It translates those needs into forms (subgoals, projects) that can be accomplished at lower levels. It identifies the resources required to meet the goals. It optimizes the relationship of the value of the goals to the effort required to reach them.

From its very nature, the bulk of quality planning must be done at levels below the corporate level. For example, the corporation may mandate to the divisions that they evaluate competitive quality annually. However, the methods for doing that must usually be left to the divisions. Some corporate staffs state it forthrightly: "You know that business better than we do."

We shall not, in this chapter, go into details of how to plan to meet specific goals. That has been done in the preceding chapters. However, two aspects of planning to meet companywide quality goals do require elaboration:

Providing resources

"Corporate interference"

Providing Resources

In the absence of some form of CWQM, a formidable obstacle to meeting quality goals has been lack of resources. That has been widely demonstrated in efforts to go into quality improvement projects. To bring such projects to completion requires various resources: time for project team members to guide the projects; support from technicians and specialists; training in several directions. With the exception of some aspects of training, those resources have not been provided adequately. In turn, lack of the resources has starved out many efforts to improve quality on a scale that might offer substantial benefits.

The CWQM approach, being tied into companywide business planning, offers a way to overcome that deficiency. Companywide business planning has long included a positive approach to bringing out into the open the resources required to meet the corporate business goals. Those who are apprehensive about "corporate interference" (see below) should note that CWQM provides a channel for dealing with the problem of securing resources.

QUALITY CONTROLS

Control is used here in its usual sense, a process for:

Evaluating actual performance

Comparing actual performance to goals

Taking action on the difference

Since the quality goals are now companywide, the controls should also be companywide.

Evaluating Actual Performance

An essential element of control is evaluation of actual performance. We looked closely at evaluation in Chapters Five and Six. Review of those chapters provides a useful input to those who are faced with evaluating performance as part of CWQM.

We saw in Chapters Five and Six that evaluation requires:

A unit of measure

A sensor that can evaluate performance in terms of the unit of measure

We saw also that there is a pyramid of units of measure that serves the needs of various levels of the organization. That pyramid (Figure 5–2) is reproduced here for convenient reference.

While CWQM demands measures at all levels of the pyramid, it is the measures at the higher levels that require the most development. Generally, the measures at the lower levels are already in place. For example, to provide a salable product has required product and process evaluation to assure conformance to specifications. In like manner, managing the affairs of the departments has required minimal information on such aspects as error rates, and process yields.

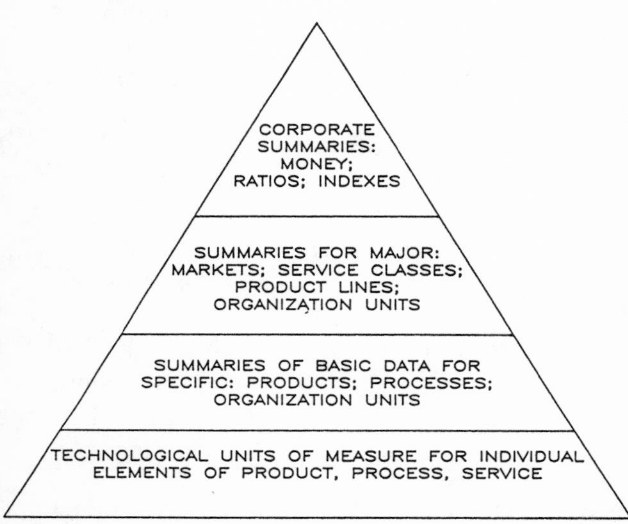

The pyramid of units of measure

Evaluation at Upper Levels

For every goal we need an associated means of evaluation, along with the basic data to serve as inputs for evaluation. Our day-to-day operations provide extensive basic data as a by-product. What is missing is processing of those data into summaries, ratios, and indexes, which then become part of the evaluation system used at upper levels. This system is an essential part of the infrastructure that supports CWQM. The Committee should see to it that this part of the infrastructure gets built. Such departments as Quality Assurance and Controller can be of considerable help in design and construction of those systems.

Figure 11–1 tabulates some typical measures derived from "by-product" data.

SUBJECT	UNIT OF MEASURE	DATA SOURCE
Office errors	Errors per volume of work	Office inspections, audits
Factory process yields	Percent yield	Inspection, test
Product conformance to specification	Percent defective; parts per million	Inspection, test, audit
Product dissatisfactions: complaints, returns, warranty charges, service calls	Number of dissatisfactions per 1000 units of product, and per $1,000 of sales; cost of dissatisfactions per $1,000 of sales	Accounting data; field service data
Cost of poor quality	Dollars; ratio to sales	Accounting data; estimates
Time to provide service	Days; weeks; etc.	Customer Order Department; Service Department

FIGURE 11–1 **Measures of performance derived from "by-product" data**

Other measures are not derived from by-product data. In such cases special provision must be made to create the data sources. Examples are:

FIELD PERFORMANCE. Performance features vary remarkably: uptime of computers, maintenance hours per 1,000 operating hours, fuel consumption. Some customers maintain good data on such features. Acquiring those data is then a matter of negotiation, persuasion, purchase, or whatever.

COMPETITIVE PERFORMANCE. The performance features are the same as in the above, and some customers (of the competitors) maintain good data on this performance. Securing the data is more complicated: Customers resist disclosing such data to competitors of their suppliers. If they do disclose such data, they resist identifying their supplier. Acquiring the data is again a matter of negotiation, persuasion, purchase, or whatever.

PRODUCT SALABILITY. To evaluate product salability requires data of a market research nature. Such data are not a by-product of day-to-day operations; they are the result of studies specifically undertaken to evaluate salability. Some of the concepts involved and methods used were discussed in Chapter Seven (pages 120–128) under the heading "Salability Analysis."

PERFORMANCE ON QUALITY IMPROVEMENT. This evaluation is important to companies that go into quality improvement on a project-by-project basis. Because of a lack of commonality among the projects, collective evaluation is limited to such features as:

Summary of *numbers of projects:* undertaken, in-process, completed

Summary of *financial results:* amounts gained, amounts invested, returns on investment

Summary of *persons involved* as project team members (Note that *a key measure* is the proportion of the company's management team actually involved in improvement projects. Ideally, this proportion should be over 90 percent. In the great majority of Western companies the actual proportion is less than 10 percent.)

In addition, individual projects are also reported on an individual basis. Typically, the project teams' final reports include a narrative summary supplemented by visual aids and supporting data. Such final reports serve as a news digest for upper managers as well as providing recognition for the team members.

PERFORMANCE OF MANAGERS RELATIVE TO QUALITY. Most companies already have in place a system for merit rating of operating managers. Those systems provide for evaluation of managerial performance relative to various criteria: cost, productivity, quality, schedule. Sometimes the criteria are weighted to permit computation of a composite evaluation. In such cases it is feasible to change the assigned weights. That has actually been done in some companies: The weight assigned to the quality criterion has been raised as a result of the quality crisis.

For some managerial functions, e.g., staff functions, the conventional criteria are less applicable. One solution has been to write out a sort of generalized evaluation. The interested managers convene and undertake to complete the following sentence: "This job has been properly done when the following state of affairs has been reached: . . . "

Through discussion, the managers identify those unique criteria which should be met in order to consider the job properly done. This approach has been widely used in "managing by objectives."

SPECIAL NEEDS. Some companies have certain goals and plans for which the conventional measures of performance seem not to apply; something special needs to be designed. In such cases the thing to do is design something special. There is always enough ingenuity in the house to create such a design.

The starting point is to secure nominations. The interested managers are assembled, and the questions are written on the blackboard:

How shall we evaluate performance against goal X?

What unit of measure shall we use?

What type of sensor shall we use?

The resulting brainstorming produces nominations, and the subsequent discussion establishes preferences. Means are then worked out to conduct evaluations in several ways, each responding to one of the leading preferences. Those evaluations are then published for a trial period. From experience gained during the trial, the most useful measures are revised and retained. The rest are discarded.

Human Sensing

In the higher levels of organization, evaluation of performance necessarily involves a good deal of sensing and judging by human beings. The goals and plans are too broad to permit evaluation solely by the numbers. Managerial performance is likewise too broad in scope to permit evaluation solely by the numbers.

The use of human sensing brings in all the failings of human sensors. We saw in Chapter Six (pages 89–96) that use of human sensing involves a formidable list of potential errors. Some of those types of errors are directly applicable to human evaluation of progress against managerial goals.

The remedies set out in Chapter Six are likewise applicable. In addition, there is the option of using *a jury of opinion*. Under this option, evaluations are secured from multiple managers. The resulting consensus avoids the extremes that can result from individual human error.

Quality Audits

We define "quality audit" as an independent review of quality performance.

The key word is "independent." To be independent, the reviewer should have no close responsibility for the adequacy of the performance. A review of performance by the immediate supervisor is not regarded as independent. A review by a supervisor several levels removed *is* regarded as independent. So is a review by an "auditor" from a totally different functional department.

Audits at Technological Levels

Most quality audits have been directed at technological subject matter, mainly:

Evaluation of adherence to quality methods and procedures. These are "procedural" audits.

Evaluation of product conformance to product specifications. These are "product" audits.

Those quality audits have served and continue to serve a useful purpose. They provide managers with information which, being independent, is free from the biases of departments reporting on their own performance. For critical matters (product safety, government regulations) the audits are an added form of assurance that performance is adequate.

At the technological levels the activities of auditing have much in common with the activities of inspection and test. A key difference is in the purpose served:

The customers for inspection and test information are mainly the operating forces.

The customers for audit information are mainly managers who are not closely involved with operations but who "have a need to know."

Audits at Managerial Levels

At managerial levels the concept of quality audit broadens to include business matters as well as technological matters. The questions to be answered by such audits relate directly to the ingredients of CWQM, such as:

Does our quality provide product satisfaction to our clients?

Is our quality competitive with the moving target of the market place?

Are we making progress in reducing the cost of poor quality?

Is the collaboration among our functional departments adequate to assure optimizing company performance?

Are we meeting our responsibilities to society?

Questions like that are not answered by the conventional technological audits. Moreover, the auditors who conduct such technological audits seldom have the managerial experience and training needed to conduct quality audits that are business-oriented. In consequence, companies that do carry out quality audits oriented to business matters do so by using upper managers as auditors. The widest use of this concept is in the major Japanese companies.

The President's Quality Audit

In those major Japanese companies it is usual to conduct quality audits that do include review of business-oriented quality matters. Those audits are typically conducted annually, either by the Companywide Quality Committee or by some other team of upper managers. Where the president personally participates in the audit, it is usually called the President's Quality Audit.

It is obvious that such audits, conducted by upper-level managers, can have powerful impacts throughout the company. The subject matter is so fundamental in nature that the audits reach into every major function. The personal participation of the upper managers simplifies the problem of communicating to the upper levels and increases the likelihood that action will be forthcoming. The very fact that the upper managers participate in person sends a message to the entire organization relative to the priority placed on quality and to the kind of leadership being provided by the upper managers—leadership, not cheerleading.

THE QUALITY REPORT PACKAGE

The adoption of CWQM and the associated controls inevitably leads to the evolution of a standardized package of reports on quality. That evolution is similar to what took place for centuries in the finance function. In that function the reports have become highly standardized. That standardization makes it possible for managers in diverse sectors of society (banking, government regulation, tax collection, suppliers) to learn a great deal about the financial condition of a company just by reading the financial reports.

Standardization on such a scale has not yet been attained in the quality function, but a similar evolution is taking place. Certain aspects of any company's quality performance are of interest to such "outsiders" as clients, insurance companies, government regulators, investors. This trend should be kept in mind during the design of the report package.

A popular approach for design of the report package is for someone (e.g., the quality manager) to "make the rounds," that is, to secure each key manager's views on what quality-oriented reports that manager requires in his role as a member of the management team. From those inputs the quality manager can prepare a report package responsive to the consensus of needs. The report is distributed, reviewed, and modified, after which it becomes the agreed report package for the next several years. All else is discontinued.

Format

Reports for upper managers should be designed to be read at a glance and to permit easy concentration on those exceptional matters which call for attention and action.

Reports in tabular form should present the three essentials: goals, actual performances, and variances. Reports in graphic form should show minimally the trends of performances against goals. The choice of format should be made only after learning what the preferences of the customers are.

Publication of managerial reports on quality is usually on a monthly or quarterly basis. The schedule is typically established to be in synchronism with the meetings schedule of The Committee or some other key reviewing body.

(For a more detailed discussion of the quality report package, see J. M. Juran, *Quality Control Handbook,* Third Edition [New York: McGraw Hill Book Company, 1974], "Executive Reports on Quality," pp. 21-20–21-32.)

"CORPORATE INTERFERENCE"

In some companies CWQM faces resistance from the autonomous divisions (or from the functional departments) on the grounds of "corporate interference." It is a fact that adoption of CWQM takes away some of the autonomy previously enjoyed by the divisions and departments. Such reduction in autonomy is never welcomed, even if the associated human relations are harmonious. Where they are less than harmonious, the problem can become severe.

Examples of Mandates

The "interference" can involve all aspects of CWQM: goal setting, quality planning, quality control, quality audits. For example, a large maker of automobiles established a corporate goal of equaling the quality of leading competitors within five years. Establishment of that goal then resulted in a number of impacts on the autonomous divisions in the corporation:

> Divisional quality goals were established. The logic could not be debated: To build "world class" automobiles required "world class" engines, transmissions, and so on from the divisions. However, the corporation had never before mandated the establishment of formal divisional quality goals. The divisions had been free to set their own quality goals or to operate without setting formal quality goals.
>
> The corporation also mandated preparation of formal quality plans by the division, and those plans were to be submitted to the corporation for review. That mandate was likewise unprecedented. Previously the divisions determined for themselves whether to prepare formal quality plans or not, and there was no review of such plans by the corporation.
>
> In addition, the corporation mandated that methods be evolved for evaluating progress against goals, and copies of the reports were to be sent to the corporation for review. That mandate was largely unprecedented.

The logic behind the corporate mandates is an important common bond among the divisions. Such common bonds take various forms. The divisions may:

Contribute inputs to a common final product

Sell their products under a common brand name or to a common clientele

Use common technology

Lacking a common bond, the concept of corporate quality goals and plans becomes more debatable. In the extreme case (a conglomerate) there is little logic to support corporate quality goals and plans. Instead, resort is had to "selling" the division general managers on the merits of including quality goals in the divisional business plans.

Mandated Methods

Probably the greatest risk of resentment involves mandating the methods used to meet goals. All suppliers, internal and external, instinctively urge their customers: "Tell us what product you want, but don't tell us how to produce it." Nevertheless, there is an abundance of specifications, which mandate methods and procedures. They abound not only in military and other government purchases, but also in specifications of industrial companies.

A recent example with widespread impact has been the mandate that "statistical process control" (SPC) be used during manufacturing operations. Actually, the concept of SPC has a great deal of merit. However, the mandates have been too broad, forcing suppliers into many uneconomic applications and breeding a great deal of resentment among internal as well as external suppliers.

Mandated Training

Still another form of corporate mandate involves training programs in such matters as basic statistical tools, or quality "awareness." The expectations are that the trainees will thereby become knowledgeable and stimulated to a degree that will cause them to solve the company's quality problems. Generally, all such programs have some degree of intrinsic merit. However, the expectations are hopelessly naïve. The training does not involve setting quality goals, planning how to meet goals, and the like, and hence cannot lead to results. Then, when pressure is applied to secure the hoped-for results, resentment and divisiveness set in.

Cultural Resistance

Some of the objections to "corporate interference" are in the nature of "cultural resistance." The objections are not based on the merits of the proposals; they are based on the social consequences, that is, the effect of the proposals on the cultural pattern of the impacted divisions or departments. Each of those organizations has built up over the years a fabric of attitudes, beliefs, habits, practices, status symbols, rituals, taboos. That cultural pattern serves useful purposes and is therefore protected by the organization. Any proposed changes are a potential threat to the stability of the pattern and thereby are a potential threat to the well-being of the members of the culture.

In the present book we shall limit our treatment of this subject to the "rules of the road" for introducing change into a going culture. The rules have been evolved by behavioral scientists, notably cultural anthropologists.[1]

1. *Provide participation:* The members of the culture should participate both in the planning and in the execution of the change.
2. *Provide enough time* for the members of the culture to (a) evaluate the merits of the change in relation to the threat to their habits, status, beliefs, and (b) find an accommodation with the advocates of the change. Providing enough time may take various forms:
   a. *No surprises:* A substantial benefit of the cultural pattern is its predictability. A surprise is a shock to this predictability and a disturber of the peace.
   b. *Start small:* Conducting a small-scale tryout before going "all out" reduces the risks—for the advocates as well as for the members of the culture.
   c. *Choose the right year:* There are right and wrong years—even decades—for timing a change.
3. *Keep the proposals free of excess baggage:* Avoid cluttering the proposals with extraneous matters not closely concerned with getting the results. The risk is that the debates will get off the main subject and into side issues.
4. *Work with the recognized leadership of the culture:* The culture is best understood by its members. They have their own leadership, and this is often informal. Convincing the leadership is a significant step in getting the change accepted.
5. *Treat the people with dignity:* The classic example is that of the relay assemblers in the "Hawthorne experiments." Their productivity kept rising, under good illumination or poor, because in the "laboratory" they were being treated with dignity.
6. *Reverse the positions.* Ask the question: What position would I take if I were a member of the culture? It is even useful to

[1]For a popularized elaboration, see J. M. Juran, *Managerial Breakthrough* (New York: McGraw-Hill, 1964), Chapter 9, "Resistance to Change—Cultural Patterns."

go into role playing to stimulate understanding of the other person's position.

7. *Look at the alternatives.* There are many ways of dealing directly with resistance to change:
   a. Try a program of persuasion.
   b. Offer a *quid pro quo:* something for something.
   c. Change the proposals to meet specific objections.
   d. Change the social climate in ways that will make the change more acceptable.
   e. Forget it. There are cases in which the correct alternative is to drop the proposal. We simply do not know how to plan so as to be 100 percent successful.

QUALITY IMPROVEMENT

CWQM covers the entire quality Trilogy of processes, including quality improvement (see Figure 1–2, page 12). However, the title of the present book is *Planning for Quality;* the book does not get into the details of quality improvement.

For a full account of how to establish and maintain quality improvement, see *Juran on Quality Improvement,* a series of sixteen color video cassettes and associated literature published by Juran Institute, Inc., 88 Danbury Road, Wilton, CT 06897-4409.

SUMMARY

Companywide quality management (CWQM) is a systematic approach for setting and meeting quality goals throughout the company.

CWQM parallels closely the approach to setting and meeting financial goals.

Companies that have adopted CWQM are outperforming companies that retain the methods of the past.

CWQM requires personal leadership by upper management. It cannot be achieved by exhortation.

The first step toward CWQM is creation of a high-level companywide quality committee to establish and coordinate the approach.

A quality policy is a guide to managerial action.

Published quality policies usually relate to customer relations, quality competitiveness in the marketplace, quality improvements, and relations with internal customers.

A quality goal is an aimed-at quality target.

Corporate quality goals can be effective only if they are deployed so that they identify specific deeds to be done and assign specific responsibility for doing those deeds.

Quality goals should extend to all functions, not just factory functions.

Quality goals should also extend to relations with clients and suppliers.

Planning for meeting goals is an inherent part of CWQM and should provide the essential resources.

CWQM includes establishment of controls for evaluating performance against quality goals.

CWQM also includes establishment of business-oriented quality audits to be conducted by upper managers.

A standardized package of reports should be evolved to serve, for the quality function, the purpose served by financial reports in the field of finance.

Institution of CWQM results in reducing some of the traditional autonomy of the divisions and departments. That reduction may be viewed by them as corporate interference.

Corporate mandates encounter cultural resistance, that is, resistance to the social consequences of the mandates.

To deal with cultural resistance, make use of the "rules of the road" evolved by the behavioral scientists.

] 12 [

Departmental Quality Planning

THE MISSION OF THIS CHAPTER

The mission of this chapter is to provide managers and supervisors with a structured approach to planning/replanning the quality of their departmental work.

For such a structured approach to be carried out by many departments in the same company requires agreement on basic concepts. It also requires standardization of the meanings of key words. The next section sets forth the basic concepts and defines the key words. Most elements in the list have already been discussed in prior chapters. Those elements are repeated here (sometimes in revised form) for convenience and to make this chapter self-sufficient.

BASIC CONCEPTS AND DEFINITIONS OF TERMS

Goal

A goal is an aimed-at target—an achievement toward which effort is expended.

Process

All company organization units are assigned responsibilities, which they carry out by performing appropriate activities (tasks, steps, operations, work cycles). We shall use the word "process" as a generic term to describe any such activity. In Chapter Nine we defined a process as "a systematic series of actions directed toward the achievement of a goal."

Processor

Whoever conducts a process is a processor.

Processor Team

Many processes are conducted by groups of individuals. We shall use the term "processor team" to represent any such grouping.

A processor team is any organization unit (of one or more persons) that carries out a prescribed process. Such organization units are found throughout the entire company hierarchy. The company is a processor team. So is each division, department, subdepartment, group. *So is each individual.* (We sometimes call an individual a one-man band.)

Note that processor teams can differ remarkably in their functional responsibility, e.g., marketing, finance, product development, manufacture, customer service, human relations. They can also differ remarkably in their level in the company hierarchy, from the office or factory worker to the chief executive officer.

Product: Output

Whatever is produced by the process—the output—is a product. Product includes goods and services.

Customer

Anyone who is impacted by a process or product is a customer. Customers include persons internal to the company as well as external.

Inputs

Inputs are all the means employed by the process to produce the product. Inputs include information, materials, components, human effort.

Supplier

Whoever provides inputs is a supplier.

Feedback

A feedback is an input from a customer relative to the impact of the product.

THE TRIPLE ROLE

Every processor team conducts a process and produces a product. To do so the processor team carries out three quality-related roles, which are in the list above:

A processor The processor team carries out various managerial and technological activities in order to produce its products.

A supplier The processor team supplies its products to its customers.

A customer The processor team acquires various kinds of inputs, which are used in carrying out the process. The processor team is a customer of those who provide the inputs.

THE TRIPROL™ DIAGRAM

We can depict the triple role by means of an input–output diagram, which we will call a TRIPROL diagram (Figure 12–1).

The TRIPROL diagram is delightfully simple. However, the realities of quality planning are quite complex:

There are usually multiple internal and external customers.

There are usually multiple steps in the process; each step is a sort of subprocess.

There are usually multiple inputs, supplied by multiple suppliers.

The resulting combinations of customers, process steps, and inputs are unique to each process. That uniqueness lends support to the contention of some department heads that "my process is different." However, the methods and tools used for quality planning are quite similar, no matter what the makeup of the process is.

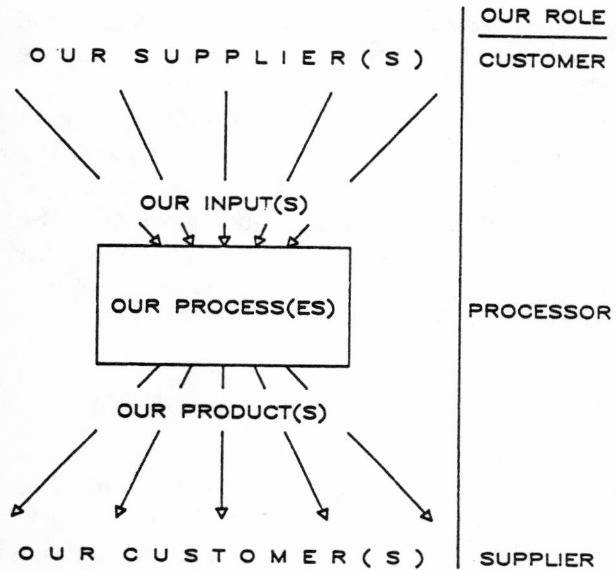

FIGURE 12–1 The TRIPROL diagram

APPLYING THE TRIPLE ROLE CONCEPT

The triple role concept provides any processor team with a logical basis for analyzing its approach to quality planning. That analysis must provide answers to such key questions as:

Who are our customers?

What are their quality needs?

Do our products meet customers' needs?

Are our products competitive?

Is our process capable of meeting customer needs?

Are our process controls adequate?

Do our products provide value commensurate with cost?

Do our products serve a useful purpose?

Where are the opportunities for improvement?

To provide answers to such questions requires an organized method of analysis. The need for such organization arises from the complexities of those numbers of customers, process steps, and suppliers. However, the tools of analysis will be quite familiar; we have used them over and over again in the prior chapters.

To provide answers to those questions also requires a lot of work, especially collecting and analyzing a lot of information. The work is not a by-product of day-to-day operations. In most companies there is no clear responsibility for getting such work done. So one of our inquiries will be: How shall we assign responsibility for doing the analysis? We shall have a look at that later, under the heading "The Triple Role Analysis—Analysis by Whom?"

THE LIST OF ACTIVITIES: FLOW DIAGRAM

A good starting point for applying the triple role concept is to list the activities currently being conducted in the department. The best tool for the purpose is the flow diagram. (See in this connection Figure 2–2, page 19; Figure 2–3, page 21; and associated discussion.) It is a good idea to number each activity in order to simplify future reference and discussion.

The flow diagram, of course, lists the activities that collectively make up the process. It also shows the sequence in which they are carried out. In addition it shows the various "loops": the cases in which the process backtracks because of deficiencies. An example of such a loop appears in Figure 2–4, page 22.

The flow diagram not only lists the activities; it also identifies some:

Products that result from the activities

Customers who are impacted by the products

Suppliers who provide inputs

The identifications are not complete, but they will grow as the analysis proceeds.

VITAL FEW ACTIVITIES: PARETO ANALYSIS

The flow diagram usually involves numerous activities (operations, tasks, steps). The more numerous the activities, the bigger the job of analyzing what is going on. We can make a sizable reduction in the work involved with only a minor reduction in the value of the analysis. The method is to apply the Pareto principle of concentrating on the "vital few."

To illustrate, a certain flow diagram includes forty-one specific activities. Those activities are not equally important. Several of them are more important than all the collective rest. This follows the familiar Pareto principle as discussed in Chapter Two. (See Figure 2–5, page 27.)

How does the planning team decide which are the vital few activities? One way is by discovering what the consensus among team members is. A consensus can be reached with the use of index cards. Each activity is written on an index card. The pack of cards (forty-one in our example) is then given to each planning team member to make his selection of the vital few, e.g., ten of the forty-one. He then ranks those ten in his order of importance. The resulting rankings are then entered on a spreadsheet to compile the totals. The totals are an indication of the team consensus.

After study and discussion of the indicated consensus, the planning team decides which activities to choose for analysis. The remaining activities (the useful many) are placed on hold. (In due course the team may decide to analyze some of the useful many as well.)

The planning team next proceeds to analyze each of the selected vital few activities, using the triple role analysis. The team's work is simplified and made more orderly by creating a spreadsheet for each activity. Figure 12–2 is an example of such a spreadsheet. The spreadsheet is headed with the name of the activity.

THE LIST OF PRODUCTS

As we have seen, all activities produce products, whether goods or services. Those products become inputs to the recipient, a customer. In addition those same products may impact other customers, internal and external.

The flow diagram provides ready identification of some of the products that emerge from the activities under study. The quality planning team will identify other products as it discusses details of the activities.

As the list of products evolves, it is entered in the spreadsheet (Figure 12–2).

CUSTOMERS	CUSTOMERS' NEEDS	VITAL FEW CUSTOMERS	VITAL FEW NEEDS	PRODUCTS	DO PRODUCTS MEET NEEDS?	ARE PRODUCTS COMPETITIVE?	DO PRODUCTS PROVIDE VALUE VERSUS COST?	DO PRODUCTS SERVE USEFUL PURPOSES?

FIGURE 12–2 **Spreadsheet for Departmental Quality Planning**

WHO ARE OUR CUSTOMERS?

Chapter Two of this text deals with the question of customers as applied to *inter*departmental quality planning. In the present chapter our mission is departmental quality planning, which is quite a simplification. We shall be dealing with fewer customers, fewer needs, and fewer complications generally. However, a quality planning team that sets out to do departmental quality planning/replanning is well advised to refer back to Chapter Two (and other chapters) for reference.

Every member of a quality planning team has customers, whether internal or external (or both). In addition, some team members are customers of other team members. Those direct supplier–customer relationships provide the team with ready identification of some customers. The team identifies other customers with the aid of the flow diagram it has worked up.

Customers: A Cast of Characters

In some cases the customer actually consists of an entire cast of characters.

> The pharmaceutical company that sells to hospitals finds that within the hospital there are multiple customers, including:
>
> The purchasing department
>
> The quality control laboratory
>
> The physicians who prescribe medication
>
> The pharmacists who fill prescriptions
>
> The nurses who administer medication
>
> The patients

In such cases the quality planning team should identify the entire cast of characters and their respective roles. That identification will prove especially useful during determination of the needs of customers (next section).

Vital Few Customers

Some quality planning teams may find that "Who are the customers?" is a long list. In that event, the team may choose to apply the Pareto principle (as it did in the case of activities). At the level of departmental quality planning, the vital few customers consist mainly of:

Supervisors of the activities under study

Supervisors of departments that are direct customers of those activities

Clients who are significantly impacted by those activities

Key employees within those activities, e.g., those who do: setup of processes, maintenance, troubleshooting, auditing

Ideally those vital few customers will be contacted individually to secure essential information and feedback. (Some of the methods are discussed in Chapter Three.)

Useful Many Customers

The activities under study may also impact various categories of useful many customers, e.g., consumers, the workforce, the public. The team may conclude that certain of those categories should also be contacted as part of the quality planning. Such contacts will be conducted by sampling or by other means, as discussed in Chapter Three.

In due course the team reaches agreement on who the vital few customers are and on which are the selected categories of useful many customers. Those are listed on the spreadsheet (Figure 12–2) in preparation for the next step in the analysis.

WHAT ARE THE NEEDS OF OUR CUSTOMERS?

The general approach to determining needs of customers is set out in Chapter Three. The quality planning team is well advised to review that chapter as part of the preparation for determining what the needs are.

Sources of Information

For any activity undergoing quality planning, the most realistic information about customer needs comes from customers, not from suppliers or processors. If no such customer is on the quality planning team, it can be risky to assume that the suppliers and processors have complete information. Their views should be respected—they usually have had long experience with the activity and have received extensive feedback from customers. Nevertheless, their views should be questioned, diplomatically, e.g., "Do you mind explaining to us the basis for your statement?" (Some people resent the blunt question, "How do you know that?")

Why must we ask people of long experience to explain the basis for their statements? Because we have learned, also from long experience, that too many of those statements are not fully valid. With the passing of time there have been changes: shifts in the marketplace, entry of new technology, lapses in memory, evolution of biases. By ensuring that assertions are backed up by facts, the planning team avoids perpetuating outdated beliefs and practices.

Users—The Key Source of Information

While "customers" may be a cast of characters, for quality planning purposes the key sources of information are the "users." By users we mean those customers who carry out positive actions with respect to the product, e.g., further processing or ultimate use. In the hospital case the physicians, nurses, and patients would obviously be users.

If the quality planning team lacks direct access to users, the question should be raised: How can we secure information about needs direct from the users? Discussion of that question will usually evolve a satisfactory answer. Failing this, the team may be forced to accept indirect information, with all the associated doubt as to validity.

As information is acquired on the needs of customers, it is entered in the "Customers' Needs" column of the spreadsheet, Figure 12–2. That sets the stage for analyzing to see if the products of the activity are properly responsive to customers' needs.

DO OUR PRODUCTS MEET CUSTOMERS' NEEDS?

Assuring that customer needs are in fact being met is one of two main purposes of departmental quality planning/replanning. (The other is to act on the opportunities for improvement.)

In addressing the question, it is important to set up valid criteria for judging whether customer needs are met. The principal criteria are:

The product gives product *satisfaction.* Its performance responds to customers' needs and is competitive with other available products.

The product gives customers minimal *dissatisfaction.* It avoids creating extraneous problems for customers, e.g., complaints, claims, returns.

Many processors judge whether customer needs are being met by the amount of product dissatisfaction. It is a treacherous basis. It evaluates dissatisfaction but cannot evaluate product satisfaction (why clients buy the product) since product satisfaction and product dissatisfaction are *not opposites*—they are two very different concepts. Being different, they require different bases for evaluation.

Ideally, the planning team is able to establish direct communication with customers to secure their views on adequacy of the product. If that is not feasible, resort must be had to indirect information and to study of customers' behavior. The latter tells us what customers do but not why they do it.

Note that contact with customers can nevertheless result in an incomplete picture. What is missing is contact with noncustomers. Why are they noncustomers? One reason may be that in their experience the product did not meet their needs.

As the information evolves, the planning team enters it in the spreadsheet (Figure 12–2). The team may choose to classify the degrees to which the products meet customer needs, e.g., customer needs are:

Fully met

Partially met

Not met

Product serves no known needs

Such entries may be made by code number in order to keep the physical size of the spreadsheet to a minimum.

IS OUR PROCESS CAPABLE OF MEETING CUSTOMER NEEDS?

The question of capability is especially pertinent in those cases where our products do not fully meet customer needs. In such cases the list of theories of causes always includes the following:

The process is inherently not capable of meeting customer needs.

The process is inherently capable of meeting customer needs, but something is getting in the way.

The concept of process capability was discussed in some detail in Chapter Nine, including methods of evaluation (see pages 173–193). The project team should review that material as part of the input for analyzing the capability of their process.

It may be discovered that process capability is adequate but process performance is not. In that event the team is faced with discovering what stands in the way. To make that discovery usually requires diagnosis: theorizing as to causes and then testing the theories through data collection and analysis.[1] In choosing theories for test, it is well to give priority to the dominant variable as discussed under "Concept of Dominance" (pages 208–209).

ARE OUR PROCESS CONTROLS ADEQUATE?

Process control was defined as "the activity of keeping the operating process in a state that continues to be able to meet process goals." Process control via the feedback loop was discussed in some detail (see page 212). A review of that discussion makes clear that the work of process control includes a good deal of adherence to repetitive procedure as well as adherence to schedules for maintenance of facilities.

Historically, adherence to planned process controls has been a weak area in managing for quality. In the decades when quality did not have top priority, it was tempting to solve problems in on-time delivery, productivity, and other areas by making short cuts in process controls. The recent trend to assign top priority to quality has tended to strengthen adherence to process controls.

[1]For a reference on the methods of diagnosis, see footnote 3 on page 289.

The triple role analysis should include a rigorous audit to determine the extent of adherence to the established quality controls. In addition, the audit should review the *adequacy* of the established controls in the light of operating experience. The review should include a reexamination of:

Adequacy of the system of self-control

Completeness of the list of control subjects

Assignment of responsibility for the various control actions and decisions

Adequacy of facilities maintenance procedures and schedules

ARE OUR PRODUCTS COMPETITIVE?

Competitiveness in quality is an obvious requirement for continuing salability in the marketplace. If the quality planning team is faced with such a requirement, it should first study "Competitive Analysis" (pages 119–120) and the related "Salability Analysis" (pages 120–128).

Competitive analysis is also applicable to products that are "sold" to internal customers. Industry maintains huge numbers of internal monopolies. Office departments prepare payrolls and financial statements to serve other departments. Factory departments make components to be assembled by other departments. Still other internal monopolies include such services as building and equipment maintenance, transportation, cafeteria.

Those monopolies are self-imposed. For the great majority of the monopolies it is feasible to find outside sources of supply. If there is enough at stake, then it is worthwhile, during a replanning project, to examine some available external alternatives from the standpoint of competitiveness in quality, price, promptness, and other attributes. Some companies do in fact make such examinations periodically. The result can be enlightening. If external sources of supply offer superior service, the customer has some new options:

1. Contract out some or much of the service
2. Improve the internal service provided by the monopoly (This option is made easier if it has been shown that outside sources offer superior service.)

DO OUR PRODUCTS PROVIDE VALUE COMMENSURATE WITH COST?

To answer the value/cost question, the quality planning team must:

1. Estimate the value of the product quality
2. Estimate the cost of providing that quality
3. Judge whether 1 and 2 are compatible

The Value of Quality

For products sold in a competitive market, comparative price data can be acquired. The usual assumption is that value is whatever external customers are willing to pay.

For products used internally, such market prices are not readily available. Instead, resort must be had to value analysis methods such as were discussed in Chapter Seven.

Value analysis estimates are usually subject to wide differences of opinion. However, some findings of value analysis leave little room for doubt. Value analysis can identify with confidence instances in which a product or process serves no useful purpose at all.

> A common example is statistical or accounting reports that are prepared and sent out in the belief that the information will be helpful to the recipients. However, the reports are in fact filed away without being read.

Value analysis can also identify instances in which the value of the product is obviously out of line with the cost.

> For example, a study of the procedure used to pay suppliers' invoices showed that the average cost to carry out one cycle of the procedure (to pay one invoice) came to about $8.50. Yet the same procedure was being used to pay many invoices for which the amount owed was less than $10.00.

Cost of Providing Quality

The cost of providing quality is the total of two very different costs:

1. The cost of the process that produces the products: the inputs, the facilities, the human effort

2. The cost of poor quality, including the chronic wastes and the sporadic firefighting

In comparing cost to value it is necessary to include both 1 and 2 in the cost figures. However, all too often, 2 is ignored. To illustrate:

In evaluating competitive bids, great stress is placed on the purchase price. However, little stress is placed on the added costs due to poor quality of the products purchased.

In evaluating productivity it is usual to base the evaluation on the total number of units of product produced instead of the total number of units of *good product.*

Good quality planning demands a thorough look at the costs of poor quality. Those costs, especially the chronic wastes, are always among the major opportunities for quality improvement and cost reduction.

DO OUR PRODUCTS SERVE A USEFUL PURPOSE?

It is quite common for a quality planning project to discover that some product or process does not serve a useful purpose. We saw an example above: the case of the reports that were filed but not read. More usually, such cases involve products that once did serve a useful purpose. Then some change came along and eliminated the need for the product. However, the planners of the change failed to follow through.

For example, a process delivers products of such poor quality that a 100 percent check is established to prevent the errors from reaching customers. Subsequently the process is replanned so well that it delivers error-free products. Now the 100 percent check no longer serves a useful purpose. However, the planners failed to grasp this opportunity to eliminate an out-of-date process.

Discovery of out-of-date products can be made in several ways:

Ask the customers what use they make of the product.

Identify recent changes in the process, and look to see whether those changes eliminated the need for some products.

Identify products for which suppliers receive no feedback from customers.

The case of "no feedback from customers" requires some elaboration. Anyone who prepares documents (data sheets, reports) regularly gets feedback from customers: questions about unclear information, requests for added information, correction of errors. If no such feedback is received, the reason may well be that no use is made of the product.

THOSE WASTEFUL "LOOPS" IN THE FLOW DIAGRAM

One of the most obvious targets for replanning is the "loops" in the flow diagram. An example we encountered was Figure 2–4. It is reproduced here for convenience.

In any such case the original work is done over again because of deficiencies in the process. If the process can be revised to eliminate those deficiencies, it becomes possible to reduce or eliminate the amount of work done in the loop.

An interesting case example of analysis of loops is related by Fuller.[2] It involved assembly of printed circuit boards from

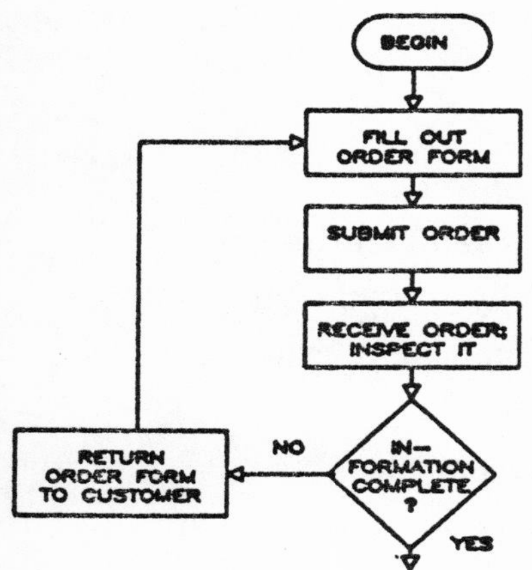

A loop—an opportunity for improvement

[2]F. Timothy Fuller, "Eliminating Complexity from Work: Improving Productivity by Enhancing Quality," *National Productivity Review,* Autumn 1985, pp. 327–44.

kits of components. The problem: Most kits were missing one or more components.

Excess Facilities

Related to the waste in loops is a whole class of cases in which excess facilities are provided because of poor quality.

For example, an office has two copying machines despite the fact that one machine has enough capacity to handle the entire demand for copies. The reason is that the copier is so failure-prone that a second machine is required to provide continuity of copier service.

In general terms, excess capacity is provided as a result of failure-proneness. The case examples abound, whether in offices, factories, warehouses, or whatever. If the failure-proneness can be driven down far enough, the operations become more efficient, and the excess capacity is no longer needed.

THE LONG LIST OF OPPORTUNITIES FOR IMPROVEMENT

Up to now, we have seen numerous opportunities for improvement that the quality planning team may have encountered:

The list of customers is not fully known.

The list of products is not fully identified.

The vital few customers have not been identified.

The needs of customers are not fully known or understood.

Customers' needs are judged by inadequate criteria.

Customers' needs are not being met.

Reactions of noncustomers are not known.

Product competitiveness is not known.

Products are not competitive.

The relationship of product value compared to cost is not known.

The relationship of product value to cost is inadequate.

Products do not serve a useful purpose.

Much work must be done over again because of deficiencies in the processes.

Every item on that long list is a candidate for a quality improvement project, which has come to light as a result of the quality planning activity.

MAKING IMPROVEMENTS

Making improvements is one of the processes of the quality trilogy (see Figure 1–2, page 12). Every chronic quality problem shows up as a symptom—the outward evidence of some deficiency. The improvement process analyzes the symptoms, theorizes as to causes, and tests the theories to find the real cause. Having found the real cause, the improvement process provides a remedy to eliminate the cause.[3]

Making improvements is also part of the replanning process.

Departmental Problems

As a quality planning team undertakes to discover causes and provide remedies, it will find that some problems are inherently departmental. In other words, the departmental quality planning team can by itself discover causes and provide remedies.

For example, a team finds that some key customer's needs are not being met. The list of theories of causes includes "process not capable." A process capability analysis demonstrates the validity of that theory. The team then is able to provide a remedy by reducing the variability of the process. All is contained within one department, but it has taken a lot of work all the same.

Interdepartmental Problems

The team may encounter other problems whose scope extends beyond departmental boundaries.

The symptoms may be such that some essential part of the diagnosis must come from outside the department, e.g., market re-

[3]For elaboration of the improvement process, see J. M. Juran, *Managerial Breakthrough,* chapters 2–11. (New York: McGraw-Hill, 1964). See also *Juran on Quality Improvement,* (a video cassette series), Juran Institute, Inc., 88 Danbury Road, Wilton, Connecticut 06897.

search, cost analysis, laboratory tests. Alternatively, the cause may be such that the remedy must come from other departments, e.g., change in product design, revision in overall procedures, new external supplier, revision in process facilities.

For such interdepartmental cases a departmental quality planning team must find ways to secure participation and/or aid from other departments. In many cases, simple discussion among the respective departmental supervisors may be adequate to work out a solution. In complex cases, with a good deal at stake, it may be necessary to create a multidepartmental team to complete the diagnosis and provide a remedy.

THE TRIPLE ROLE ANALYSIS: ANALYSIS BY WHOM?

Numerous options for getting analysis done have been tried out. Some of the results have been published. Other results, though not published, are known. Based on those experiences, we can list the principal options along with the associated benefits and limitations.

Full-Time Analysts

In one approach a full-time analyst (systems analyst, quality engineer, procedures analyst, industrial engineer) is assigned to conduct the analysis. He "makes the rounds." He interviews the cognizant people: managers, supervisors, the workforce. He observes the activities. Based on those inputs he prepares the flow diagrams, spreadsheets, and so on. He then prepares a report and makes recommendations for revisions.

This approach largely solves the problem of providing the time to do the analysis. The operating forces already have full-time responsibilities: produce quality products, meet schedules, meet the budget. To be sure, the operating managers and supervisors do have the time to attend a few meetings and to review a few reports. However, a project to review departmental planning for quality goes well beyond a few meetings.

Use of the full-time analyst delegates the bulk of the work to someone whose full-time job is analysis. It is the analyst who takes on the time-consuming tasks of making the rounds, working up the flow diagrams and spreadsheets, preparing reports and recommendations.

While use of the analyst helps to solve the problem of time for analysis, this approach has deficiencies that some companies are no longer willing to accept:

The approach retains much of the concept of separating planning from execution. That concept is inherently divisive, especially at departmental levels.

The analysts exhibit the biases inherent in their culture. Their biases then enter their recommendations.

Use of full-time analysts tends to confer "ownership" of the process on the analyst. Companies are increasingly moving in the direction of shifting the sense of ownership to the line personnel.

Line managers whose jobs are impacted by recommendations prepared by someone else tend to feel that there has been a lack of full participation. The feeling reduces their willingness to support the resulting recommendations.

To give line managers greater responsibility for quality planning requires that the line managers acquire proficiency in use of the tools of analysis. This acquisition is delayed if full-time analysts continue to do the analysis.

Managerial Teams

The departmental manager, together with his subordinate managers, takes full responsibility for the analysis and the resulting recommendations. Some of the detailed work may be delegated to analysts or technicians, but the managers retain the direction, which means they make such determinations as:

The questions to which we need answers

The priorities

The costs we are trying to optimize

Generally, the use of the managerial teams has met such objectives as:

Arming the line managers with the tools and skills of quality planning

Increasing the line managers' sense of participation in quality planning

Shifting the function of quality planning to the line managers

Minimizing the effect of biases of full-time planners

Increasing the willingness of line managers to support the recommendations of the analysis

Increasing the line managers' sense of "ownership" of the process

The big disadvantage of using managerial teams is the time it takes. Multiple people (teams) must do what could be done by one trained individual. In addition, the added work is superimposed on the time of people who already are carrying a full-time load.

We do know that as the line managers acquire experience in use of the quality planning tools they become more proficient. But to reach a state of proficiency does require finding the time to participate in the work of the teams. The record on this is mixed.

Workforce Participation

The urge to increase worker participation in quality planning is part of a broader movement to involve workers in decisions that impact their jobs. The premises are these:

All workers have contributions to make, thanks to their intimate knowledge of job conditions.

Those contributions can include ideas for improvement as well as identification of problems.

Many workers want to contribute.

Such contributions increase worker morale, provide a sense of ownership, and improve management–worker relations generally.

To date, organized methods to provide for worker participation have consisted largely of:

Provision for *individual* contribution in such forms as suggestion systems

Provision for group contribution by *teams of workers* in such forms as QC circles

In the case of planning for quality, worker participation appears to require yet another form: teams consisting of a mixture of exempt and nonexempt people. The reason is the mixture of inputs needed. The workers have much expertise on the details of "their" operations, but the impacts of those operations usually extend well beyond departmental boundaries.

As yet we have no clear picture of the effectiveness of such teams. The experiments have been few, and the results have been inconsistent. The jury is still out.

In this chapter we have generally assumed the assignment of work to be as follows:

1. The analysis will be carried out by a team of managers and supervisors, making use of the time of analysts as needed. We have referred to the team as a *quality planning team.*
2. The analysis will include securing inputs from the workforce as needed. Whether that is done by including workers in the planning team structure or by other means is a matter to be decided locally.

THE END RESULT OF DEPARTMENTAL QUALITY PLANNING

The end result consists of an information "package" containing:

The conclusions reached by the analysis

Proposals (recommendations) relative to products, processes, inputs

Supporting information: flow diagram, spreadsheets, data

The proposals will generally be presented in the standard formats used in the company for describing products, processes, procedures.

Some of the proposals will concern matters over which the department itself has full jurisdiction. In such cases the departmental manager can adopt them forthwith. Other proposals require concurrence by or action from other departments. Such proposals then require follow-up until (1) the recommended action is taken or (2) there is a decision by cognizant authorities not to adopt the proposals.

DEPARTMENTAL QUALITY PLANNING: CAN WE STANDARDIZE?

Departmental quality planning can make use of some extensive commonalities:

The triple role concept (supplier, processor, customer) applies to every processor team.

The flow diagram is a universal aid in determining who the customers are.

The spreadsheet is a universal aid to orderly arrangement of findings.

Application of those and other commonalities to the team project soon runs into uniqueness: Nothing else has the particular combination of customers, needs, products, processes, suppliers. However, the departmental quality planning team has the know-how needed to deal with that uniqueness. With respect to that "particular combination," no one else has so much depth of knowledge or so much experience as the quality planning team.

SUMMARY

The quality planning road map is applicable to departmental quality planning.

Each processor team carries out the triple role of processor, supplier, and customer.

The triple role analysis is the basis for departmental quality planning.

The flow diagram and spreadsheet are essential tools for triple role analysis.

The analysis should identify and concentrate on the vital few activities.

Customers can constitute an entire cast of characters.

Departmental quality planning should identify and concentrate on the vital few customers and selected categories of useful many customers.

Customers, especially users, are the most important source of information on customer needs.

Inputs on customer needs should be secured from nonclients as well as from clients.

Assuring that customer needs are met is a primary purpose of departmental quality planning.

Customer needs include both product satisfaction and freedom from product dissatisfaction.

Product satisfaction and product dissatisfaction are not opposites.

If customer needs are not being met, it is essential to determine whether the process is inherently capable of meeting those needs.

Departmental quality planning should always reexamine the adequacy and the state of adherence to quality controls.

Departmental quality planning should ensure that, for internal and external customers alike, the products:

Are competitive with available alternatives

Deliver value commensurate with cost

Serve a useful purpose

All "loops" in the flow diagram should become nominations for replanning.

Departmental quality planning will disclose numerous opportunities for quality improvement, some of which can be acted on within the department.

Improvement projects of an interdepartmental nature require use of interdepartmental teams.

Departmental quality planning by staff analysts solves the problem of providing the time needed for the analysis, but has deficiencies arising from lack of full participation by line managers.

Departmental quality planning by managerial teams meets the principal objectives of the triple role analysis but demands the expenditure of substantial amounts of managerial time.

The triple role analysis should provide for securing inputs from the workforce.

Use of joint teams of exempt and nonexempt people is still in the experimental stage.

The end result of departmental quality planning is an information package consisting of conclusions, proposals, and supporting information.

] *13* [

Introducing *Planning for Quality*

WHAT DO WE MEAN BY "INTRODUCING *PLANNING FOR QUALITY*"?

In the title of this chapter the words "Planning for Quality" refer to the name of this book. In the literal sense, "Introducing *Planning for Quality*" means bringing to a company the ideas contained in this book. Let us look at those ideas from two viewpoints:

The viewpoint of some advocate who feels the ideas have enough merit to warrant their adoption by the company

The likely viewpoint of those within the company who will be impacted

THE VIEWPOINT OF THE ADVOCATE

The advocate's viewpoint is the result of perceptions plus logical theories from those perceptions.

Dissatisfactions with Prior Results

The advocate typically is dissatisfied with the results of the prior approaches to quality planning. Those results are perceived as follows:

A continuing procession of planned products and processes that contained unacceptable levels of deficiencies

A quality crisis, created in large part by those deficient products and processes

No end in sight, unless the quality planning is improved

Theories of Causes

The advocate typically has also thought about what may have caused the prior planning to turn out such deficient products and processes. The resulting theories are based on perceived recurring defects, such as:

Some important customers were not identified

Some important customer needs were not identified

There was lack of participation by important parties in interest.

There was failure to optimize.

The defects collectively added to the time and costs, creating a shortage of time and money, which in turn resulted in still more defects.

The Supercause

The advocate then typically concludes that behind those causes is a common supercause: the lack of a systematic, structured approach. By that theory the remedy is to introduce a structured approach to planning for quality, an approach that will result in:

Systematic identification of customers

Systematic identification of customer needs

Structured participation of those who are impacted (through use of councils, teams)

Use of planning tools that "mark the trail" and reduce planning errors (e.g., flow diagrams, spreadsheets, quantified process capability)

The Remedy

The advocate's remedy follows logically from the theories of causes and supercause: adopt a comprehensive structured approach to planning for quality. As set out in this book, such an approach is then applicable at multiple levels in the company:

Quality planning for interdepartmental projects, as set out in Chapters Two to Ten.

Companywide quality management as set out in Chapter Eleven

Departmental quality planning as set out in Chapter Twelve

THE VIEW FROM THE RECEIVING END

From the receiving end the view is quite different. The viewers consist of a spectrum of explorers, conservatives, and inhibitors.

The Explorers

Many managers can point to defects in the present approach to planning for quality. Among those problem identifiers are a few who go beyond the stage of identifying and complaining; they are open to ideas for changing the approach. Those few managers are in the nature of explorers, and thereby they are potential allies of the advocates. In consequence, the advocates should take steps to identify who the explorers are. It is the explorers who will provide the testing ground for the new approaches.

The Conservatives

All managers would like to see improvement in the approach to quality planning. However, most managers are wary about going into changes based solely on theory and logical reasoning. They are wary, because they have endured too many prior experiences in which the results did not come up to what the advocates had promised. We shall classify these managers as "conservatives."

The conservatives (who constitute most of humanity) do not oppose change on principle. They are quite willing to change once it has been demonstrated that the change does in fact produce results. Their insistence on results before change is actually a valuable stabilizer. (It is an essential ingredient in maturing industries.)

The advocate may well be impatient with the seeming inertia of the conservatives. However, once the results have been demonstrated, the conservatives are open to persuasion.

The Inhibitors

A few managers occupy the negative end of the spectrum of attitudes toward improvement. They are not convinced by logical reasoning or even by demonstrated results. They are the last to accept change. When they do accept change, it is because they cannot openly remain so small a minority.

The advocate is well advised to leave the inhibitors for the last.[1]

Stated Objections

The stated objections of the conservatives have a good deal of logic and plausibility to support them:

> We are experienced, competent planners. Our present approach has evolved through years of facing hard realities.
>
> During those years we have tested various features of what is now asserted to be a "new" approach.
>
> The planning concept is obviously not new.
>
> The principal tools (flow diagram, spreadsheet, process capabilities) are not new. We have known about them for years, and we do make some use of them.
>
> The participation concept is not new. We make some use of it now.
>
> The concept of companywide quality management *is* new, but it is untried in our company.
>
> Based on our experience, to mandate a formal structured approach would involve more work and more delay.
>
> Similarly, to broaden and formalize participation will lengthen the quality planning cycle because of the need for all those joint meetings and the associated responses required.
>
> The asserted benefits of the proposed structured approach are untested theories as applied to our company. We have in the past mandated a number of programs (such as drives) based on untested theories. Collectively the results have been so limited that we should be skeptical about mandating a new program until we have demonstrated that it will produce useful results in our company.

Some stated objections may not be plausible at all, e.g., "Our business is different." Also, the stated objections will not necessarily include some important real objections, e.g., loss of status due to loss of some prior monopoly. However, the list of stated

[1]For a more extensive discussion of the attitudes of explorers, conservatives, and inhibitors, see J. M. Juran, *Managerial Breakthrough* (New York: McGraw-Hill, 1964), Chapter 3, "Breakthrough in Attitudes," pp. 29–40.

objections can effectively neutralize the effort to "sell" the new approach by logical reasoning.

BRIDGING THE VIEWPOINTS: PILOT TESTS

In many companies the differences in viewpoints (advocates versus those on the receiving end) will preclude reaching a meeting of the minds solely through discussion. In such companies, barring an unlikely mandate from the upper managers, progress will depend on the results of a pilot test. If the results are favorable, the new approach is scaled up.

Companies Move in Single File

Companies are normally unable to move in a new direction on a broad front. Instead, they move in single file, one division after another, one department after another. That tends to be true even if there has been an upper management mandate requiring all to move. In part, the single file results from bottlenecks in essential services, e.g., capacity for training. In part, the single file results from differences in priorities and enthusiasm among the various parts of the organization.

The single file phenomenon means that little is lost by deliberately designing a pilot test to be conducted in the departments of the "explorers." The explorers are likely to be at the head of the single file anyway. The resulting pilot tests become the means for converting the skeptics into believers.

Pilot Tests at Different Levels

Planning for Quality is directed at three different levels of quality planning. Those levels call for different strategies in design of pilot tests. The strategies may be tabulated as follows:

LEVEL IN COMPANY	PILOT TESTS ARE CARRIED OUT IN:
Functional departments	A sample of functional departments
Multidepartmental quality planning projects	A sample of multidepartmental quality planning projects
Companywide	A sample of specific business units

Let us look at these more closely.

Departmental Pilot Tests

The approach to departmental quality planning, set forth in Chapter Twelve, is based on the triple role concept. When *Planning for Quality* is the subject of an in-house seminar, it can be expected that a call for volunteers (to test the concept in their departments) will bring out some favorable responses.

The organization for such tests can be simple. Typically the undertaking is by a department head and a selection of his subordinates. (It is feasible to include selected members of the workforce as well.) It is helpful to provide facilitator assistance, as discussed below under "Training."

Multidepartmental Pilot Tests

Multidepartmental pilot tests involve multifunctional projects, as discussed in detail during Chapters Two through Ten. To conduct such tests requires multifunctional teams. The associated organization becomes more complex, and the workload can be significant.

It is quite important to carry out some such multifunctional pilot projects. Our quality deficiencies are largely traceable to the causes mentioned earlier: failure to identify some important customers, failure to identify some important customer needs, lack of participation by some important parties in interest, failure to optimize. Those are precisely the areas best dealt with by multifunctional teams.

Business Unit Pilot Tests

The need for business unit tests arises when we undertake to establish companywide quality management (CWQM). That concept is business-oriented, so the pilot tests should be conducted in business units—specific divisions, product lines, market segments. The subject matter as set out in Chapter Eleven relates to the corporation as well as to the business units. However, even if the corporate heads mandate a corporate approach, the concept of single file will still apply as to the business units.

To establish CWQM requires creating some organization structure that is probably not yet in existence. We shall discuss this below under "Organization."

Workforce Pilot Tests

Whether the structured approach of *Planning for Quality* can be carried out at the workforce level remains to be seen. It is certainly feasible to bring workforce members into departmental quality planning, as discussed previously. Undoubtedly many QC circles have carried out quality planning projects using the conventional ways of the past. However, the concepts and tools set out in *Planning for Quality* are quite extensive. For workforce teams to apply those concepts and tools will require special training and assistance. We shall look at those below under the heading "Training."

ORGANIZATION

In all companies there is already in place some form of organization for quality planning. In the case of multifunctional projects the responsibility is usually assigned to staff planners who do the overall project planning: systems analysts, product designers, process designers. For high-technology goods it is also usual to make use of quality specialists from Quality Assurance.

The relationship of those planners to the operating managers is generally expressed as follows:

	RESPONSIBILITY	
ACTIVITY	STAFF	LINE MANAGERS
Prepare the plan	X	X
Execute the plan		X
Audit execution versus plan	X	

Of the above responsibilities, the least clear has been the line managers' participation during the planning. The extent of that participation has varied widely among companies and even within companies. Under the concepts in *Planning for Quality,* that participation grows and acquires greater formality. In those companies where line manager participation has been very limited, the new approach may have the outward appearance of a change in organization, since it involves extensive use of multifunctional teams.

To introduce CWQM does require creating some new organization structures. As noted in Chapter Eleven, there is need to establish:

1. A companywide quality committee (If a high-level quality committee is already in existence, it may be feasible to add CWQM to its functions.)
2. The quality equivalent of the financial controller

The Immune Reaction

All large organizations exhibit some of the features of a biological organism. Invariably one of those features is the immune reaction when something alien is introduced. The organism senses the intrusion of the alien and mobilizes to reject it.

In biological systems the immune reaction can be lessened by:

Introducing only those transplants which are genetically alike, e.g., from one's self or from an identical twin

Chemically altering the response of the immune system

The introduction of CWQM is analogous to an alien transplant, and it stimulates an immune reaction. That reaction can be reduced in ways similar to those used for the biological organism:

Design CWQM so it resembles one's self, that is, closely parallels the existing business planning structure

Alter the merit rating system in ways that will stimulate the managers to accept the new quality goals

TRAINING

This book is designed to serve as a text for seminars on the subject of planning for quality. Some seminars are "open": The participants come from various industries and companies. Such participants obviously acquire inputs from the text and from the instructor. In addition, the participants learn from each other. Such cross-fertilization is an important aid in grasping those concepts and principles which have universal application.

Other seminars are of the in-house type. Now the participants are all from one company. They usually have known each other for years. For them the seminar provides a means of unifying the company's approach to planning for quality through a common thought process, a structured methodology, universal concepts and tools, a common language.

Training Requirements

Some companies may conclude that they should put into practice much of what is set out in *Planning for Quality.* Such an undertaking will require training at all levels.

At the upper management level the training will involve in-house sessions that concentrate on establishing CWQM and on creating the infrastructure needed to introduce the new approach to other levels.

For the remaining levels the training will require an array of training materials such as:

Video cassettes to provide summarized instruction in interesting, digestible form

Workbooks that can help teams of company managers to tackle pilot projects in planning/replanning

Manuals to enable facilitators and instructors to help the project teams carry out their assignments

As of September 1986, those training aids were not yet in existence.[2]

Facilitators

Companies that prepare some or all of those training aids will also need to designate "facilitators" to aid the project teams. Facilitators are usually full-time supervisors or specialists. They are selected to become facilitators on a part-time basis and are then trained to carry out the roles of facilitator. Those roles are some combination of the following:

EXPLAIN THE MISSION. The facilitator has attended meetings at which there has been explanation of what the company is trying to accomplish. The facilitator is thereby able to communicate to the project team the details of what the company is trying to do:

[2]Juran Institute Inc. has in progress a project to develop these training aids. In all likelihood they will be published by the end of 1987.

to improve quality planning so as to avoid creating deficiencies in the resulting products and processes. The facilitator is also able to explain how that mission differs from prior company endeavors: a structured approach, participation by parties in interest, use of designated planning tools.

PROVIDE ASSISTANCE IN TEAM BUILDING. The facilitator helps the team members to act as a team: to contribute ideas, to challenge ideas of others, to share experiences, to propose lines of inquiry.

ASSIST IN DISCUSSION OF THE TRAINING MATERIALS. The facilitator has already gone over the training materials in advance. He may already have guided other teams through their first project. Such experiences enable the facilitator to play an instructor role.

RELATE EXPERIENCES OF OTHER PROJECT TEAMS. The facilitator has multiple sources from which to draw other teams' experiences:

Project teams for which he has served as facilitator

Meetings of facilitators at which they share the experiences of their respective teams

Final reports of project teams, as published in-house

Projects reported in the literature

ASSIST THE PROJECT TEAM CHAIRMAN. The facilitator is not a member of the project team and thereby avoids getting into the substance of the project. However, the facilitator is helpful to the project team chairman in such respects as stimulating attendance and improving human relations among team members.

INTRODUCING A MAJOR PLANNING TOOL: LESSONS LEARNED

There is no known way for us to perfect our quality planning solely through logical reasoning. We must in addition provide the planners with proper tools. A key planning tool, which we have not yet discussed, is *lessons learned:* the source of the planners' data base.

Countdowns are in wide use, mainly to control changes of various sorts, e.g., startups or shutdowns of processes, geographical moves, maintenance actions. Some countdowns provide for decision-making at various forks in the road. For example, a program for developing and marketing a new product is usually carried out in a structured series of steps or phases. At certain steps in the sequence, business decisions must be made on whether to proceed further with the program or not.

Yet another form of lessons learned is the list of *needed breakthroughs:* identification of systematic obstacles to good quality planning. Those obstacles go by various names: inhibitors, deterrents, disincentives. What they have in common is their chronic nature; they are built into the system, so that only a change in the system can root them out. In turn, such a systematic change does not come about unless the problem is put on the agenda in its own right—not as incidental to some other problem.

For example, during the process of launching a new product "T" we encounter delays and waste due to incomplete prior marketing research. We set up a meeting to deal with this crisis. During the meeting someone brings up the need for better marketing research in the early stages of new product launchings. "We had a similar problem during the launching of products G and K." Generally nothing will happen, because the real topic under discussion is how to deal with the crisis in the new product T. Only when we put "Marketing Research for New Products" on the agenda as a topic in its own right are we on the road to a solution.

Merits of Lessons Learned

Once available, the above (and other) forms of lessons learned exhibit some useful, built-in features:

They make available to any user the collective experience and memories of numerous individuals, organized in ways that permit ready retrieval.

They are of a repetitive nature. They can be used over and over again for an indefinite number of planning cycles.

They are impersonal. They avoid the problems created when one person gives orders to another person.

The Concept

"Lessons learned" is a catchall phrase describing what we have learned from experience. From experience outside the workplace we learn not to touch poison ivy or to overheat milk. From experience within the workplace we also learn: We learn which decisions and actions have brought us good results and which have brought us grief. The value of those lessons is obvious, and it is universal for human beings to store those lessons learned in their memories as guides to action in the future. Human beings go further. They extend their memories through records and libraries; through systems of beliefs, rituals, and taboos; through the design of their products and processes. Collectively, human use of the concept of lessons learned has been decisive in human dominance over all other animal species. So awesome a result suggests that the degree of use of lessons learned can also play a significant role in competition in the market place.

Forms of Lessons Learned

There is no debate about the merits of the concept of lessons learned. The problem is how to assemble the myriad bits of human experience into forms that can be readily used by human planners and decision-makers. Those forms are well known. They consist principally of data banks, checklists, countdowns, and needed breakthroughs. We can look briefly at each of those before we discuss how to organize to create them.

The *data bank* is a compilation of numerous facts specially organized to facilitate retrieval. We have looked closely at one example widely applied in quality planning: data banks on process capability (see pages 191–193).

The *checklist* is an aid to human memory, a reminder of what to do and what not to do. The frequent traveler is well advised to maintain a list of the items his experience has shown to be needed when he arrives at his destination. This list then serves as a repetitive aid to his planning.

Checklists abound. They are widely used by those who have long lists of things to keep in mind: workers, auditors, inspectors.

The *countdown* consists of a list of deeds to be done in a predetermined sequence. Usually, technological safeguards are built in to require adherence to the planned sequence. A very elaborate example is the countdown associated with launching of space vehicles.

Obstacles to Compilation of Lessons Learned

A serious obstacle to compiling lessons learned is that there is a price to be paid. It takes a good deal of work to:

Identify with precision the specific data banks, countdowns, or whatever needed

Design and carry out a plan for data collection and analysis

Compile and publish the resulting lessons learned

None of those tasks is accomplished as a natural by-product of "regular" job assignments. "Extra" work is required specifically to establish lessons learned.

A second obstacle is delayed return on investment. The sequence is work now, benefit later. All of that work must be done before the lessons learned can be put to use.

A further obstacle is our inability to quantify return on investment (ROI) for work done to establish lessons learned. Projects of unknown ROI are handicapped when competing for support against projects for which ROI can be estimated.

Finally, company merit rating systems tend to discourage planners from spending time on lessons learned. Planners who undertake to create data banks do not greatly benefit their current job assignment. Instead, they benefit the common good, and not now, but later. Most company merit rating systems are designed to reward performance that meets current goals, not performance that benefits the common good later.

Collectively those obstacles help to explain why the concept of lessons learned is so seriously underemployed. To make adequate use of the concept requires *a special design of organization* for the specific purpose of establishing lessons learned.

ORGANIZATION TO DEVELOP LESSONS LEARNED

"Lessons learned" consists of a loose collection of specific data banks, checklists, and so on. Each is the result of a specific undertaking—a project, a problem scheduled for solution. In addition, each is interdepartmental by nature: the input data come from multiple sources; the use is by multiple customers. Such interdepartmental projects are best assigned to interdepartmental project teams.

(If lessons learned is to be undertaken on a grand scale, there will be many projects and hence multiple project teams. In that event it is useful to set up a council to coordinate the work of the project teams. Such a council then establishes priorities for projects, appoints project teams, provides support, follows progress, and so on.)

Any project team is given the responsibility of producing "lessons learned" over a defined scope of activity. The team carries out that responsibility by following the planning sequence set out in this textbook: identify customers and their needs, and so forth. However, some aspects of that sequence deserve elaboration here.

ACQUIRE THE INPUT DATA. In part, input data are gathered by "making the rounds." Interviews are conducted to learn from the experience and memories of persons in a position to make useful contributions. Individuals are urged to contribute their "squirrels' nests" of data to a common pool. But in part the data are acquired by systematic analysis of prior history. (See "Retrospective Analysis," next section.)

ANALYZE THE DATA. The extent of input data varies remarkably from project to project. In some cases the project team itself conducts the analysis. In other cases the data are so voluminous that the team must secure the assistance of technicians to do the details of analysis.

CONVERT TO LESSONS LEARNED AND PUBLISH. The final steps transform the data into countdowns and other forms that are usable by the customers.

LESSONS LEARNED THROUGH RETROSPECTIVE ANALYSIS

Retrospective analysis to uncover lessons learned has the greatest potential for innovative discoveries. At the same time, it is seldom used. The likely reason is that it is the extreme form of "work now, benefit later."

A simple example of retrospective analysis is that of replaying the video recording of human performances, e.g., theatrical plays or sports contests. Such reviews permit identification of strengths and weaknesses. If the data base is large enough, the analysis can go further: Pareto analysis to discover the vital few weaknesses, for example.

The concept of retrospective analysis has wide potential application in industries of all kinds. A comparatively simple example is the analysis of federal income tax returns to determine the extent to which taxpayers' errors are due to the design of the forms and the associated instructions.

> The tax form has numerous lines to be filled in by the taxpayer. The instruction provides information as to how to fill in the respective lines. Through analysis of prior returns the Internal Revenue Service has found that a "vital few" lines on the form exhibit far greater error rates than the average for all lines. Those vital few cases then raise a presumption: The high error-proneness is due to the design of the form and the wording of the instruction rather than to taxpayers' errors.

On a larger scale is retrospective analysis of a very complex process such as is used for:

- Developing and marketing a new product
- Establishing a new, comprehensive management information system
- Design and construction of major military system

Such processes are repetitive, but the projects are few in number—perhaps one per year. Each project is lengthy; the cycle time can run to several years. With so much time between cycles it is easy for the same quality problems to recur, cycle after cycle. That is in fact what takes place. To illustrate:

- New systems are devised, but they carry over wastes that were present in the predecessor systems.
- New products are put on the market despite embodying a carryover of failure-prone features of prior products.

Nevertheless, the process (e.g., for developing and marketing a new product) is quite similar from one cycle to another. That being the case, it is perfectly feasible to carry out retrospective analysis.

Of course, the scale of analysis becomes considerable, much greater than replaying the video tapes of sports contests. On such a scale, special organization is needed to carry out the analysis.

That special organization consists of:

1. A project team of managers assigned to direct the analysis and to propose remedies based on the findings
2. A "historian" assigned to study prior cycles of the process

Under this arrangement the historian does the equivalent of reviewing the videotapes of the sports contests. The historian reviews prior cycles of the process through study of the records (minutes of meetings, correspondence, reports of tests). That study is supplemented by interviews to fill in the gaps and take out the biases. The historian also performs analysis as directed: identification of recurring symptoms, test of theories of causes, estimates of time lost.

The project team meets periodically with the historian to direct the analysis, identify questions for which answers are needed, propose theories of causes of symptoms, review the findings of the historian, propose remedies.

Note that lessons learned is widely practiced *informally.* Experienced, older planners have lived through multiple prior cycles. Their memory has registered problems encountered, and they draw on that memory when they go into new projects. They also transfer some of the knowledge (orally) to subordinates and peers. Collectively, all that memory is a form of lessons learned. However, it is a very loose form. It is subject to human biases, lapses in memory, and other ailments of human sensors. It does avoid the cost of a systematic analysis, but it cannot compete in quality of analysis.

SUMMARY

Introducing *Planning for Quality* can seem very logical to advocates but is viewed quite differently by most managers who are faced with adapting to new ways.

A few managers—the explorers—are readily open to testing the new ways.

Most managers—the conservatives—want to see results demonstrated before departing from the existing order.

The stated objections of operating managers are generally quite logical from their perceptions.

Most companies adopt change in single file rather than across a broad front.

Pilot tests are an important means of bridging the viewpoints of advocates and conservatives.

Pilot tests should first be undertaken in the departments headed by "explorers."

Pilot tests are feasible at all levels of the company.

The structured approach to planning for quality requires use of multifunctional teams to assure adequate participation.

Introduction of companywide quality management (CWQM) requires establishment of:

1. A companywide quality committee
2. The quality equivalent of the financial controller

Introducing CWQM also requires dealing with the company's immune reaction by:

Designing CWQM to be similar to the existing business planning system

Revising the merit rating system so that it stimulates the managers to accept the new quality goals

Extensive introduction of *Planning for Quality* requires an array of training materials, including video cassettes, workbooks, and leaders' manuals.

Such extensive introduction also requires use of facilitators to assist the project teams.

Lessons learned is the concept of summarizing prior experience into repetitive-use aids for planning.

Lessons learned consists of data banks, checklists, countdowns, and lists of needed breakthroughs.

Lessons learned is a key aid to introducing a structured approach to planning for quality.

Lessons learned is not a by-product of day-to-day operations. It requires special organization and special efforts.

Lessons learned requires work to be done now for benefits to be realized later.

Retrospective analysis is a form of lessons learned, derived from analysis of prior cycles of operation.

For complex processes, retrospective analysis requires special organization:

A team of managers to direct the analysis and propose remedies

An historian to conduct the analysis

] *Appendix* [

The Roll of Honor

Planning for Quality has evolved through an uncommonly extensive series of collaborations with practicing managers. The extent of the collaboration may well be unprecedented in the annals of managerial literature.

The first phase of the collaboration was the critique of the first draft of *Planning for Quality*. The following provided such critiques:

PERSON	COMPANY	LOCATION
Arciniaga, G. M.	General Motors Truck & Bus	Pontiac, MI
Atkinson, Ron	General Motors Truck & Bus	Shreveport, LA
Aubrey, Charles A. II	Continential Illinois Bank	Chicago, IL
Balash, Frank J.	Avco Management Services	Houston, TX
Ball, David	Becton Dickinson & Co.	Paramus, NJ
Barnes, G. E.	AT&T Technologies	Greensboro, NC
Besgrove, Dorris	McDonnell Douglas Electronics Co.	St. Charles, MO
Black, John	Boeing Aerospace Co.	Seattle, WA
Britton, Marvin	Corning Glass Works	Corning, NY

PERSON	COMPANY	LOCATION
Collins, Calvin W.	Borg-Warner Corporation	Ithaca, NY
Conti, T.	Ing. C. Olivetti & C., S.p.A.	Ivrea, Italy
Dmytrow, Eric D.	Bureau of Labor Statistics	Washington, DC
Early, John F.	Bureau of Labor Statistics	Washington, DC
Graham, Ed	Avco Corporation	Washington, DC
Greer, David	Caterpillar, Inc.	Peoria, IL
Gust, Lawrence J.	Mobil Chemical Company	Macedon, NY
Harris, M. C.	Avco Financial Services	Irvine, CA
Hawthornthwaite, Brian	Union Carbide Corporation	Greenville, SC
Herlich, M. E.	Paul Revere Insurance Companies	Worcester, MA
Hines, J. E.	AT&T Teletype Corporation	Lisle, IL
Hrapkiewicz, Steve	First Tennessee Bank	Memphis, TN
Huizenga Thomas	Perkin-Elmer Corporation	Norwalk, CT
Hulse, James	Becton Dickinson & Co.	Paramus, NJ
Janney, H. L.	AT&T Technologies	Hopewell, NJ
Judy, Hal	Apollo Computer	Chelmsford, MA
Laurent, Jacques	AFNOR	Paris, France
Lerch, B. H.	AT&T Technologies	Springfield, NJ
Loeser, Ross C.	E. I. DuPont de Nemours	Wilmington, DE
Lowe, Ted	General Motors Truck & Bus	Pontiac, MI

PERSON	COMPANY	LOCATION
Marchal, E. F.	Avco Lycoming	Williamsport, PA
Marks, John	P-E Consulting Group	Johannesburg, South Africa
Mazzeo, J. M.	General Motors Truck & Bus	Pontiac, MI
Mazzola, J.	Avco Specialty Materials Division	Lowell, MA
Munsey, James R.	E. I. DuPont de Nemours	Wilmington, DE
Olsson, Dexter	Bethlehem Steel Corporation	Bethlehem, PA
Onnias, Arturo	Texas Insruments–France	Villeneuve–Loubet, France
Perry, Robert L.	McDonnell Douglas Electronics Co.	St. Charles, MO
Rosati, Ralph	Eastman Kodak	Rochester, NY
Ross, T. G.	IBM	Atlanta, GA
Schwartz, Otto	Internal Revenue Service	Washington, DC
Smith, H. Douglas	BMC Industries, Inc.	St. Paul, MN
Sterett, W. Kent	Florida Power and Light Company	Miami, FL
Tabley, Ron W.	Management Frontiers Pty. Limited	North Sydney, Australia
Thornton, P. A.	AT&T Technologies	Berkeley Heights, NJ
Towse, James	Avco Financial Services	London, Ontario, Canada
West, Royce	Dana Corporation	Ottawa Lake, MI
Wier, J. M.	AT&T Technologies	Holmdel, NJ

The second phase of the collaboration was the Stamford conference, August 27–28, 1985. Those participating were as follows:

PERSON	COMPANY	LOCATION
Ackerman, Roger	AT&T Technologies, Inc.	Berkeley Heights, NJ
Atkinson, George	Eastman Kodak Company	Rochester, NY
Ball, David	Becton Dickinson & Co.	Paramus, NJ
Besgrove, Dorris	McDonnell Douglas Electronics Co.	St. Charles, MO
Black, John	Boeing Aerospace Co.	Seattle, WA
Britton, Marvin	Corning Glass Works	Corning, NY
Burbank, J. R.	IBM	Atlanta, GA
Clos, Robert	Boeing Aerospace Co.	Seattle, WA
Collins, Brendan	Florida Power and Light Company	Juno Beach, FL
Collins, Calvin W.	Borg-Warner Corporation	Ithaca, NY
Croft, Stephen	E. I. DuPont de Nemours	Wilmington, DE
Danek, Bob	General Motors	Warren, MI
Dmytrow, Eric D.	Bureau of Labor Statistics	Washington, DC
Early, John F.	Bureau of Labor Statistics	Washington, DC
Erdman, John P.	E. I. DuPont de Nemours	Wilmington, DE
Essinger, Ted	Florida Power and Light Company	Miami, FL
Godfrey, A. Blanton	AT&T Bell Laboratories	Holmdel, NJ
Greer, David	Caterpillar, Inc.	Peoria, IL
Hamood, Ally	General Motors Truck & Bus	Pontiac, MI

PERSON	COMPANY	LOCATION
Houser, Bill	Tenneco, Inc.	Houston, TX
Hulse, James	Becton Dickinson & Co.	Paramus, NJ
Judy, Hal	Apollo Computer	Chelmsford, MA
Lowe, Ted	General Motors Truck & Bus	Pontiac, MI
Marchand, Gerald	Bethlehem Steel	Chesterton, IN
McArthur, Dan	Tenneco Inc.	Houston, TX
McWeeney, P. Kevin	Boeing Aerospace Co.	Seattle, WA
Mead, Robert	Borg-Warner Corporation	Ithaca, NY
Nickell, Warren L.	IBM	Atlanta, GA
Olsson, Dexter	Bethlehem Steel Corporation	Bethlehem, PA
Palmer, Terry	General Motors of Canada, Ltd.	Oshawa, Ontario, Canada
Perry, Robert L.	McDonnell Douglas Electronics Co.	St. Charles, MO
Pleasants, William W.	Burlington Industries	Greensboro, NC
Plsek, Paul	AT&T Technologies, Inc.	Berkeley Heights, NJ
Reed, Ken	McDonnell Douglas Electronics Co.	St. Charles, MO
Schwartz, Otto	Internal Revenue Service	Washington, DC
Stevens, Eric	General Motors of Canada, Ltd.	Oshawa, Ontario, Canada
Tilley, Brian	David Hutchins Associates, Ltd.	Berkshire, United Kingdom
Vanderstoop, Nick	General Motors of Canada, Ltd.	Oshawa, Ontario, Canada
Vlach, Kenneth	Xerox Corporation	Webster, NY
West, Royce	Dana Corporation	Ottawa Lake, MI

The third phase of collaboration was the field tests. The following were designated by their organizations to provide leadership to the project teams:

PERSON	COMPANY	LOCATION
Brokke, Harris	Juran Institute, Inc.	Wilton, CT
Galvin, John	Bureau of Labor Statistics	Washington, DC
Grace, Thomas E.	Packaging Corp. of America	Trexlertown, PA
Hamood, Ally	General Motors Truck & Bus	Pontiac, MI
Hoogstoel, Robert	Juran Institute, Inc.	Wilton, CT
Houser, Bill	Tenneco, Inc.	Houston, TX
Huizenga, Thomas	Perkin-Elmer Corporation	Norwalk, CT
McArthur, Dan	Tenneco, Inc.	Houston, TX
Poirier, Chuck	Packaging Corp. of America	Evanston, IL
Polca, Andy	Packaging Corp. of America	Trexlertown, PA
Scanlon, Robert	Caterpillar Inc.	Peoria, IL

The project team members and the titles of their projects were as follows:

at THE AMERICAN SOCIETY FOR QUALITY CONTROL (AUTOMOTIVE DIVISION), planning an annual conference:

Hamood, Ally (facilitator)	General Motors Truck & Bus Group
Eureka, William	General Motors
Frank, Thornton F.	General Motors
Hayhow, Betsy	General Motors
Komarzec, Walter	General Dynamics
Lowe, Ted (chairman)	General Motors Truck & Bus Group
McBean, Gerald	General Dynamics
Seasor, Ann	TRW

Tomlinson, Charles	Chrysler Corporation
Troy, John	Chrysler Corporation
Troyanovich, Jack	Chrysler Corporation

at the BUREAU OF LABOR STATISTICS:

Galvin, John (facilitator)

Project Team 1, replanning the CPI price listing review process:

Ford, Kay (team leader)
Fortuna, Charles
Isaksen, Frances
Kamalich, Richard
Kerr, Cheryl
Konny, Chrystal
McMichael, Mary
Stewart, Ken

Project Team 2, replanning the CPI checklist revision process:

Adkins, Bob
Allen, Sheila
Chelena, Joe
Cooke, Shaw III
Isaksen, Frances
O'Leary, Michael
Ternes, Robert
Weyback, Don (team leader)

at CATERPILLAR, INC.:

Scanlon, Robert (facilitator)
Project Team 1, development of the best alternative for design, manufacture, and sourcing of small wheel loader axle arrangements (Aurora Plant):

Burkiewicz, Jim (team leader)
Couch, Art

Davis, Dan
Deltenre, Robert
DuVall, Jim
Hendron, Ray
Hopkins, Mike
Lewis, John
Nelson, Lenny
Pfotenhauer, Gene
Sanuki-San, G.
VanDell, Don

Project Team 2, planning the quality improvement steering process (Aurora Plant):

Braatz, John
Elliott, Jerry
Hair, Cliff
Keeran, Chuck
Koschnitzke, Karl
Peabody, Dave
Reddish, Larry
Rice, Roger
Rinkel, Glenn
Schmidt, Gerry
Smith, Chuck
Tunt, Tim
Valentine, Howard (team leader)
Van Winkle, John

Project Team 3, replanning the process for release of new part numbers (East Peoria Plant):

Bianchi, Steve
Brown, Rick
Galbreath, Chuck

Lamprecht, Jerry
Monge, Myron (team leader)
Nicholson, Ernie
Voros, John
Welker, Gerry

at GENERAL MOTORS ADVANCED ENGINEERING STAFF, replanning the process of technology transfer for the Factory of the Future:

Hamood, Ally (facilitator)
Baker, George (chairman)
Brooks, Joe
Carter, Mike
Lasecki, JoAnne
Roeland, Ed
Smith, Paul

at JURAN INSTITUTE, INC., replanning the preparation of the annual catalog:

Brokke, Harris (facilitator)
Hoogstoel, Robert (facilitator)
Asrelsky, Hope
Blackiston, G. Howland
Cioppi, Patricia
Ellis, Linda
Tedesco, Frank
Ventrella, Scott
Wilson, Robert
Yeager, Bob (Integrated Marketing International)

at PACKAGING CORPORATION OF AMERICA, replanning the production scheduling process:

Polca, Andrew (facilitator)
George, Robert F.

Grace, Thomas E.
Kimes, Roy G.
Mickey, Sophia
Pausinger, Siegfried
Tisi, Peter, D.

at PERKIN-ELMER CORPORATION:

Project Team 1, replanning the product development process:

Huizenga, Thomas P. (facilitator)
Cahill, Jerry E.
Conlon, Ralph D.
Fyans, Richard L.
Liepins, Kaspar
Olbert, John A.
Pisano, Daniel J. (team leader)
Savino, Ben C.
Saturno, Ralph
Vesciglio, Robert P.
Yates, Dennis

Project Team 2, planning the transfer of machining jobs to the Niigata Machining Center:

DeFeo, Joseph A. (facilitator)
Huizenga, Thomas P. (facilitator)
Adinolfi, J. Richard
Brennan, Donna M.
Coppola, Robert V. (team leader)
Groeschner, Donald L.
Hager, Timothy
Horesco, Ronald A.

Lipka, Teddy K.
Trembicki, Sharon R.
Wesolowski, Dennis F.
Zamolsky, Peter J.

Glossary

Accuracy accuracy of a sensor is the degree to which the sensor tells the truth; the extent to which its evaluation of some phenomenon agrees with the "true" value as judged by an accepted standard.

Activity symbol (of a flow diagram) rectangle, which designates an activity.

Assembly "tree" a process form widely used by the great mechanical and electronic industries that build automotive vehicles, household appliances, electronic apparatus. The roots (or leaves) of the tree are numerous suppliers or in-house departments making parts and components. Those elements are assembled by still other departments.

Autonomous department a process form that receives basic "materials" and converts them into finished goods and services, all within a single self-contained department.

Bias a tendency or inclination of outlook which is a troublesome source of error in human sensing.

Biological process a process form in which a cell divides into multiple cells, which differentiate to create an organism with multiple organs all coordinated by a nervous system. An enterprise created by a single founder and then "franchised" follows a similar process of growth.

Breakthrough see *Quality improvement.*

Capability index (also known as the process capability index) the ratio of tolerance width to process capability.

Carryover features carried over to new processes or products from existing processes or products.

Central tendency the tendency of data gathered from a process to bunch around a value somewhere between the high and low values.

Checklist an aid to human memory, a reminder of what to do and what not to do; a form of "lessons learned."

Coloration a deliberate distortion of data sensed by a human, for a variety of (usually) self-serving human purposes.

Companywide quality management (CWQM) a systematic approach for setting and meeting quality goals throughout the company.

Competitive analysis analysis of product and process features and performance against those of competing products and processes.

Connector (of a flow diagram) a circle, which is used to indicate a continuation of the flow diagram on another page.

Conscious errors human errors that are intentional and witting.

Control subjects specific things to be controlled; a mixture of product features, process features, side-effect features.

Compromise a means for resolving differences in which each party meets some desired goals at the price of taking some unwanted actions.

Conservatives managers who are wary about going into changes based solely on theory and logical reasoning.

Constructive conflict Follett's term for a teamwork approach to discover the optimum.

Coonley–Agnew process a process for resolving differences in which the parties to the difference must (1) identify their areas of agreement and their areas of disagreement; (2) agree on why they disagreed; (3) decide what they are going to do about it.

Countdown a list of deeds to be done, in a predetermined sequence.

Criticality analysis a tool for dealing with proliferation and complexity in which a product feature may be classified as critical for a variety of reasons, including: essential to human safety, legislated mandates, essential to salability, demanding as to investment, demanding as to continuity, long lead time, instability.

Criticality analysis spreadsheet a spreadsheet of product features and criticality, which ensures that appropriate action is taken with respect to all critical features.

Critical processes processes that present serious dangers to human life, health, and the environment or risk the loss of very large sums of money. Critical processes usually require numerous safety features to be built into the operational quality control system.

Cultural needs include needs for job security, self-respect, respect of others, continuity of habit patterns, and still other elements of what is broadly called cultural values.

Customer anyone who is impacted by our processes and products.

Data bank a compilation of numerous facts specially organized to facilitate retrieval; a form of "lessons learned."

Decision symbol (of a flow diagram) a diamond, which designates a decision.

Decreed quality standard a quality standard imposed on us by forces that are largely beyond our control, e.g., client, government agency, society.

Deployment (of corporate goals) subdividing the goals and allocating the subgoals to lower levels in the organization.

Design review a process originally evolved as an early warning device during product development. The method is to create a *design review team,* which includes specialists from those classes of customers who are heavily impacted by the design—those who are to: develop the manufacturing process, produce the product, test the product, use the product, maintain the product, and so on. Their responsibility is to provide early warning to the designer: "If you design it this way, here are the consequences in my area."

Document symbol (of a flow diagram) a symbol that denotes a document pertinent to the process.

Dominance a means for resolving differences in which a customer imposes his or her terms on the supplier. Dominance of this sort is common when supplies are plentiful. When a supplier has a monopoly, he may practice dominance over customers.

Dominance, concept of (of a process): the phenomenon that among the numerous variables that impact a process, one usually dominates; it exhibits an influence greater than all the rest combined. Common forms of dominance include setup-dominance; time-dominance; component-dominance; worker-dominance; information-dominance.

Dry run a test of a process under operating conditions.

Early warning advance notification of upcoming problems, derived (usually) from customers' participation in suppliers' planning: "If you plan it this way, here is the problem I will face."

Engineering study scientific collection and analysis of data.

Explorers managers who, in addition to being problem identifiers, are open to ideas for changing the approach to the problem.

Facilities control the form of process control that provides for maintenance of the physical facilities: equipment, tools, instruments.

Failure rate a measure widely used to quantify the frequency of failures in manufactured products. In *service industries* and nonmanufacturing processes the term "failure rate" is seldom used. Instead, terms like "error rate," "defect rate," "discrepancy rate," or "outage rate" are used.

Feedback an input from a customer relative to the impact of the product.

Feedback loop a systematic sequence for communicating information on process performance as an input to maintenance of process stability.

Flow diagram a graphic means for depicting the steps in a process.

Flow line (of a flow diagram) a line that links together the sequential steps of a process.

"Foolproofing" building safeguards into the technology of a process to reduce inadvertent human error.

Frequency distribution the mathematical relationship between the value of a variable and the relative frequency with which that value occurs; also, the graphic representation of the relationship.

Frequency histogram the graph resulting when an envelope is drawn around a frequency distribution.

Glossary a list of terms and their definitions.

Goal an aimed-at target; an achievement toward which effort is expended.

Inadvertent errors human error due to inattention; these errors are unintentional, unpredictable, and often unwitting.

Inhibitors those few managers who occupy the negative end of the spectrum of attitudes toward improvement. They are not convinced by logical reasoning or even by demonstrated results. They are the last to accept change.

Input all the means employed by a process to produce its product.

Internal failures product failures that occur before product is delivered to external customers.

Joint planning planning carried out across organization boundaries to reduce adverse effects of suboptimization; also, a form of optimizing internally through use of interdepartmental planning teams.

Juran Trilogy® the processes of quality planning, quality control, and quality improvement.

"Lessons learned" a catchall phrase describing what has been learned from experience. Examples are data banks, checklists, countdowns, lists of needed breakthroughs.

"Making the rounds" the approach to internal marketing research in which a specialist is assigned to contact departments significantly impacted by the project undergoing planning; also, visiting each customer to secure input for planning purposes.

Marketing research research to discover the quality needs of customers.

Misinterpretation a human error resulting mainly from imprecise communication.

Needed breakthroughs, list of a list of frequent obstacles to good quality planning.

Optimum (as applied to a quality goal): that which meets the needs of customer and supplier alike, and minimizes their combined costs.

Pareto principle the phenomenon whereby, in any population that contributes to a common effect, a relative few of the contributors account for the bulk of the effect.

Perceived needs customers' needs based on their perceptions.

Phase system a means of dividing a complex process (usually the product development process) into a definable series of steps or phases. The phase system usually provides for business decisions to be made at several key points during the progression.

Pilot test a test of process capability based on an intermediate scaling up between the planning phase and full-scale operations.

Policy a guide to managerial action.

Precision a measure of the ability of a sensor to reproduce its results on repeat test.

President's quality audits audits that include review of business-oriented quality matters. In some Japanese companies these audits are typically conducted annually, either by the Companywide Quality Committee or by some other team of upper managers in which the president personally participates.

Process a systematic series of actions directed to the achievement of a goal; the activities (tasks, steps, operations, work cycles) by which an organization unit carries out its assigned responsibilities.

Process capability a standardized evaluation of the inherent ability of a process to perform under operating conditions; the performance of a process after significant causes of variation have been eliminated; in manufacture, process capability usually is equated to six standard deviations of the variability.

Process capability index see *Capability index.*

Process control the systematic evaluation of performance of a process, and taking corrective action if performance is not according to standard; the application of the feedback to maintaining stability of a process.

Process performance what a process *actually does.*

Process validation a documented program that provides a high degree of assurance that a specific process will consistently produce a product meeting its predetermined specifications and quality attributes (quoted from an FDA guideline).

Procession a process form in which the product progresses sequentially through multiple departments, each performing some operation which contributes to the final result.

Processors those who run the process; customers who employ our product in their processes.

Processor team any organization unit (of one or more persons) that carries out a prescribed process.

Product a generic term for whatever is produced by a process, whether goods or services.

Product breakdown see *Product subdivision.*

Product control a form of process control that takes place after some amount of product has been produced. The purpose of product control is to make the decision as to whether or not the product conforms to product goals.

Product development the process of providing product features that respond to customer needs.

Product dissatisfaction adverse customer reaction to product in such forms as complaints, returns, claims (including lawsuits).

Product satisfaction positive customer reaction to product; why customers buy the product.

Product subdivision (or product breakdown) a process of product analysis from the system design level down to lower levels in the product hierarchy.

Pyramid of needs a system that organizes customers' needs into a logical interrelated hierarchy of needs: primary, secondary, tertiary, and so on.

Quality (1) product performance that results in customer satisfaction; (2) freedom from product deficiencies, which avoids customer *dis*satisfaction. (A shorthand expression that conveys both meanings is "fitness for use.")

Quality audit an independent review of quality performance. (See also *President's quality audit.*)

Quality goal an aimed-at quality target.

Quality improvement the organized creation of beneficial change; improvement of chronic performance to an unprecedented level. (See also *Breakthrough.*)

Quality planning the activity of developing the products and processes required to meet customers' needs. (Quality planning follows a universal sequence of steps elaborated in Chapters Two through Ten of this book.)

Quality standard a mandated quality model to be followed.

Quincunx a device in which beads, dropping through an orderly maze of pins, simulate, in the variability of arrival location at the bottom of the maze, the variability of an operating process.

Real needs those fundamental needs which motivate customer action, e.g., a real need of a car purchaser is transportation.

Rehearsal a means to provide the key operating personnel with the needed experience *before* the process goes into operation. Rehearsals include drills to acquire experience in dealing with crises.

Retrospective analysis analysis based on feedback of information from operations.

Running control the form of process control that takes place periodically during the operation of the process. The purpose is to make the decision to "run or stop."

Salability analysis evaluation of product salability. The analysis is typically based on a study of customer behavior, perceptions, and opinions, and on competitive product differences.

Self-control (of an individual) that state in which an individual possesses (1) the means of knowing what actual performance is, (2) the means of knowing what target performance is, and (3) the means for changing performance in the event actual performance does not conform to target performance.

Sensor a method or instrument that can determine the presence and intensity of a phenomenon.

Setup (startup) control a form of process control, the end result of which is the decision whether or not to "push the start button."

Simulation a form of planning that makes use of mathematical models or small scale models; also, a means of providing operating personnel with experience prior to conduct of operations.

Spreadsheet an orderly arrangement of planning information consisting (usually) of (1) horizontal rows to list needs and (2) vertical columns to list the means for meeting those needs.

Spiral of Progress in Quality a graph that shows a typical sequence of activities for putting a product on the market.

Standard deviation a widely used measure of variability. For data from a large sample of product, the standard deviation, σ, is expressed as:

$$\sigma = \sqrt{\frac{\Sigma d^2}{n}}$$

d = the deviation of any unit from the average
n = the number of units in the sample
Σ means "the sum of"

Stated needs needs as seen from customers' viewpoint, and in their language.

Suboptimization pursuit of local goals without regard to the goal of the larger enterprise.

Suppliers those who provide inputs to a process.

Teamwork a form of cooperation among multiple departments, e.g., design review or joint planning. (See also those entries.)

Technique error a species of human error traceable to lack of knowledge of some essential "knack."

Terminal symbol (of a flow diagram) a rounded rectangle, which unambiguously identifies the beginning or end of a process.

Transfer to operations the shift of responsibility from planners to the operating forces.

Trilogy the managerial processes of quality planning, quality control, and quality improvement.

Triple role the three roles carried out by every processor team: processor, supplier, and customer.

TRIPROL™ Diagram an input–output diagram that depicts the triple role of processor, supplier, and customer.

Unintended use use of the product in a manner different from that intended by the supplier.

Unit of measure a defined amount of some quality feature that permits evaluation of that feature in numbers.

Upper managers the managers who constitute the upper layer of a company, including the corporate officers and staff, and, in a divisionalized structure, the division general manager and staff.

User (of a product) a customer who carries out positive actions with respect to the product, e.g., further processing or ultimate use.

Value analysis a process for evaluating the interrelationships among the functions performed by product features, and the associated costs.

Variability the dispersion or scatter exhibited by evaluations of successive events resulting from a common process, e.g., measurement of successive units of product emerging from a process.

Zero defects (1) a term denoting defect-free product; (2) a slogan sometimes used during "drives" to improve quality.

Biographical Note

J. M. Juran has since 1924 pursued a varied career in management as engineer, industrial executive, government administrator, university professor, impartial labor arbitrator, corporate director, and management consultant. That career has been marked by a search for the underlying principles common to all managerial activity. Applied to the specialty of management for quality, the search has produced the leading international reference literature and the leading international training courses, training books, and video cassettes. He is the author of *Quality Control Handbook* (Third Edition, 1974), the international standard reference work on the subject.

In the field of general management, Dr. Juran's book *Managerial Breakthrough* generalizes the principles of creating beneficial change (breakthrough) and of preventing adverse change (control). His book *The Corporate Director* (with J. K. Louden) generalizes the work of the corporate Board of Directors. His book *Upper Management and Quality* (Fourth Edition, 1982) is the pioneering training manual on that subject. Beyond his eleven published books, he has authored hundreds of published papers.

A holder of degrees in engineering and law, Dr. Juran maintains an active schedule as author and international lecturer while serving various industrial companies, governmental agencies, and other institutions as a consultant. He has been the recipient of more than thirty medals, fellowships, honorary memberships, and other honors awarded by professional and honor societies in twelve countries. The latest is the Order of the Sacred Treasure, awarded by the Emperor of Japan for "the development of Quality Control in Japan and the facilitation of U.S. and Japanese friendship."

Index